England: an elegy

ENGLAND: AN ELEGY

ROGER SCRUTON

Chatto & Windus

LONDON

Published by Chatto & Windus 2000

2 4 6 8 10 9 7 5 3

Copyright © Roger Scruton 2000

Roger Scruton has asserted his right under the
Copyright, Designs and Patents Act 1988 to be identified
as the author of this work

First published in Great Britain in 2000 by
Chatto & Windus
Random House, 20 Vauxhall Bridge Road,
London SW1V 2SA

Random House Australia (Pty) Limited
20 Alfred Street, Milsons Point, Sydney,
New South Wales 2061, Australia

Random House New Zealand Limited
18 Poland Road, Glenfield,
Auckland 10, New Zealand

Random House (Pty) Limited
Endulini, 5A Jubilee Road, Parktown 2193, South Africa

The Random House Group Limited Reg. No. 954009
www.randomhouse.co.uk

A CIP catalogue record for this book
is available from the British Library

ISBN 1 85619 251 2

Papers used by Random House are natural,
recyclable products made from wood grown in sustainable forests;
the manufacturing processes conform to the environmental
regulations of the country of origin

Typeset by Deltatype Ltd, Birkenhead, Wirral
Printed and bound in Great Britain by
Biddles Ltd, Guildford.

Contents

Preface

'The owl of Minerva spreads its wings only with the gathering of the dusk.' Hegel's words ring true of every form of human life: it is only at the end of things that we begin to understand them. And understanding them, we know that they are lost. Which comes first – the understanding or the losing? Often it seems that we kill things by examining them; and then again, that understanding is a way to keep what we value, when all other means have vanished.

What follows is a memorial address: I speak of England as I knew it, not as the country might appear to the historian. My intention is not to add to the store of factual knowledge, but to pay a personal tribute to the civilisation that made me and which is now passing from the world. Since the Second World War the Owl of Minerva has hovered uninterruptedly above my subject: book upon book has appeared, describing, denouncing, analysing, and anatomising England – whether or not under this, its true and proper description. I cannot add to, still less compete with, the work of diligent historians, and if the names of Sir Geoffrey Elton, Alan Macfarlane, Jonathan Clark, David Cannadine, Linda Colley, A.D. Harvey and the late Raphael Samuel appear rarely, if at all, I hope that I will be forgiven for making so little acknowledgement of their influence. My aim is that of all funeral orations: to praise the dead, and to cheer the survivors.

This is not the first such oration. Lamentations over England's passing have been a feature of English literature throughout the twentieth century – so much so that one can be forgiven for questioning their sincerity. From George Sturt's *Change in the Village* (1912) to Peter Laslett's collection devoted to *The World We Have Lost* (1984), writers have brooded on the destruction caused by social and material progress, to a country which a century earlier had made 'progress' its motto. But these lamentations, often dismissed as nostalgia, and criticised on all sides for their failure to compare the fate of England with the fate of everywhere else, have been superseded by a newer and more genuinely valedictory literature, in which the uniqueness of England is recognised, and its mortal nature shown. In a work packed with historical knowledge (*In Memory Of England*, London, 1998), Peter VanSittart has given an account of our disappearing country whose erudition I could not hope to rival. In more lyrical vein Linda Proud has evoked the spirit of England in a book – *Consider England* (London, 1994) – whose message is powerfully reinforced by the watercolours of Valerie Petts, and which makes an unanswerable case, both literary and visual, for the Old England of our dreams. Some, like Philippe Daudy in *Les Anglais* (Paris, 1991), have said their farewells from abroad. Some, like Jeremy Paxman in *The English* (London, 1998), have picked up the pieces (a few of them at least) while pieces remain. Others have documented, whether in anger, in sorrow or in secret or not so secret satisfaction, the passing of some aspect of our culture – of the countryside (Graham Harvey, *The Killing of the Countryside*, London, 1996), of the education system (George Walden, *We Should Know Better*, London, 1998), of our political institutions and political independence (John Redwood, *The Death of Britain?*, London, 1999), of the class system (David Cannadine, *The Decline and Fall of the British Aristocracy*, Yale, 1990, and *Class in Britain*, London, 1999), of the ritual and liturgy of the Anglican Church (Brian Morris, ed., *Ritual Murder*, Manchester, 1980), or of the entire English culture and settlement (Clive Aslett, *Anyone for England?*, London, 1997, and Peter Hitchens, *The Abolition of Britain*, London, 1999). Unique among the many obituaries is that of Julian Barnes, whose witty account of a represented and re-presented England (in *England, England*, London, 1998) contains a strangely moving evocation of the old tranquillity.

My excuses for this book are two: first, that it is a personal tribute; second, that it is an attempt to understand, from a philosophical perspective, what we are now losing as our form of life decays. England furnished us with an ideal, and the English people acquired some of the gentleness, amiability and civilised manners which that ideal prescribed. What the English people have since become is, to my mind, a proof that ideals are important.

Malmesbury, 2000

Chapter One

What on Earth was England?

What was England: a nation? A territory? A language? A culture? An empire? An idea? All answers seem inadequate; in this chapter I attempt to say why.

The English enjoyed the strange privilege of knowing exactly *who* they were, but not *what* they were. In moments of crisis they would reach for abstract ideas. Asserting his sovereignty against the Pope, Henry VIII described England as an 'empire, entire unto itself'. His subjects called it a kingdom, but were astonished to discover, when James VI of Scotland ascended the throne, that the kingdom stretched to the Outer Hebrides. Under Cromwell, England became a 'protectorate', though protected from what it was impossible to say. Following the Glorious Revolution of 1688, the English spoke first of empire, then of union and finally of a United Kingdom. Meanwhile, they accepted a foreign king, George I, who spoke no English, and they learned to revise the geographical description of their country. It was no longer England but Great Britain and Ireland – the latter dragged in protestingly and with a just grievance that has never been answered or atoned for.

The English began to call themselves British and the most popular of their patriotic songs affirms that 'Britons never never never shall be slaves!'[1] Their empire – having been acquired, as Sir John Seeley

---

[1] Although 'Britain' was contained in the royal title after the Act of Union of 1707, the use of the word 'Briton' was subsequently an object of satire – especially from

famously put it, 'in a fit of absence of mind', in other words not by political planning but by private enterprise in which the Scots, the Welsh and the Irish played an equal part[1] – was not the English but the British Empire. Even at the height of imperial splendour, however, England was the focus of their loyalty. Macaulay gave his countrymen the canonical image of their past in an unfinished work entitled *History of England* (1849–55). France had defined itself already as a nation; Germany and Italy were following suit, in each case with no small measure of violence, revolutionary upheaval and intoxicated speechifying.[2] But still the English had no real equivalent of the national idea. Vague notions of 'kith and kin' animated the builders of empire; but who was included and why remained uncertain. When politicians appealed for support, they addressed not the nation or the kingdom but 'the country' – meaning all those people who were represented in the Parliament of Westminster. But what these people had in common, and what had brought them together under a single crown, remained wholly obscure. The Scots were still governed by their own laws, and possessed institutions, offices and ceremonies that made little sense to those brought up south of the Border. When politicians appealed to the country it was as though they were waving vaguely from the Palace of Westminster, towards territory that stretched without definition until falling, in some distant and unvisited region, into the sea. That territory was England – and it was an enchanted territory, which called to its children in every far-flung corner of the globe, furnishing them with the idea and the love of home.

It was therefore as the home country that England was most easily

Wilkes, in his *The True Briton* – and Scots and Irish soldiers were still referring to themselves as 'English' (being in service to the English crown) in the 1800s. See A.D. Harvey, *Collision of Empires: Britain in the Three World Wars, 1793–1945*, London, 1992, p. 6n.

[1] Sir John Robert Seeley, *The Expansion of England in the Eighteenth Century*, London, 1883.

[2] See Adam Zamoyski, *Holy Madness: Romantics, Patriots and Revolutionaries, 1776–1871*, London, 1999.

defined. But the definition made less and less sense as the empire dwindled, and slowly and uncertainly the English revised their self-description, pretending like the rest of Europe that they were a nation. But what nation? Why, the British of course: for they were British nationals. No such thing, however, was written in their passports, which referred instead to 'the United Kingdom of Great Britain and Northern Ireland', and which 'requested and required', in the name of Her Britannic Majesty, that the bearer should be allowed to pass freely. Legally speaking, they were subjects of the Queen – or rather, of the Crown, which is not a person or a state or a government but a 'corporation sole', a collective with at most one member: an entity recognised only by the common law of England, an ancient product of the English imagination interred like some adamantine relic in the subsoil of our culture.

The idea of Britain was invented to give credibility to the Union, to sustain the Protestant religion of England and Scotland, and to fortify Great Britain against continental power. So argued Hilaire Belloc, in a genial old history of battles and kings. And so argues Linda Colley in a brand-new history full of the sounds and smells of the common people.[1] Their story of the British nation is fast becoming orthodoxy. Philosophically speaking, however, it is flawed. It is true that there was a British Empire, that the English learned to describe themselves as Britons, and that Britain and Britishness became the common currency of sovereign claims. But still, there never was a British nation. The Scots continued to describe themselves as Scots; the Irish as Irish – or, if they rejected the Republic, as 'Unionists', meaning adherents to the strange legal entity described in their passports. The Welsh, who provided us with our most determinedly English kings, the Tudors, were still, in their own eyes, Welsh. The English remained English, and in their hearts it was England that secured their loyalty, not Scotland, Ireland or

[1] Hilaire Belloc, *History of England*, London, 1915; Linda Colley, *Britons: Forging the Nation, 1707–1837*, Yale, 1992.

Wales. Only one group of Her Majesty's subjects saw itself as British
– namely, those immigrants from the former Empire who seized on
the idea of British nationality as a means of having no real nationality
at all, certainly no nationality that would conflict with ethnic or
religious loyalties, forged far away and years before. There were black
British or Bangladeshis, but not black or Bangladeshi English; and
there were few black British who saw themselves primarily as
subjects of the English Crown.

Nations are, in Benedict Anderson's illuminating phrase,[1] 'imagined communities' – communities formed through their own
storytelling, shaped by language, culture and consciousness into a
form that will prepare their members for a common fate. Nations are
not the 'natural' communities implied by their name: seldom if ever
do they arise from a common stock or a web of kinship. They are as
much the products as the producers of the states which govern them,
and even if they are sanctified by a common language and a common
religion, these things may exist because administrative convenience
requires them. Hence the theory – exaggerated in detail, but
persuasive in outline – that the nation is a creation, or at any rate a
consequence, of the modern state, and nationalism the ideology upon
which at least some modern forms of political order draw for their
legitimacy.

The theory was first advanced by Lord Acton;[2] since then it has
become a commonplace among historians, and one that is seized
upon with glee by those who find the simple loyalties of simple
people both dangerous and unattractive. The recent experience of
nationalism in Germany, the Balkans and the Soviet Empire inspires

[1] Benedict Anderson, *Imagined Communities: Reflections on the Origin and Spread of
Nationalism*, London, 1983.
[2] J.E.E. Dalberg-Acton, Lord Acton, 'Nationality', in *The History of Freedom and
Other Essays*, eds J.N. Figgis and R.V. Laurence, London, 1907, pp 273–4. The thesis
has been presented in other, more modern, and more eccentric versions by Anderson, *op.
cit.* (whose study concerns the emerging 'nation-states' of post-imperial Asia and Africa),
Eric Hobsbawm, *Nations and Nationalism Since 1780*, Cambridge, 1990, and Ernest
Gellner, *Nations and Nationalism*, Oxford, 1983.

little affection for the national idea. And the anti-British history of recent decades – whether mild-mannered and half amused in the manner of David Cannadine, or sneering and bitter like Tom Nairn and Perry Anderson – can be seen as a sustained rejection of British nationalism, and of the pride and loyalty that made Britishness into a coherent project and a serious ideal.

In fact, however, this ideal was made in England. There was no process of 'nation-building' in the United Kingdom, which was founded on a loyalty that preceded and transcended the modern state. This was the loyalty to England: not a nation or a doctrine or a state, but a *country*, the place where we belong. There are those who argue, like Liah Greenfeld, that nations emerged in Renaissance Europe, with the England of Henry VIII as the first clear example.[1] But rather than use the term 'nation' so boldly, I prefer to distinguish loyalties nurtured on ideas of a shared national identity – as in post-Romantic Germany[2] – and those formed in other ways, either through religion, or through dynastic authority, or, as in our case, through the experience of home.

'Our case', yes. But who are we? This is the question that the English never needed to ask themselves – not because they had a ready answer, but because England exerted so strong a hold over their imaginations that they instinctively knew who they were, without recourse to those concepts of nationhood, *Volk* and culture which have played such a large and questionable part in continental politics. England defined their membership. As to England itself –

---

[1] Liah Greenfeld, *Nationalism: Five Roads to Modernity*, Cambridge, Mass., 1992. The controversy here is endless and boundless. The Germans as described by Tacitus had a kind of national identity; the Jews have always described themselves as a nation, even in their millennia of wandering – and the term 'nation' came into common usage through the Jewish Bible. Still, it is the distinctions, and not the similarities, that matter for my purpose.

[2] Fichte's *Reden an die Deutsche Nation* (1807–8) illustrate the new concept of 'nation', invoked here as a summons: the Germans are being invited to *become* a nation, to define themselves as a unity, and to discover the grounds that would make this self-definition believable.

who could say what it was? Home, yes. But what was that? And what distinguished home from all those other places, known collectively as 'abroad', to which the English ventured and from which they returned in mild surprise at their good fortune?[1]

Political communities exist only if they can assert and defend themselves against their enemies and rivals; only if they can call upon a fund of patriotic sentiment; only if, in times of crisis, their members are prepared to sacrifice themselves for the common good. Without this shared sense of membership a community will disintegrate, like the artificial states left in their wake by collapsing empires. Of course, liberal thinkers, seeking the foundation of political order, have looked for something more rational, more free and less incipiently belligerent than the experience of membership. Their theories of the social contract make rational choice, rather than irrational sentiment, into the primary social fact. But all theories of the social contract begin from an assumption that *we* are deciding on our collective future. And if we are in a position to decide on our collective future, it is because we already have one – because we already belong together, as members of a social entity, bound by historical obligations at least some of which we did not choose. In other words, the social contract makes sense only on the assumption of an historical community, a 'first-person plural', which is not the result of a contract at all.

Nations are useful, because they enable people to rationalise their common fate, to *define* themselves as a 'we', and to prepare themselves for the competition – which may, at the limit, become a life-and-death struggle – between 'us' and 'the others'. But not all ways of forming a first-person plural are so conscious. There are other, more instinctive and more immediate, forms of membership which serve the purpose just as well or better, and which have the desired result of making it possible for people to live together in a state of mutual support.

[1] Thus it was that, in the last concerted effort of English writers and artists to revive the idea of England, they travelled to foreign parts, to enjoy their 'home thoughts from abroad'. See Paul Fussell, *Abroad*, Oxford and New York, 1980.

For example, there is the tribe, in which people think of themselves as bound by kinship and common descent. Members of the tribe join together instinctively in the face of external threat, and the idea of blood relationship – which may be little more than a myth – sustains their sense of mutual obligation. Religion provides a comparable criterion of membership and is, in its elementary forms, scarcely separable from the 'rites of passage' which form the 'unity across generations' of a tribe.[1] In modern communities, which are communities of strangers, religion and kinship sink behind the façade of the administrative state. But in times of emergency they may be used once again to conscript the people to a common purpose. Kinship then appears as 'race', and religion as a form of national loyalty.

Ideas of race, tribe and religion, which have played a dangerous part in continental politics, have also shaped English identity. But they were qualified and moderated by the concept of home. England was first and foremost a *place* – though a place consecrated by custom. There thus grew on English soil a patriotism not unlike that from which the word 'patriotism' derives – the patriotism of the Romans, in which the homeland, rather than the race, was the focus of loyalty. For seven centuries there was no other official test of Englishness than the fact of being born here. The Nationality Acts of the twentieth century were emergency measures. They built upon and modified the ancient loyalty of the English by extending citizenship to people who had come 'here' from 'abroad'. These new citizens were 'naturalised British subjects' – in other words, not really Englishmen at all, but people who had become *British*, by a strange process which overcame the *unnaturalness* that distinguishes foreigners. The disquiet over immigration was the result, it seems to me, not of racism, but of the disruption of an old experience of home, and a loss of the enchantment which made home a place of safety and

---

[1] See the exemplary argument of Emile Durkheim, in *Les formes élémentaires de la vie religieuse*, Paris, 1912.

consolation. Until this fatal disenchantment, immigrants were regarded by the English as newcomers to the home, entitled to hospitality while they found their feet. It was thus, for example, that the Huguenots were received, following the revocation of the Edict of Nantes in 1685; likewise the Dutch and German immigrants, who came in such numbers when the English borrowed foreign princes and recycled them as kings. And to this day the right of asylum is an untouchable provision of the English law, and one that survives despite widespread and criminal abuse of it.[1]

Of course, the experience of home is not exclusive to the English. Goethe's *Wilhelm Meisters Lehrjahre*, Hölderlin's 'Die Heimat', Eichendorff's 'Heimweh' (in *Aus dem Leben eines Taugenichts*), the landscapes of Caspar David Friedrich, Schubert's setting of Müller's *Winterreise* – such works paint an incomparable picture of man's need for home, and of the longing which is our destiny when home has been left behind. Hegel's dialectic describes thought itself as a venture into alienation, and homecoming as the redemptive goal – though a homecoming which 'knows the place for the first time'. Hegel set the pattern for German Romantic philosophy, and a century later we encounter in Heidegger the melancholy fragments of an idea which has its roots in national feeling, and which was to survive the experience of defeat only in distorted and guilt-ridden form.

That idea of home is, however, not the English idea, even though educated Englishmen used to warm to it spontaneously. The German *Heimkehr* is too mystical, too drastic, too much divorced from old and tried and customary things. The English idea of home was more down to earth and commonsensical. Yet it too was endowed with its own kind of unassuming magic.

---

[1] Recent hostility to immigration is surely to be explained in the same way. Disenchantment of the homeland is experienced as a loss of control. England, the English believe, is no longer 'ours'. In such circumstances hospitality (which implies ownership) becomes impossible. It is not *we* but *they* who are inviting these newcomers to stay. Resentment follows as a matter of course.

Home is not just a place; it is also what goes on there. A place *becomes* a home, by virtue of the habits that domesticate it. The English habits began with people who came to England from Jutland, Saxony and Scandinavia, and who were distinguished by their litigiousness. They established in their territory a remarkable system of law, which was to become the 'common' law of England, and which has survived into the twenty-first century. This system of law is sometimes described as 'judge-made' law – since it derives from individual cases, decided by the courts, rather than from decrees laid down by the sovereign. But the description is inaccurate. The common law is not an invention but a discovery. The judge's decision does not make the law: it applies the law, even when the law cannot be stated as a principle. Common law was understood from the beginning as the *law of the land*. That is, it belonged to *England*, and not to any resident – not even to the sovereign. William the Conqueror was accepted as king because he promised to uphold the law of England. This law remained the true sovereign of the country and, in some peculiar mystical way, was embodied in the land itself. The law of England was the habit, the 'being at ease', which turned the place into a home.

In the course of their history the English accepted monarchs of Norman, French, Scottish, Welsh, Dutch and German origin, even monarchs like George I who spoke no English, or monarchs like Cromwell who were not monarchs at all. They accepted them largely because they viewed their monarchs as creatures, and not creators, of the law. With the exception of Cromwell, each sovereign represented himself as entitled by law to his dominion, and – more importantly – as *subject* to the law and bound to uphold it. The point was made by the thirteenth-century judge Henry de Bracton, in his *De Legibus et Consuetudinibus Angliae* ('Of the Laws and Customs of England', *c.*1220, revised *c.*1250). The king, Bracton argued, lies below the law, since it is the law that appoints him. Bracton was not philosophising: he was transcribing the rooted English understanding of law, as something objective, permanent, and part of the furniture

of England, something to be not invented and imposed but
discovered and obeyed.

Many of the peculiarities of the English can be traced to this
conception of law. What is sometimes known as their 'individualism'
– that is, their disposition to affirm the right and responsibility of
individual action in all spheres of social life – is surely to be
attributed to their sense of being protected by the law from those
who might otherwise coerce them. Alan Macfarlane has shown that
this individualism has been a feature of English society from
medieval times.[1] And he reminds us of the extent to which the
Marxist caricature of history – according to which 'feudal' tenure
gives way to 'bourgeois' forms of ownership – misrepresents the
history of England, which was one of uninterrupted enterprise and
ownership. But perhaps Macfarlane does not go far enough, so as to
see English individualism for what it was: a common-law creation,
going hand in hand with forms of government that have their origin
in Anglo-Saxon times.

The common law endorses custom and tradition – indeed, it *is* a
kind of tradition. And it unites the land and the law in a manner that
gives human contours to both. A piece of earth is made safe by the
common law; and because it is common – in other words, coextensive
with the land itself – it becomes a familiar companion, an unspoken
background to daily dealings, an impartial observer who can be called
upon at any time to bear witness, to give judgement and to bring
peace. The common law therefore played an important part in the
sense of England as a home. It was the root cause of the law-
abidingness of the English, and of their ability to live side by side as
strangers in a condition of trust. All communities depend upon trust:
but in few communities does trust extend beyond the family; in
almost none does it embrace the stranger, while conceding his right
to *remain* a stranger, and to go about his business undisturbed.

[1] Alan Macfarlane, *The Origins of English Individualism: the Family, Property and
Social Transition*, Oxford, 1986.

England, however, was a society of reserved, reclusive, eccentric individuals who constantly turned their backs upon one another, but who lived side by side in a common home, respecting the rules and procedures like frosty members of a single club.[1]

But there were other factors contributing to the domestication of the English territory. Perhaps the most important among them, though it is the one least often written about today, was the easy-going magic attached to day-to-day observances. The English lived in a world that had been mystified, and they accepted this mystification as an evident improvement on the natural order. Ordinary things and everyday customs possessed a nimbus of authority, a quasi-divine and in any case mysterious *given-ness*, which was all the more remarkable in being accepted as a human artefact. The world of the English was a world of rituals, uniforms, precedents and offices. In any serious business they would spontaneously adopt another and higher tone, borrowing legal and biblical words, addressing their colleagues not directly but through some real or imaginary chairman, and creating a mystical body out of a mere gathering of people. Schools had their uniforms and began their days with an assembly in which hymns were sung, solemn words uttered and the spirit of the school invoked from the daïs. Their institutions were marked by ceremonies and offices, and housed in buildings clad in Gothic arches, barbicans and fairy pinnacles. Each defined not just a function but a form of membership. Barristers dined in their Inns and dons in their colleges; each village had its cricket team, its darts club and its Women's Institute. The English accepted titles, coats of arms and insignia of office as endowed with their own special magic, and the Royal College of Heralds was kept busy year upon year by their claims for privilege and precedence of a purely symbolic kind. Class, for them, was not an economic but a spiritual fact, and through their tenacious titles of nobility they rendered social differences by and

---

[1] This is not to say that the common law was sufficient to control the English during times of rebellion and riot, otherwise the Riot Act of 1725 would not have been necessary. Since that time, however, and until very recently, the law-abidingness of the English has been a constant object of admiration.

large acceptable, even to the losers. Titles, forms and the mystique of noble birth are costumes, through which the upper classes can display their difference and safeguard their privileges without flaunting their power. The English aristocrat was not a courtier, kowtowing to his sovereign in the city, but the heart and soul of the landscape where he resided, bearing a title that ennobled the country as much as it ennobled himself.

Monarchy was, for the English, not a form of political power, but a work of the imagination, an attempt to represent in the here and now all those mysterious ideas of authority and historical right without which no place on earth could be settled as a home. The English never suffered the transition described by Weber, from traditional to legal-rational forms of authority. For they held the law to be a part of what they loved – not something that would replace the charisma of monarchy and the magic of tradition, but a permanent condition that was intricately connected with both. Indeed, the English were a living refutation of Weberian sociology: the distinction between traditional and legal authority was inapplicable to a country in which law was a living tradition.

When human beings cease their wandering and mark out a place as their own, their first instinct is to furnish it with things which have no function – ornaments, pictures, knick-knacks – or with things which, while possessing a function, are valued for other reasons: for their associations, their beauty, their way of fitting in. This instinct for the purposeless has a purpose – namely to make these objects into an expression of ourselves and our common dwelling place, to endow them with the marks of order, legitimacy and peaceful possession. In other words objects, when they form part of the home, are endowed with a soul. This 'subjectivity of objects' lingers on after human deaths and departures, which is why:

> Home is so sad. It stays as it was left,
> Shaped to the comfort of the last to go
> As if to win them back. Instead, bereft

Of anyone to please, it withers so,
Having no heart to put aside the theft

And turn again to what it started as,
A joyous shot at how things ought to be,
Long fallen wide. You can see how it was:
Look at the pictures and the cutlery.
The music in the piano stool. That vase.[1]

The enchantment of things in the home is part of a larger spiritual project. Home has its customs, its rituals, its special times and places. Or if it does not, it is so much the less a home, so much the less a place to look back upon in adulthood, when anger and rejection have intervened. A kind of authority attaches to the way things are done at home, and to the roles of mother and father as they divide the labour between them. We take this experience of authority with us into later life, and the images of father, mother and the rituals that haloed them shape our subsequent emotions. All attempts to find solace in ritual and faith in some supreme parental love have their origins here, and the enchantment of religion should be seen not as the cause but as the effect of another and deeper enchantment, which is the natural inheritance of childhood.

Enchantment is a personalising force: it endows objects, customs and institutions with a moral character, so that we respond to them as we respond to one another. The English were more than normally alert to this and filled their lives with local forms of membership. Indeed, they related more easily to clubs, regiments, schools and teams than to human beings. Or rather, they found human relations more natural, more easy to conduct without embarrassment, when they occurred between people already joined by some shared form of membership. However far back we look into English history, we find those 'little platoons' of which Burke wrote:[2] focal points of local but

---

[1] Philip Larkin, 'Home is so Sad'.
[2] *Reflections on the French Revolution.*

durable loyalties. The English public school was a particularly clear example of this. Unlike the French lycée, it had a distinct and local personality. Its uniform, rituals and private language; its sacred precinct and invented games; its chapel, playing fields and hall – all these were so many forms of consecration, through which the 'we' of membership was created and the mind of the child shaped according to a corporate idea.

Corporate personality is a recognised concept in law, and one that the Romans, rather than the Saxons, might plausibly claim to have invented. But the legal concept merely ratifies a prior moral reality. Corporate bodies are, or become, persons, in the very real sense that we relate to them in a personal way. They are objects of praise and blame, of love and hatred, of gratitude and resentment. They do things and take responsibility for things, they flourish and decline as you and I do, and they too aim at happiness, longevity and peaceful coexistence with others. The English had a genius for creating corporate persons and their law was uniquely designed to encourage the habit. This, indeed, was the principal means whereby they domesticated their island. From the guilds to the trade unions, from the cathedral chapters to the colliery brass bands, from the public schools to the Boy Scouts and the Women's Institute, from the Worshipful Company of Farriers to the Institute of Directors, you will find the same 'clubbable' instinct, which prefers custom, formality and ritualised membership to the hullabaloo of crowds, and which imposes a quiet and genial discipline in place of spontaneous social emotion. The game of cricket was the eloquent symbol of this experience of membership: originally a village institution, which recruited villagers to a common loyalty,[1] it displayed the reticent and

---

[1] See the beautiful invocation of the cricket match in Mary Russell Mitford, *Our Village* (1824–1832), Folio Society edition, London, 1997, p. 69, in which participation is a sign of acceptance in the parish, so as 'to be authorized to say *we*'. Writing over a century later, Francis Brett Young describes the unchanged centrality of cricket in village life: *Portrait of a Village*, London, 1937, pp. 137–8. Young's survey of village institutions and clubs should dispel any scepticism that my remarks provoke.

understated character of the English ideal: white flannels too clean and pure to suggest physical exertion, long moments of silence and stillness, stifled murmurs of emotion should anything out of the ordinary occur and the occasional burst of subdued applause.

Home, too, is a moral person, and England was no exception. The English thought of their country – the place itself, and not just the people – in personal terms. They loved, hated, resented and praised it in equal measure. 'England, my England'[1] was a persistent theme of their literature; and already, in the history plays of Shakespeare, the corporate character of England took the central role in the drama. And it is precisely because they had this attitude to their *country* that the English found it so difficult to describe what they were. Their identity was formed through a *personal* relationship with a *place* – a place enchanted precisely by that personal relationship. Famously – notoriously – in an essay entitled 'England Your England', George Orwell defined his country as a bundle of sensations:

> The clatter of clogs in the Lancashire mill towns, the to-and-fro of the lorries on the Great North Road, the queues outside the Labour Exchanges, the rattle of pintables in the Soho pubs, the old maids biking to Holy Communion through the mists of the autumn morning – all these are not only fragments, but *characteristic* fragments, of the English scene.[2]

Forget that the particular impressions upon which Orwell seizes have disappeared, and were in any case no more than one man's special flavour. Is it not obvious that Orwell is describing not a people but a

---

[1] The phrase comes from the famous patriotic poem by W.E. Henley, entitled 'Pro Rege Nostro': 'What have I done for you, / England, my England?' D.H. Lawrence took it for the title for one of his most subtle short stories, exploring the ambivalence that nests in this innocent-seeming phrase.

[2] George Orwell, *The Lion and the Unicorn*, Harmondsworth, 1982, p. 36. It is interesting to observe that T.S. Eliot, faced with the problem of defining Englishness in *Notes Towards the Definition of Culture*, also embarked on an eccentric list of ephemera, including Derby Day and boiled cabbage cut into segments.

place, and at the same time identifying that place as a person? For Orwell too, England was not a nation or a creed or a language or a state but a home.

Things at home don't need an explanation. They are there because they are there. It was one of the most remarkable features of the English that they required so little explanation of their customs and institutions. They bumbled on, without anyone asking the reason why or anyone being able, if asked, to provide it. Continental observers often accused the English of a disrespect for reason, and an unwillingness to think things through. But if the result of thinking things through is paradox, why should reason require it? The French thought things through at their Revolution, and the result was accurately summarised by Robespierre: 'the despotism of liberty'. Impenetrable contradiction is what you must expect, when you try to start from scratch and refuse to recognise that custom, tradition, law and what Burke called 'prejudice' are the best that human beings can obtain in the way of government. So for many centuries the English were content with an unwritten constitution, a Parliament whose powers remained undefined, a form of sovereignty that could be traced to no specific institution and no single person, a system of justice in which the most important laws were not written down, and patterns of local administration that could not be explained even by those who operated them.

Home is a place where you can be yourself and do your own thing. Respect the rituals and the household gods, and for the rest you can please yourself. Therefore, when people feel at home, they allow themselves freedoms, hobbies and eccentricities. They become amateurs, experts and cranks. They collect stamps, butterflies or biscuit tins; they grow vegetables so large that nobody can eat them, and breed dogs so ugly that only an Englishman could look them in what might charitably be called the face. The eccentricity of the English follows as a matter of course, once it is recognised that they were at home in their world and safe there.

So too does their amateurism. The empire was acquired by roving adventurers and merchants who, trading with natives whom they could not or would not trust, summoned the law of Old England to conclude the deal and, in the wake of the law, the sovereign power that would enforce it. But it was not only the empire that was acquired in this way. Almost the entire social order of the country arose from private initiatives. Schools, colleges and universities; municipalities, hospitals, theatres; festivals and even the army regiments, all tell the same story: some public-spirited amateur, raising funds, setting out principles, acquiring premises, and then bequeathing his achievement to trustees or to the Crown, with the state appearing, if at all, only after the event, in order to guarantee the survival and propagation of good works that it would never have initiated by itself. Even the sovereign, embarking on some charitable enterprise, did so, as a rule, as a private individual, creating another autonomous institution outside the control of the state. That is the English way. It is the way of people who are at home, and who refuse to be bossed about by those whom they regard as outsiders. Their attitude to officialdom reflected their conviction that, if something needs doing, then the person to do it is you.

Of course the English received institutions from outside, and in particular from the Church of Rome, which Christianised them in the early years of their home-building. It is a striking fact, however, that, long before the Reformation, the Church *in* England had become the Church *of* England, and was chafing against papal authority in the name of ancient customs and home-made forms of mystery. The Church acquired the same dispersed and homely quality as the system of law courts, sheriffs and shires. It had two archbishops, both situated outside the capital. Its cathedrals were scattered around the country in small market towns. Its priests were appointed by private patrons, colleges or the sovereign, and when Henry VIII declared that it was he and not the Pope who was head of the Church, this was accepted by many people as entirely natural and in no way incompatible with the fundamental tenets of the Catholic faith. Even today the Church of England calls itself Catholic, and its Protestant credentials are like the Protestantism of England generally – not so much a protest at the Apostolic succession, as a refusal to be governed from elsewhere.

Put very briefly, the Church was *domesticated* in England, defined, like everything else, by a place rather than a doctrine or a chain of command. It adapted to the core religious experience of the English, which was of the consecrated nature of their island. Its ceremonies and liturgies sanctified the English language, the English landscape, the English law and institutions and the English Crown – the mysterious corporation sole which is also the supreme fiction in this fairy tale.

But enchantment breeds disenchantment and home invites rejection. From the outset, therefore, England was a place of dissent. Important sections of English society have scorned its traditions, its compromises and its aristocratic ways, seeing only the bare bones of power and oppression and the hypocrisy that has kept these things in place. Lollards, Luddites, Puritans, Dissenters and Roundheads stood always in the wings of English society, moving centre stage in times of crisis. Chartists, trade unionists and republicans have relayed their dissenting message to the modern world, and their imprint is as much to be discerned in the paragraph I quoted from Orwell as is that of the Crown or the Anglican Church.

But that only reminds us of the fact that English dissent, like the English Church, was domesticated. The violence of the Reformation once over, there was to be only one major disruption in the law and institutions of the country, and that was the Cromwellian interregnum, the meaning of which is the subject of deepest controversy among historians precisely because it is unique. The England that I knew in its twilight years was a country in which orthodoxy and dissidence lived side by side, sharing the same lodgings, the same diet, and even the same relaxation, like tetchy old bachelors who nevertheless prefer each other's company to the company of strangers. The Anglican Church stood in the same street as the Nonconformist chapels, sharing with them its Bible, its language and its repertoire of hymns. Republicans and monarchists sat side by side in the House of Commons, and trade unionists shot sarcasms at industrialists across the floor of the old House of Lords. Class resentment inhabited the same suit of clothes as social snobbery, and the most radical of gatherings might open with a reading of the minutes and close with a prayer.

To be sure, the English contained among their number a great many sneerers and scoffers: but they formed an accepted part of the organism, a chafing away from inside which created the comfortable impression that England itself was impregnable, since its quarrels were purely internal. And however furious those quarrels, the prevailing belief was that a solution could always be found to them, since common sense and compromise were the norms of English politics. In the light of this it is surely unsurprising that it is now over three hundred years since the last violent change in the form of government in England, and that only Denmark has had a longer record of peaceful political evolution.

Home is a focus of loyalty; it is also a place to live up to. Values and ideals adhere to it, and although these ideals develop, adapt and diversify, they are shaped by the core experience of refuge, which imparts to them an enduring national character. The sublime chivalry of Chaucer's 'parfit gentil knyght' survives in the modern idea of the gentleman, and the ethic of *Piers Plowman*, with its emphasis on godliness and honest toil, lives on in the Nonconformist conscience. Although the Germans, the French, the Greeks and the Turks (to name but four) have their versions of those ideals, there is a recognisable Englishness attached to our own and home-grown versions.

This does not mean that the English always had the *same* ideals. On the contrary, their corporate moral life was in a state of continuous flux. The English were amiable and even admirable in some periods, devious and manipulative in others. During the civil war, many reconstrued their patriotism in tribal and religious terms, influenced by Foxe's *Actes and Monuments* to view England as the

New Israel, carrying God's message to the world. Nevertheless, in England such sentiments exist in their violent form only briefly. By the end of the eighteenth century the tribal fervour had been domesticated, and William Blake, returning to the old puritan vision, invoked not Israel but Jerusalem, and not the English race but England's 'green and pleasant *land*'. His famous verses, set to music by Parry, became after the First World War the anthem of the brass band movement (which had already been in existence for a century), of the Suffragettes and finally of the Women's Institute. What had begun as a martial call to arms, threatening the overthrow of everything, ended, in a typically English manner, as a choral anthem for ladies.

Meanwhile, England had been moralised in another way, as the land of the free. Such was the England celebrated by Henry Fielding and Samuel Johnson, and the description was plausible, so long as you confined your attention to England, and ignored those places like Ireland and the Scottish Highlands which, while subject to the English Crown, were hardly protected by it. The swashbuckling adventurers spread across the globe, many of them making fortunes from the African slave trade. But no such condition as slavery was recognised by the laws of England – so it was established in the eighteenth-century case of James Somerset, an escaped Negro slave whose master unsuccessfully sued for his recovery in the English courts.

Subsequently, with the expansion of the empire and the war on slavery, the moralisation of England as the land of the free became the everyday theme of politics. The 'England expects' of Nelson echoed down the years of Victoria's long reign, and its last whispers reached the ears of those, like me, whose parents had served in the Second World War. The England that I knew was not merely to be enjoyed, it was to be *served*. A remarkable culture of service had been inculcated by its schools and clubs and professions. England was also a place of public spirit, charitable initiatives and institution-building, and although it contained its sponges and idlers, who demanded their 'rights' with the cavilling self-righteousness of Dickens's Mr Boffin, they were identified as people who were not 'doing their bit' for the country. England, I was taught, preferred duties to rights, and quiet cooperation to the obstinate demands of idleness.

At least, that was what I was taught at school. But it was not what I was taught at home. Nor was it what I learned in later years from the books of history and social criticism written by people of my parents' generation. I listened for the last breath of England amid the clamour of voices which denounced her. To many of the post-war writers the ideals of freedom and service were mere ideological constructs – 'ruling illusions' which, by disguising exploitation as paternal guidance, made it possible to ship home the spoils of empire with an easy conscience. All those features of the English character which had been praised in wartime books and films – gentleness, firmness, honesty, tolerance, 'grit', the stiff upper lip and the spirit of fair play – were either denied or derided. England was not the free, harmonious, law-abiding community celebrated in boys' magazines, but a place of class divisions, jingoism and racial intolerance. Look beneath every institution and every ideal, I read, and you find the same sordid reality: a self-perpetuating upper class and a people hoodwinked by imperial illusions into accepting their dominion. Some of those who wrote in this way were from the Celtic fringe – Raymond Williams, for example, and Tom Nairn, who expressed the old grievance against the English in an updated Marxian idiolect. Others, like E.P. Thompson, were quintessentially English, giving secular utterance to emotions which had once found outlet in the sermons of Nonconformist preachers. Anthony Sampson attacked the self-perpetuating élite of England – and in doing so became part of it. Perry Anderson dismissed English culture as a sham, fabricated by a wave of 'white emigrés' – a thesis taken up in other terms by Terry Eagleton. Correlli Barnett, in book after book, told of the price paid for an education system which promoted boyish virtues over scientific expertise, and for a political system which made honour and service into the highest values, at a time when cunning and brute force were the only conceivable defence. English culture was ransacked for its myths and hypocrisies, and the old English virtues made to look like worn-out theatrical costumes, designed for a farce which had long ago vanished from the stage.[1]

I was brought up amid this derision, in which some of the most intelligent voices of English post-war culture took part. And I began to think that there must be some other, gentler sound that the anti-imperialist, anti-capitalist, anti-aristocratic, anti-monarchical, anti-bourgeois, anti-authoritarian and, in short, anti-English hullabaloo was intended to drown. Although I was from the earliest age an intellectual and a troublemaker, something in me wished, even as a schoolboy, to be reconciled with the thing that everyone denounced, which some called England, some Britain, some the ruling classes and most just 'them'. Before proceeding with this elegy, it is worth revisiting those early years of doubt, for they were also the last years of England.

---

[1] Among the seminal works devoted to the debunking of England, the following are of special importance: Raymond Williams, *The Country and the City*, London, 1973; E.P. Thompson, *The Making of the English Working Class*, London, 1963, and *Whigs and Hunters: the Origin of the Black Act*, London, 1975; Perry Anderson, 'Components of the National Culture', in *New Left Review*, vol. 50, 1968; Anthony Sampson, *The Anatomy of Britain*, London, 1962 (a book that has been several times updated, in search of new grievances whenever the old ones have been answered); Correlli Barnett, *The Collapse of British Power*, London, 1972, and *The Audit of War: the Illusion and Reality of Britain as a Great Nation*, London, 1986.

Chapter Two

First Glimpses

Only towards the end was the English educational system controlled by the state, and even then it owed its character to private initiatives such as these: the grammar schools, established after the destruction of the monastic educational network, in order to teach grammar (i.e. Latin) to local children; the 'public' schools, some of them very ancient, founded with a view to providing education to the public at large; and the charity schools which sprang up in the seventeenth, eighteenth and nineteenth centuries, usually under the auspices of church or chapel.

Many of the public schools were intended to provide for the poor. The oldest of them, Winchester College, founded in 1387 by William of Wykeham, Bishop of Winchester (who had risen to that eminence from peasant origins), provided in its statutes for seventy 'poor and needy scholars', sixteen choristers and only ten 'commoners' (i.e. sons of the rich). However, as the schools expanded, they were rapidly colonised by an upper class which could afford to send its children away for their education. (This habit was greeted with amazement by an Italian visitor in 1500, who took it as a sign that the English were devoid of parental affection.) In the mid-nineteenth century the schools underwent extensive reforms, championed by Dr Thomas Arnold, headmaster of Rugby, who expanded their curriculum to include mathematics, modern languages and history, and who placed organised sport and evangelical Christianity at the centre of their social ethos. Thereafter, the public schools provided a model for secondary education in England, and one that was loved and resented in equal measure.

The England that I knew had been more profoundly influenced by the public schools than by any other educational institution. They provided its social and political élite, its army officers, a large part of its legal establishment and the more flamboyant and outspoken of its intellectuals. Documenting these facts, Anthony Sampson argued for the existence in English society of a self-perpetuating power structure based not on merit but on class: networks established at school were maintained in later life, with the public schoolboys acting in concert to retain the pickings for themselves.[1] Such a conclusion could be drawn only on the assumption that the public schools provided an education no better than the schools which had been taken over by the state. And this assumption was false.[2] When an education is available, the effect of which is to train an élite in the arts of government and public service, then it is scarcely surprising if the top positions in society are occupied by people who have enjoyed it. Still, it cannot be denied that the public schools had an upper-class image, and for those who resent such things, this was sufficient to condemn them.

My father was one of those who resent such things. Having been born and bred in industrial Manchester, and snatched away from school, despite intellectual promise, before completing his education, he acquired the full emotional repertoire of the unwilling underdog. He was conscious of his superiority, while trapped in a position where his gifts were not rewarded. In consequence he became an egalitarian: this alone enabled him to bear the humiliation of occupying the lowest rung in the teaching profession, while self-interested dunces grinned down at him from above. He raised his children in the Old Labour doctrine. England, we were taught, was

---

[1] Anthony Sampson, *The Anatomy of Britain*, London, 1962.

[2] For some of the arguments, see W.D. Rubenstein, *Élites and the Wealthy in Modern British History*, London, 1987, and especially the chapter entitled 'Education and the Social Origins of British Élites, 1880–1970'.

in the hands of an unscrupulous upper class, which owned the factories, controlled the government, monopolised the judiciary and exploited the workers. This aristocracy was maintained by an education system designed to perpetuate social inequality, and by an Anglican Church which offered social promotion to the conformists and the snobs. The only hope for the working class (of which my father remained, in spirit, a member, long after he had left it, and long after it had disappeared) was to nationalise the industries, disestablish the Church, abolish the monarchy and introduce a new educational system, with equality rather than privilege as the goal.

By and large, therefore, when it came to education my father was against it, just as his own father had been. Certainly, he believed, children should acquire the basic skills; but they should not be taught to 'get above themselves'. The public schools were responsible for the enduring social divisions in England, and the state ought to destroy them. But state schools produced their own form of social snobbery. The eleven-plus examination divided children into successes and failures; it therefore exacerbated the class conflicts that were undermining English society. There would be no hope for the English until the grammar schools too were abolished. That, roughly speaking, was the philosophy which I had imbibed, not with my mother's milk, but with my father's gall, which was distributed in equal abundance.

Early in the seventeenth century, Archbishop Laud initiated the search for an effective system of examinations, arguing that it would give poor scholars the opportunities that might otherwise be monopolised by the rich. The archbishop was subsequently executed by the puritan Parliament; had the indictment named examinations as the main offence my father would have regarded this judicial murder even more favourably than he did. Thanks in part to the legacy of Laud, the eleven-plus had been adopted as the most efficient way to advance the educational opportunities of the lower classes. It did not contribute to domestic harmony that I passed the exam and went to the local grammar school. But it contributed immeasurably to my chances in life, opening up prospects that few people without money now enjoy, and granting a vision of a world from which my father believed himself to have been excluded, and which he therefore wished to destroy.

High Wycombe Royal Grammar School had been founded in 1562; the ruins of its original building – a carcass of Gothic arches in flint and limestone – still stood by the London Road near the centre of town. The school had been several times rehoused, and was now contained in a neo-Georgian building of brick, dating from the 1920s. It stood on the crown of Amersham Hill, fronted by a stretch of green lawn and surmounted by a white clock tower which imparted to the façade a vaguely nautical appearance. The classrooms had tall sash windows, sturdy old-fashioned desks of beechwood, in which many generations of schoolboys had scratched their names, and panelled doors with brass handles. The masters wore gowns and the head, Mr Tucker, would take assembly in a mortarboard, the tassel of which dangled next to his glasses like a twirling spider on its thread.

Mr Tucker was ambitious for the school, and had consciously redesigned it on the model of Eton. Of course, the raw material being what it was, the school could never actually *be* another Eton. Still, that was Mr Tucker's goal, and the result was as near to a public school as chimpanzees could make it. There were rival 'houses', with boarders under the jurisdiction of housemasters. We had 'rugger' rather than football; there was a cricket pavilion and fives courts and all the military apparatus associated with a flourishing cadet corps. The full paraphernalia of public-school discipline was also imposed on us. The prefects had the ancient right – of which they took full advantage – to beat us with gym shoes; Mr Tucker and his deputy wielded the cane, while the head of juniors – a man with an impeccable Nonconformist conscience – would, on overcoming his scruples, lash his victim with enthusiastic swipes from a leather strap. We did not go so far as Eton in the way of uniforms, but any boy seen wearing the school blazer out of school without the cap was liable to punishment.

But it was not in these outward trappings of imperial Britain that the school excelled. Its real virtue lay in its teachers, two of whom were responsible for my first real glimpses of England, in those days when (though we did not know it at the time) last glimpses were the only glimpses to be had.

Mr Chapman taught physics in the upper sixth. He had read natural sciences at Cambridge, and even done research under the great Lord Rutherford, who imparted to him a passion for atomic theory. However, he was not cut out for a university career, having absorbed from his public school – Charterhouse – the love of adventure and service which was there counted higher in the scheme of things than knowledge. He joined the colonial service, was called up to defend various outposts of the empire against imaginary Germans, and then, after the war, found himself Assistant District Commissioner in Nigeria, responsible for the administration of the Ibo territories.[1]

Mr Chapman was one of many high-ranking colonial officers who had come home after decolonisation, in search of jobs compatible with their real but fragile self-esteem. Many of them entered the teaching profession, but not all of them could find the post they were seeking in a public school. High Wycombe Royal Grammar School was the next best thing, and Mr Chapman brought to it a personality and an experience that helped to give substance to Mr Tucker's fantasy of a suburban Eton. This is not to say that they liked each other: Mr Chapman, I learned, despised the headmaster as a snob and a philistine. But for both of them the old ideal was still alive, and in Mr Chapman it achieved a poignant embodiment which all his pupils acknowledged, even if they could not put it into words.

[1] The policy of recruiting public schoolboys to the highest positions in the colonial service was not, *pace* Sampson, endemic to the system. On the contrary, it was deliberately initiated in 1910, by the then chief Under-Secretary for the Colonies, Sir Ralph Furse, in order to place men of character and principle at the head of the service, which had been too often discredited by adventurers and profiteers. The policy was followed until the end of the colonial era, in 1948. See Robert Heussler, *Yesterday's Rulers*, Oxford, 1963.

It would be easy to caricature him as the archetypal British imperialist, 'the sweet, just, boyish master' of the world described by Santayana.[1] And it is true, there was something ineffably boyish about him, as he strode about the school with quick, nervous glances, as though hoping for someone to throw a ball at him. He had a deep chest, regular features, a clipped military moustache, and a complexion reddened and hardened by the tropics. His expression was challenging, but with his head held always slightly back from the thing he encountered. He had a slight shortness of breath as though from lungs hampered by exotic diseases, and he spoke with a moist public-school accent, never wasting words and often pausing to look around him as the silence resurged. In everything he seemed to betray those solitary habits of which it is impossible for the true colonist to divest himself, even after he has settled again in the country which he had mythologised as 'home' and which invariably disappoints him with its brash indifference to the sacrifice he has made on its behalf.

In time, however – and it took time to know Mr Chapman – the old imperialist caricature seemed less and less appropriate. My first inkling of this came when I stayed behind after a lesson, to express my puzzlement over something in our physics book. He seemed greatly relieved at my fumbling remarks, and told me that the A-level curriculum was in his view completely absurd, that he found himself compelled to teach physics entirely the wrong way round, and that mathematics and differential equations should come first. He also recommended a book – Tolansky's *Atomic Physics* – which he promised to lend to me if I took special care of it. Astonished by these confidences I retreated in confusion. But the next day he waylaid me in the 'quad', as our playground was pretentiously called, and placed the book in my hand. It was my first encounter with systematic science, and I was impressed by it. Most of all I

[1] George Santayana, 'The British Character' in *Soliloquies in England and Later Soliloquies*, London, 1922, p. 32.

appreciated the book's tone: not talking down like a school textbook or cheating its way to conclusions that it did not prove, but examining the truth impartially, as though conversing with an equal. It was one of the virtues of the English educational system that the higher forms of learning could from time to time descend upon the lower and remove the dross of condescension.

When I returned the book, Mr Chapman informed me that he had invited some of the senior boys to his house for dinner, and that he would like me, although still a junior, to be one of the party. By 'dinner' he meant the evening meal, which we at home called 'tea'. Later I learned that these contrasting idioms belonged to two different sociolects, and that the relation between them enshrined the entire comedy of the English class system. At the time, however, I was intrigued by the master's words. The invitation, and the language used to express it, seemed like two expressions of a single fact: Mr Chapman's loneliness. No one in our school accosted him without sensing this loneliness, and without experiencing a sentiment of involuntary respect, such as you might entertain towards a monk or an explorer who had detached himself from worldly things for the sake of a good that could not be explained in the world's tainted language, and which you could therefore merely acknowledge in silence.

Mr Chapman lived in a modern block of flats, amid lawns and shrubs, bordered on one side by an elegant Victorian house, and on the other by a busy road. It was a dreary development, wholly characteristic of the new suburban England – a plain brick tower with draughty concrete staircases and metal-framed windows, enjoying generous views over the neighbouring townscape, and also spoiling it. It occurred to me later that Mr Chapman had chosen this place for its anonymity: only this characterless tenement, which could be built anywhere and which would always look like nowhere, suited his spirit, destined as it was to wander without roots in a country which neither acknowledged nor remembered the mission which it had sent him abroad to perform.

The living room consisted of a dining table and a few not very comfortable modern armchairs arranged in front of an electric fire. In the corners stood carved figures of teak and ebony, which poked their grim faces into the unfamiliar air of England with a mute refusal to belong. Tribal masks stared from the white plaster walls, and elephant tusks jousted on the mantelpiece. To Mr Chapman these objects were trophies which would always, in his own eyes, distinguish him. For me, in my juvenile snobbery, they were kitsch. The same was true of the only object which seemed not to belong with them – a nineteenth-century oil painting of Beethoven, with blazing red-rimmed eyes and greenish skin, chord upon chord knocking inside his leonine skull and threatening to burst out at any moment with a blare of brass and timpani.

Teachers who entertain their pupils to dinner run a great risk of appearing ridiculous, especially if, like Mr Chapman, they have no wife to take charge. But Mr Chapman was not ridiculous as he waited on those four tongue-tied louts at table, serving unfamiliar delicacies like smoked salmon and duck in orange sauce. He treated us as men, and even referred to us as men. Such, I later learned, was the public-school idiom – an idiom fraught with moral and historical significance. It seemed entirely natural that this middle-aged person with rolled-up shirtsleeves, who went back and forth between kitchen and dining room, pausing every now and then to sip from a tumbler of whisky and soda, should be talking to us of lessons, problems, A-levels and the daftness of an educational system which couldn't have been daft at all if it provided an opportunity like this one. He told us stories of Lord Rutherford and explained the experiments that led to the splitting of the atom. He introduced us to wine and the vital difference, which none of us had known, between claret and burgundy. He mentioned his days in Africa, and even told us a story or two, full of humour and irony, of his happy times in the jungle, mapping for the first time the territory of the Ibo-speaking tribes. He was not showing off, but simply helping us to understand that the world is larger by far than High Wycombe, and deeper by far than any A-level textbook. And then, after dinner, he sat us down to listen to the gramophone which he had just acquired and of which he was very proud.

Those were the early days of long-playing records, and the Hungarian String Quartet had just issued their complete set of Beethoven. He played the F major *Rasumovsky*. I was only just beginning to discover music, and was hearing this piece for the first time. But it made a profound impression: the slow movement in particular seemed to crystallise and beautify the loneliness that I sensed in Mr Chapman. He encouraged me to stay after the others had left and, when we were alone, explained how much Beethoven meant to him. He particularly cherished the string quartets – so serious and religious and thoughtful. I had read books in which music was described in that way; but I had never heard it said. And once again I sensed the vast fund of fertile solitude which made Mr Chapman something more than a man.

After this I would often call on him. I ate his food, drank his whisky and listened to his records – while he moved in the background, reading, marking, washing dishes and persisting, my presence notwithstanding, in his solitary ways. He listened to my troubles, offered kind advice, but about himself was reticent, with the peculiar splenetic reserve that was so often admired in the English. Only one subject would prompt him to hold forth and that was Africa. He had seen his role as ADC in altruistic terms: he was bringing civilisation to the uncharted jungle. The taxes he collected, often in the teeth of rebellious elders, were to be justified by schools, clinics and the necessities of modern life. He had learned the Ibo language, befriended the local chieftains and witch doctors, devoted days and nights to the well-being and advancement of a people whose need for protection evidently pleased him greatly. He had also found himself in hair-raising scrapes, which he related with a calm objectivity as though they had happened to someone else. You sensed his streak of heroism the moment he withdrew from mentioning it.

Although I had been brought up to sneer at the British Empire, I could not sneer at Mr Chapman, for whom the empire was not a commercial enterprise but a moral task, the only reward of which (although this, to him, was sufficient) lay in the satisfaction of doing his duty. If that makes him sound naive, so be it. But his naivety was of the sublime kind that idealises what it touches. The Ibo tribes appeared in his narratives as endowed with a childlike innocence and a touching eagerness to please. They learned and unlearned daily, like children, and, again like children, they visibly grew into manhood under his care. He loved them with the severe just love of a Victorian father. And because he had an enquiring mind he recorded their habits, their gods, their sacred tales and rituals. He let me read what he had written and it made a deep impression on me. I decided to become an anthropologist. The ambition did not last long; nevertheless, Mr Chapman encouraged it and guided my reading. Soon I was familiar with Frazer, Malinowski, Lévy-Brühl and Radcliffe-Brown, and often we would discuss the 'elementary forms of the religious life', as Durkheim had described them.

To my astonishment I discovered that Mr Chapman was a Christian. His scientific interest in pagan customs had not tarnished the Anglican vision which dawned on him at Charterhouse, and which had persisted through his sweaty adventures like a cool quiet angel preceding him down jungle paths. I had lost my little faith and not regained it, and I became aware that he disapproved – although without expressing it. Nothing would have prompted him to speak openly of something so intimate as God the Father. Nevertheless, a slight tension arose whenever I applied the methods of comparative anthropology to the rituals and doctrines of the English. For Mr Chapman, I realised, the Church of England was sacred and untouchable, like England itself. The fact that England had, during his absence, changed beyond recognition, only enhanced its holy ambience in his memory. England for him was no longer a real place, but a consecrated isle in the lake of forgetting, where the God of the English still strode through an imaginary Eden, admiring His works.

And another thing too astonished me. In a rare moment of

confidence, after an evening of quartets and whisky, Mr Chapman confessed that he was married, with a son at public school – I forget which. Except, he added, that his wife, defeated by the tropics, had left him and successfully petitioned for a divorce; nor did he see his son. In his own eyes, however, he was still married, the vow of marriage being eternal and unbreakable. He made the point with an emphatic sniff, so as to place it beyond discussion. And that was all he ever said about his failed domestic life.

As time went on, however, he would betray more and more of his inner feelings. He let me understand that I was not his favourite pupil; this place being reserved for another boy whom I did not know, but who had impressed Mr Chapman as a model of youthful promise – handsome, fair, blue-eyed, well-mannered, well-spoken, clever but not too clever, a sportsman, and in fact the kind of manly all-rounder who had been the public school ideal. Mr Chapman began to refer more and more frequently to this paragon. By so doing he was able to convey obliquely what he would never have said to my face, namely, that I was too uncouth, too rebellious, too much of an intellectual, too much given to darkness and poetry and mystical things to be wholly likeable. But he also conveyed the astounding fact that he loved this boy with a distant but unquenchable passion, and that he poured into this passion all the pent-up idealism of his nature.

In the England that I am trying to evoke, the platonic love of boys was not merely frequent; it was part of the idealisation of schooldays which fed the illusions and the disillusions of the upper class.[1] Single-sex schools were the norm and so were romantic relations between boy and boy and girl and girl. And when, as was inevitable, a teacher felt a strong attraction for one of his pupils he was not afraid to let it show itself – provided, of course, it showed itself in chaste and honourable ways. Plato argued that homosexual love, when it achieves physical release, sullies both subject and object. When,

[1] See the once popular 'David' books by E.F. Benson, focusing on life at school and university, in which love never escaped from the charmed circle of adolescent boys: *David Blaize* and *David of King's*.

however, it is sublimated in discourse, so as to impart knowledge and culture to the young, it becomes one of the highest of human goods, higher in its way than the love between man and woman. Plato was not altogether wrong. But the lesson he taught has been forgotten. For such as Mr Chapman homosexual desire was an abomination, and the thought of it was banished from his world. And because of this there grew that other and more mysterious thing – the love of a boy on the verge of manhood, not as the object of desire but as the recipient of knowledge and prowess, the one to whom all hard-won gifts should be conveyed in tribute, the inheritor who would redeem through his beauty the sacrifice of a life lived honourably and sadly and well. This was the English version of Plato's ideal, and if it was so often betrayed, it was not by such as Mr Chapman.[1] On the contrary, he showed why 'repression', which had become, thanks to the vulgarisers of Freud, a term of abuse, was really the name of our highest virtue and the one on which all other virtues depend.

The English took repression to heroic lengths, however – to such lengths as sometimes to negate its benign purpose, which is to make people lovable. Mr Chapman retired from the grammar school and went to live in an equally dreary block of flats in Horsham. I would visit him there and continued to take comfort in his austere disapproval, which contrasted so vividly with my own satirical flippancy. At last it seemed right, there being no professional relation between us, to address him by his Christian name. At school I was Scruton to both masters and boys – such was required by the public-school etiquette. Mr Chapman had begun to call me Roger, though not without a lengthy apprenticeship in formality. One day, after a glass or two, I asked him whether I could call him Guy – for this, I had discovered, was his name. He coloured and looked away. To only one person, he said, was he Guy. There was an awkward silence. Then he added that his name was not really Chapman, but Granville-

---

[1] For some of the facts, written from a hostile perspective, see Alisdare Hickson, *The Poisoned Bowl: Sex, Repression and the Public School System*, London, 1995.

Chapman, and that sometimes, out there in Africa, when he had made some particular friend, and it felt right, which it sometimes did, to be on first-name terms, he would let the other chap call him Granville. If I liked, I could call him Granville. Needless to say, I never did. He remained Mr Chapman, a figure drifting inexorably into solitude, a sad captain of the empire who guarded behind his stiff exterior a tender, vulnerable and dutiful heart.

The other teacher who afforded a glimpse of England was one whom I never studied with, though I knew enough of him to guess that he was in many respects the opposite of Mr Chapman. His name was Derek Broadbridge, and his favourite pupils called him Derek. He taught English and because I was in the science sixth it was only by hearsay that I could enjoy his lessons. Nevertheless, I had particular friends who were studying A-level English; they told me what they were reading and I followed suit. They imitated Derek Broadbridge's manner, his severity of judgement, his frowning refusal to be pleased by works of literature which lay outside the Great Tradition. It was my first encounter with so-called Leavisism, and even at two removes the effect was devastating. I read *Revaluation* and *New Bearings in English Poetry* before I had anything better than a casual acquaintance with the works discussed in them. I don't say that this was a good thing. But it was not wholly a bad thing either. I discovered literature not as a realm of pleasure but as a realm of judgement; it really mattered – so my friends told me, with much sorrowful shaking of the head – that popular culture was trash, that sentimentality had rotted the heart of literature, and that only here and there were works to be come across in which *felt life* was still acknowledged as the final and inescapable value.

It is easy to caricature Dr Leavis's position, and in time I rebelled against its killjoy attitudes and its puritanical sniffing after errors of taste. Nevertheless, it afforded one of the last glimpses of the high culture of England. Perhaps it is significant that this champion of high culture was a product of the lower-middle class, who devoted himself to undermining the credentials of the patrician literary establishment, as typified by Bloomsbury. For this gave him a Bunyanesque authority for those, like me, who came from the same occluded background.

Derek Broadbridge was only one of a generation of teachers who had been influenced by *Scrutiny* – the learned journal of which Dr Leavis was editor – and by the book *English in Schools*, edited by Leavis's collaborator Denys Thompson, which brought together a devout following of English teachers in order to relay the message of *Scrutiny* to the generation that emerged from the war.

Later, at Cambridge, I had the good fortune to meet young men who had been educated at King's College School Wimbledon, a fee-paying school connected with King's College London, to which Victorian bohemians like the Rossettis and Sickert had been sent in order to escape the harshness of the old public schools.[1] King's College School had acquired a similar ethos to High Wycombe RGS, and its intellectual life was dominated by Frank Miles, a Leavisite master who had instilled the quiet conviction that art matters because life matters, and that life is nothing without art – the very same conviction which radiated from the distant wing of the RGS where Derek Broadbridge held court among his disciples. Two of these Wimbledon men are among my closest friends, and our mutual understanding owes everything to those formative years. However much we smile now at the excesses of our teachers, they opened a door on to the moral and spiritual landscape of England. Nothing was ever the same again, and even the inevitable work of mourning, which Dr Leavis himself accomplished so badly, was a joy to us, once we had seen and understood the grandeur of the vanishing realm which he mapped out.

Mr Broadbridge had founded an intellectual society among his keener pupils; it was called 'The Thirteen' since its members were

---

[1] This discipline was perhaps not so much harsh as easily abused. It was later to be described in *Tom Brown's Schooldays*, the novel by Thomas Hughes, published in 1857, describing the Rugby of Dr Arnold (whom Hughes revered), where the tyrannical bully Flashman negated the 'muscular Christianity' that was the true purpose of the school.

limited to that number. He himself had ceased to attend, believing that young people should learn the art of 'practical criticism' as it had been taught in his Cambridge days, by experiment and discussion among themselves. One or two girls from Wycombe High School had been invited to join. And when the thirteen found itself reduced for some reason to twelve, I too was invited.

The meetings usually took place outside school, in living rooms from which family and friends had been excluded. The discussion was introduced by someone reading a short paper on some novel, story or poem, in order to show that it was or was not part of the tradition. There was a tense and troubled atmosphere, as in the bunker of high command on the eve of battle. Defeat and victory hung by a thread, and each out-of-place remark jeopardised the world's survival. No particular member was responsible for this atmosphere; it arose like a cloud of steam from our mental exertions and from our sense of being watched. Derek Broadbridge kept vigil over us; so too did Dr Leavis. And behind them stood the ranks of heroes – Shakespeare, Lawrence, Wordsworth, Eliot (both T.S. and George) – all brim-full of interest in our words and feelings, as we stumbled to do justice to their great bequest.

Of course, our discussions were pretentious and naive. What else could they be? When called upon to deliver a 'paper', I spoke about Rilke's *Duino Elegies*, which I had come across by accident, and of which I understood hardly a line. My words were met by stony faces, broken by occasional knowing smirks, since it had been discovered – whether by Mr Broadbridge or Dr Leavis or some other Scrutineer I couldn't tell – that modern German literature is no good, no good at all. It lacks the precious commodity – felt life – without which every written word is wasted.

I set out in search of this felt life that Dr Leavis recommended, and which was contained, apparently, in the novels and stories of D.H. Lawrence, in the Great Tradition of the English novel and in those poets – Blake and Wordsworth, for instance – whose moral vision would put us in touch with ourselves. And I was granted another glimpse of England. Although the Leavisites put their faith in life, and pointed to fictional characters who embodied it, they did not actually find life in the world around them. What they found was a machine, run on 'technologico-Benthamite' principles. True culture had been wiped out by a mass-marketed substitute, and real feelings replaced by sentimental fakes. As for 'life', you could find it only in the records of a vanished age. Prominent among these records were the descriptions of village society by George Sturt, whose *Change in the Village* (1912) and *The Wheelwright's Shop* (1926) commemorated the 'organic community' of nineteenth-century rural England at the moment when it was disappearing for ever.

I read these books, as I tried to read everything that Dr Leavis recommended. And I found myself converted to a way of thinking which was fundamental to the English idea. My father too was a convert, won over not by George Sturt but by rural idealists who wished to return the land to the common people, and who wrote illustrated books about green fields, shire horses, stone walls, wooden lathes and hedgerows – the very same hedgerows so many of which had been planted to enclose the common land. My father had come south in order to turn his back on mills, warehouses, factories and unending grimy terraces, and to discover the 'real' England – the green and pleasant land which the capitalists had destroyed elsewhere. Of course, they were busy destroying it in High Wycombe too. But – and in this he was quintessentially English – my father did not accept the fact. He wandered through our ruined town hunting out the visible tokens of its past – the old watercourses and silted mill-races, the half-timbered lofts which had housed the turners, joiners and polishers of the furniture industry, the cobbled yards where horses once had dozed and the coppiced scrublands which supplied the basket trade.

Later I was to encounter another kind of socialist, who perceived the world in the hard-headed terms prescribed by Marx, and who dismissed the whole rural theme as nostalgia or worse: an ideological construct which erased the workers from the picture of England, a veil drawn over realities far from green and far from pleasant.[1] For Raymond Williams, who taught English at Jesus College, Cambridge, where I went from school, the rural idyll was a usurpation of the landscape, a means whereby the upper class immortalised its possession of England, while banishing the industrial hell which financed its indolence.[2]

When at university I listened to such arguments with respect. But I could not help noticing that the people who expressed them tended to live either in wistaria-clad colleges, or in villages beyond the commuter belt, where horny-handed farmers would sit beside them in the pub and from time to time include them in a round of drinks. Not one of them lived by choice in a modern city, unless it were some salubrious and cultivated neighbourhood of London. When, in his fiction, Raymond Williams took time off from his grievances, it was to give his own version of English pastoral, with descriptions of a 'border country' where rural rhythms accompany the vanished decencies of working-class life. True, Williams was Welsh (sort of). But that only served to remind me of the book (subsequently made into a film) which had done most to inspire my father's revulsion against the industrial townscape – Richard Llewellyn's *How Green Was My Valley* (1939). Wherever you turned, you found the English wedded to an idealised and idyllised version of their country, in which the towns had either been removed from the picture, or else reduced to the manageable version which Trollope had immortalised – the cathedral city organised around the market and the church.

The England that I knew cannot be understood without this strange and enduring attitude to the countryside. During the two world wars of the twentieth century there sprang up a crop of patriotic literature designed to recall what we, as a country, were fighting for. Even when the word 'Britain' appeared in the title – and this was rarely – the text and the illustrations made it clear that it was

---

[1] Notable, and eminently sensible, is John Barrell's *The Dark Side of the Landscape: the Rural Poor in English Painting 1730–1840*, Cambridge, 1980, which analyses the systematic exclusion of the rural poor from English landscape painting.

[2] See especially *The Country and the City*, London, 1972.

England which was at stake, England being, first and foremost, the countryside.[1]

This literature was not the invention of war, but the continuation in urgent form of a long-standing project. It drew upon the works of such real and self-imagined countrymen as Richard Jefferies, W.D. Hudson and H.J. Massingham; it took up the themes of Lady Eve Balfour and the Soil Association (still active today in defence of organic farming); it harked back to Ruskin and the pre-Raphaelites, and further to the Lakeland poets and the idylls of Shakespeare. It achieved influential but soggy embodiment in the post-First-World-War speeches of Prime Minister Stanley Baldwin – speeches designed in some way to justify the otherwise senseless slaughter that had deprived the country of its bravest youth.[2]

However, it would be wrong to see these pastoral invocations only as responses to war. Nor are they a mere continuation of the lament over industrialisation and the destruction of landscape, which began in the early nineteenth century. The roots go back much further in time – at least to Spenser and even, with a stretch of the imagination, to the Anglo-Saxon poem, *The Phoenix*. Moreover, the principal texts *precede* the real destruction and create an inimitable sense of England as a society rooted in a landscape, growing from topography and climate under the protection of a unique religion and law. The turning points in English literature can be seen as attempts to *re-enchant the land*, as it was re-enchanted in Shakespeare's Arden, in Milton's Eden, in Gray's Elegy, in the poetry of John Clare, in the novels of Fielding, in Blake's lyrics and mystical writings and – pre-eminently – in the *Prelude* of Wordsworth. Housman's 'land of lost content' is mourned because the poet's impoverished imagination

---

[1] Notable are: Harold Nicolson's *England: an Anthology*, London, 1944; the series of pamphlets published by the English Association; OUP's collection on Shakespeare's England (1916); Ernest Barker's *The Character of England*, London, 1947 etc. The build-up to the First World War and the inter-war period also produced such books, for example, Esmé Wingfield-Stratford's *History of English Patriotism*, London, 1913, and J.B. Priestley's *English Journey*, London, 1934.

[2] Stanley Baldwin, *On England*, London, 1926.

could fill it only with substitute people, postcard peasants who had no place on the living earth. The *real* tradition of English literature continued in its ancient way – not grieving over a Merrie England that had never existed, but re-enchanting the landscape, as Hardy and Hopkins did, as Lawrence did and as Eliot did in *Four Quartets*. Those writers turned to the landscape not in order to sentimentalise it, but in order to discover another order, a hidden order, which had been overlaid by history but which was, nevertheless, the true meaning of that history and the deep-down explanation of our being here.

Even when writers turned their attention to the urban realities, it was very often with a view to endowing them with some of the soulful permanence that had been written into the landscape. The 'Five Towns' of Arnold Bennett, for example, are not temporary excrescences thrown up by industry, but places of deep settlement, with their own glamour and domesticity, even with some of the tranquillity of those 'sweet especial rural scenes' in Hopkins. Lowry showed the industrial towns to this effect in his paintings, and Betjeman in a similar way glamorised the suburbs. The crucial point is not that English art and literature took refuge in the pastoral and the idyllic, but that it was an art and literature of *place*. Its inner goal was to internalise the topography of England, to remystify it and to deliver it up as a home.

Of course, there is more to it than that. But it is this vision of English art and literature that we find in Leavis – not always in his literary criticism, which gave pride of place to such urbane and urban sensibilities as those of Donne, Carew and Marvell, but in his social criticism, and in his prescriptions for the spiritual health of the common reader. This vision was communicated to me, in however oblique and distorted a way, by the broadcasts from Broadbridge. Henceforth I walked through the streets of High Wycombe, and along the towpaths of Marlow (where we had recently moved), with a new and exhilarating sense of treading sacred ground. And henceforth the English countryside – which hardly existed in our neighbourhood except as a rumour – was an immovable part of England as I imagined it, to be fought for before all lesser things.

How strange and sudden and solitary were those glimpses of England I know only now. At the time they were like revelations: in a certain measure they told me who I was, and why; and their very fragmentariness inspired me to complete the picture – to complete it not in the ruined world around me, but in myself. I knew I could never be like Mr Chapman; I was by formation a rebel, a dissenter, a bohemian, and besides, Mr Chapman's world had vanished. And I came to suspect that, Dr Leavis notwithstanding, French and German culture would mean more to me than English. But those facts confirmed me as an exile. When later I travelled far from home it was in order to understand it as home; England was the place to which I had never truly belonged, and to which I could belong only by returning from foreign regions, inspired by my own 'home thoughts from abroad'.

Chapter Three

English Character

A century ago there appeared a book by Charles H. Pearson called *National Life and Character*. Subtitled 'a forecast' the book predicted that the distinctive features of the English – notably their independence and dutifulness – would disappear under the impact of socialism, that the state would gradually replace the family as the guardian of social reproduction, and that a habit of dependency would extinguish the ancient virtues and the old improving risks. Pearson had been Minister of Education in the Australian province of Victoria, and viewed with alarm the impending retreat from the empire and the erosion of the pride and self-discipline which made empire possible. His book – despite the accuracy of its main predictions – would now be dismissed as rambling, inconsequential and even racist in its distinction between lower and higher breeds of people.

At the time, however, it created a stir, and the subsequent decades saw a spate of writings devoted to the English character – writings twice made urgent by the need to explain and justify war in England's defence. Ernest Barker's *National Character and the Factors in its Formation* (1927) offers a comprehensive answer to Pearson, tracing the still living virtues of the English to their geographical, institutional and cultural sources, in what is surely a *tour de force* of imaginative (and sometimes fantastical) scholarship. Arthur Bryant (*The National Character*, 1934) argues that the Englishman is distinguished by an intense 'at-oneness' with his environment, which Bryant traces to the three basic factors of race, geography and climate. Some, like W. Macneile Dixon (*The Englishman*, 1931) emphasise the ideal of the gentleman and the aristocratic style which rises above adversity with so little apparent effort, while E.M. Forster ('Notes on the English Character' in *Abinger Harvest*, 1936) suggests that the Englishman is 'essentially middle class' and therefore solid, cautious and efficient, though with an undeveloped heart and a lack of imagination. J.B. Priestley (*The English*, 1973) identifies the essence of Englishness (the 'English secret') as the habit of depending upon instinct and intuition rather than abstract reasoning. Stanley Baldwin (*The Englishman*, 1940) emphasises self-government, and the virtues of tolerance, compromise and considerateness which supposedly made it possible, while George Orwell (*The Lion and the Unicorn*, 1941) finds his paradigms of Englishness among the old working class, with their grumbling acquiescence in arrangements which they did not choose and their unflappable stoicism in emergencies.

Surveying this literature, much of it written with passion and conviction, and most of it gathering dust in unvisited sections of unscholarly libraries, one is struck by the almost universal belief that there is, or was, such a thing as the English character, however hard it may be to define it in words or illustrate it through a clear example. Interestingly enough, Macneile Dixon comes up with such an example in the person of Shakespeare, an inspired choice, given that we know little about Shakespeare the man, and are not all convinced that the person whom we know by that name is the real author of the plays.[1]

Still, these books would not have existed without a subject, even if they were also to some measure inventing it. The English were recognised not only by themselves but by visitors and travellers as a distinct human type. Some of the best books about this type were

[1] Macneile Dixon was, of course, a Scot, Professor of English at Glasgow University; it never occurred to him, however, that this disqualified him from writing as an Englishman.

written by foreigners, as they endeavoured to understand a phenomenon which seemed to defy the known laws of human nature. The
Spanish-American philosopher George Santayana, the French psy-
chologist Emile Boutmy, the Belgian critic Emile Cammaërts, the
Indian sage Nirad Chaudhuri and the Czech novelist and playwright
Karel Čapek all wrote interestingly during the twentieth century
about the English, and they all agreed on two fundamental
observations: that the English were in their mutual dealings both
kind and remote, and that this feature was owed partly to human
institutions and partly to the cool, dull, uniform weather of their
country. Two representative quotations, one from Čapek, the other
from Santayana, will serve to illustrate the theme:

> . . . if you get to know them closer, they are very kind and gentle; they
> never speak much because they never speak about themselves. They
> enjoy themselves like children, but with the most solemn, leathery
> expression; they have lots of ingrained etiquette, but at the same time
> they are as free-and-easy as young whelps. They are hard as flint,
> incapable of adapting themselves, conservative, loyal, rather shallow
> and always uncommunicative; they cannot get out of their skin, but it
> is a solid, and in every respect excellent skin. You cannot speak to
> them without being invited to lunch or dinner; they are as hospitable
> as St Julian, but they can never overstep the distance between man
> and man. Sometimes you have a sense of uneasiness at feeling so
> solitary in the midst of these kind and courteous people; but if you
> were a little boy, you would know that you could trust them more
> than yourself, and you would be free and respected here more than
> anywhere else in the world; the policeman would puff out his cheeks
> to make you laugh, an old gentleman would play at ball with you, and
> a white-haired lady would lay aside her four-hundred-page novel to
> gaze at you winsomely with her grey and still youthful eyes.[1]

Instinctively the Englishman is no missionary, no conqueror. He

---

[1] Karel Čapek, *Letters from England*, tr. Paul Selver, London, 1925, popular edition
1927, pp. 174–5.

prefers the country to the town, and home to foreign parts. He is rather glad and relieved if only natives will remain natives and strangers strangers, and at a comfortable distance from himself. Yet outwardly he is most hospitable and accepts almost anybody for the time being; he travels and conquers without a settled design, because he has the instinct of exploration. His adventures are all external; they change him so little that he is not afraid of them. He carries his English weather in his heart wherever he goes, and it becomes a cool spot in the desert, and a steady and sane oracle amongst all the deliriums of mankind. Never since the heroic days of Greece has the world had such a sweet, just, boyish master.[1]

Of course, those are the words of accomplished writers, and writers impose form and order even where form and order are not to be found. Nevertheless, I recognise in their words a polished and idealised version of the England I knew, and they prompt a deep and difficult question. When we have enumerated the characteristics of the English, how do we distinguish between the essential and the accidental, the real causes of the human type, and the temporary and local effect of it? The question could be asked of any people on earth and does not often admit of an answer. But it is an interesting question, and can always be usefully pursued, even when no answer is forthcoming. For it is the very same question that we have for one another, when we strive to know what can be varied, and what must stay the same, in the people with whom we live.

There have been visitors to England, like Alexander Herzen and Richard Wagner, who wrote damning indictments of the national character. There have been Englishmen, in our century especially, whose distaste for their country has driven them into exile, there to rail like D.H. Lawrence against vices too deeply rooted to be cured. By and large, however, those who have written of the English have been favourably impressed by them, finding fault usually with qualities that the English themselves condoned – the coldness which

---

[1] George Santayana, *Soliloquies in England and Later Soliloquies*, London, 1922, p. 32.

is reserve, the hypocrisy which is compromise, the snobbery which is decorum and the stubbornness which is also pride. In their overseas adventures the English could be insolent and cruel. In Ireland, in North America and sometimes in India, Englishmen behaved like despicable criminals. Yet they were schooled in self-criticism, and unwilling to excuse a crime, merely because it was theirs. The narrative of their crimes was itself written by Englishmen and their excesses were no sooner committed than condemned.[1]

Of course, England changed over time. Foreign visitors in Elizabethan times came away with the impression of a fiery, devious and intemperate people, who stood greatly in need of both outer and inner control.[2] Voltaire, Montesquieu and their contemporaries praised the institutions of government, as these had emerged after the Glorious Revolution of 1688; they also admired the toleration, freedom and individualism of the people. Visitors to Victorian England (Hawthorne and Emerson, Berlioz and Taine) were impressed by the wealth and industry, as well as the stolidness and priggishness, of the expanding middle class. Or else, like Marx and Dostoevsky, they focused on the surrounding poverty and on the seeming hypocrisy of the Christian capitalists who did nothing to rectify it. Only in the twentieth century, after the legacy of Victorian capitalism had been finally overcome in ways that would have been inconceivable to Dickens or Mayhew or Carlyle, did the character I describe in this chapter emerge. It was related by genealogy and temperament to its predecessors – to the 'freeborn' Englishman of

[1] Witness Shaftesbury, Owen, Mayhew, Dickens and a hundred more on the condition of the industrial poor; Leonard Woolf on Ceylon and George Orwell on Burma; or the critics of British administration in India, from Burke and Sheridan in the eighteenth century through J.A. Hobson and E.M. Forster to Paul Scott in the post-imperial aftermath. The great exception to this is the treatment of Ireland. The worst crimes against the Irish, however, were committed during that bleak interregnum when the body politic was ablaze with self-righteousness. It is surely reasonable to see those times as pathological, and certainly not as representative of the English character in its normal and tranquil condition.

[2] See Willard Farnham, *The Medieval Heritage of Elizabethan Tragedy*, Berkeley, California, 1937.

the civil wars, to the stubborn but peaceable yeoman farmer
celebrated by Macaulay, to the stuffy suburban bourgeois of
Galsworthy. But it was also different – less sure of itself, less
belligerent, more quiet, sad and poetical. Before looking for its
essence, it is worth summarising what has been written, by both
defenders and detractors, of the English character in the twentieth
century, the century which saw it dwindle and diversify, as it melted
away in the stream of time.

The English, it is generally agreed, were distant, cool, reserved.
They had friends, but they did not make them easily. And when they
made them, they held them at a distance, embarrassed at the natural
flow of human affection, and taking steps to avoid it whenever it
might erupt. This reserve was part of loyalty; their affections were
cool but steady. They deplored the volatile humours of Mediterranean people, and the fickle sentimentality, as they saw it, of the Irish.
Because their attachments were slow to form they were also slow to
dissolve: for one attachment must be driven out by another, and
meanwhile takes up its place with the same discreet informality as a
member takes his armchair in his club. This reserve was observed not
only between friends, but also between lovers, spouses and members
of a family, where it could coexist with the deepest love and a mutual
identification of aims and interests. It amounted not to a lack of
feeling, but rather to a lack of self-regard – a refusal to display a
feeling just because it happened to be yours. It was the most
important cause of the fact that astonished Nirad Chaudhuri when he
first visited England in 1955 – the fact that the normal condition of
the English, in both public and private, was one of silence.[1]

Reserve therefore went hand in hand with a respect for form. The
English were given to formal clothes, formal modes of address,
formal meetings; they had an innate respect for offices, minutes and
agendas; they loved to address each other in the third person,
through the intermediary of a chairman, who could be 'madam

---

[1] Nirad Chaudhuri, *A Passage to England*, London, 1959, pp. 81–6.

chairman' but never 'chairperson' or 'chair'. At the same time, their forms were in a certain measure relaxed. Costumes and uniforms were loosely worn; ironical laughter would interrupt their most solemn deliberations; titles and forms of address would be quickly brushed aside when business required it, only to be reassumed when the time for passing resolutions arrived. They loved rituals, but would enter them in a spirit of respectful scepticism, admitting variations, imperfections and mistakes, and assuming that even the most sacred ceremony could be adjusted to meet the needs of the moment. Schools, churches, colleges, regiments, guilds, trade unions and Inns of Court all had their rituals, which were performed respectfully but inexactly. The purpose was to establish a right to be at ease: the first thing to form between Englishmen was ice; and this ice had to be broken. God too was an Englishman, and the Anglican rite was designed to help him relax, so that he could settle without embarrassment among his gruff but retiring countrymen.

This sceptical but real respect for ceremony had something to do with the empiricist tendency in English thought. The English did not reject mystery; they rejected the desire to explain it, to rationalise it, to replace it with abstract principles. Reason seemed to them unreasonable – the imposition of a standard to which no human thinking could attain. The reasonable person does not solve the problems of morality, religion, politics or gardening by consulting a priori rules, but by consultation, negotiation and compromise with those who seem to disagree with him but who might nevertheless be right. Tradition and example are far more reliable than abstract argument; rituals and ceremonies, because they exist without an explanation, are far more likely to contain the truth of things than any intellectual doctrine. This attitude led to a spontaneous preference for monarchical over republican government, and for aristocratic titles over professional degrees. It also led to a habit of understatement: the important things, it was assumed, 'went without saying', and the deeper emotions could only be debased by their

expression. The English specialised in an undemonstrative patriotism, a refusal to get worked up about events or people, and a habit of
shrugging off their own heroism. Those who lived through the
Second World War remember this attitude as a vital factor in helping
them to survive it; and the television series *Dad's Army*, which ran
from 1968 until 1977 without a break, helped them to relive some of
the self-deprecating humour that had sustained them through those
years.

There were other aspects to the English reserve, however. One of
them was puritanism, which had survived into the modern era
purged of its religious exaltation, its iconoclastic fervour and its anti-
aesthetic excesses. Puritanism lingered on as a quiet suspicion of
sensuality, reflecting the deeply buried thought that the world, the
flesh and the Devil are not three things, but one. Being incarnate was
an embarrassment, a design-fault that God may have intended in the
Italians but surely not in the English. For physical existence exposes
you to the danger of contamination. Strangers must remain strangers,
lest they pollute you with their intimacy. This pollution could be a
matter of lowering the tone, the class, the standing or the
respectability of the one whom it touched. But it could also be sexual
– and it always carried a sexual risk. This fear of contamination is,
paradoxically, what made the English into such intrepid adventurers
and explorers. They could go anywhere, encounter anyone, suffer
anything and emerge unpolluted. For they had become untouchable,
as Mr Chapman was untouchable during all his adventures in the
bush. The people among whom they wandered were essentially *other*,
and interesting for that very reason. But since they were other, they
did not belong with us.

Naturally, this attitude had its unpleasant side. The English made
themselves especially offensive to the Indians by treating all of them,
even the Brahmins, as though they were of a lower caste than
themselves, and by allowing them to share their domestic lives only
as servants and never as equals. The intricate connection between this
attitude and the fear of sexual contamination is well brought out by

Paul Scott, in his anti-English novels of the Raj.[1] But Scott also illustrates a virtue in the colonial English: that they could from time to time imaginatively identify with the natives, and see their own affectation of superiority as a sham.

Sexual puritanism is an attempt to safeguard possessions more valuable than pleasure. The good that it does outweighs the evil, and the English knew this. They were seriously repressed, largely because repression prevented them from carelessly throwing away those things – chastity, marriage and the family – which slip so easily from the grasp of people whose natural tendency is to keep each other at a distance. The repression of the English extended into all those areas where pleasure might overwhelm discretion, and the personal give way to the animal. The English were not joyless; but they took their pleasures sceptically, anxious not to care more than they should. This led to one of their least celebrated triumphs – a cuisine in which ingredients were systematically deprived of their flavour, so that everything tasted roughly the same and manly stoicism prevailed over sensory enjoyment. 'Nursery food' they called it, so referring it to a peculiarly English institution and endowing it with a peculiarly English authority: it was the food on which they had been raised, the food which had made them into Englishmen. This flavourless stodge was the matter to which English eccentricity gave its many forms. And it was dutifully served up in all those institutions – public schools, Oxford and Cambridge colleges, gentlemen's clubs – which had the reproduction of Englishness as their tacit social goal.

Repression caused them to value privacy more than any other social gift. To the English there was no more valuable freedom than the freedom to close a door. The Englishman's home was not just a castle, but an island of 'mine' in an ocean of 'ours'. The English saw their country as home and the land as their entitlement; hence they could not be content without a piece of it. They were unhappy in

---

[1] Paul Scott: *The Jewel in the Crown*, 1966; *The Day of the Scorpion*, 1968; *The Towers of Silence*, 1972; *A Division of the Spoils*, 1974.

apartments or barracks or dormitories, and underwent these harsh experiences as an exercise in self-denial, always yearning for the freedom of the householder, who could shut his front door on the world and hide away in the garden. Their passion for gardening was as great as any they had, and they would decorate their houses with lawns, shrubs and floral borders not in order to please their neighbours, but in order to establish an inalienable right of possession to the plot of land that was theirs.

This attitude to the household meant that, in pursuit of their assumed birthright, the English littered the countryside with ugly suburban houses and so eventually destroyed it. The tendency in this direction began with the Industrial Revolution and accelerated at the end of the nineteenth century. For Čapek nothing was more remarkable in the England that he glimpsed from the train than row upon row of identical houses. J.B. Priestley, not a countryman but a child of the manufacturing North, warned against the destruction of the countryside, as he observed it in his *English Journey* of 1934. Three years later, leading intellectuals contributed to *England and the Beast*, a collection edited by Sir Clough Williams-Ellis, with contributions from J.M. Keynes, E.M. Forster, H.J. Massingham and others, lamenting the unsightly spread of exurbia across the landscape.[1] The National Trust had been in existence for half a century, and now began fighting in earnest to preserve what could not be preserved as a living community but only as a varnished replica. Since the war the last-ditch battle for England has been fought as a battle for the landscape – a battle now lost, but one in which the English glimpsed for the last time what they were and why it mattered, while still insisting, each and every one of them, on their indefeasible right to a house of their own.

Privacy engenders eccentricity, and the English were famous

[1] The lament over industrial housing and its aesthetic consequences began early, in the eighteenth century. See Macaulay's scathing response to Southey's version of it, in 'Southey's Colloquies of Society', in Thomas Babington, Lord Macaulay, *Critical and Historical Essays*, London, 1874, pp. 104–6.

eccentrics.[1] In every city in the world people dress and behave crazily; they show off, play the fool, disguise themselves with masks and affectations. English eccentricity, however, was the opposite of showing off, and quite without theatrical intentions. It was in fact a kind of punctiliousness. The Englishman, by his very mixture of reserve and adventurousness, found himself living among strangers, with nothing to guide him besides customs and rituals invented in another place and another time and for another purpose. With scrupulous regard for some real or imaginary precedent he would dress for dinner in the tropics or wear plus-fours in the lecture hall; he would invite uncouth teenagers to dinner and treat them like gentlemen, as Mr Chapman did; he would travel to Cockfosters on the tube in his hunting pink, like Enoch Powell, and there take a taxi to the meet of foxhounds; he would walk after Sunday lunch to Hyde Park Corner, deliver a passionate sermon in the rain, and then return to his tea and biscuits as though nothing untoward had happened.

Such eccentricity is not the functionless by-product of leisure, but a crucial ingredient in a free and risk-taking society. John Stuart Mill warned against the pressure to conformity, as he saw it, in Victorian England. 'That so few now dare to be eccentric,' he wrote, 'marks the chief danger of our time.'[2] For Mill eccentricity was both the expression of freedom and its ultimate guarantee, the character-building force which resists coercion and turns the world to human uses. The eccentric is the object of wonder and the source of ideas, as Mr Chapman was to his pupils. He is tutor and example to others who prefer to be less noticeable.

Eccentricity was fed by another and more important aspect of the English reserve, which was an underlying attitude to authority. Perhaps more than any people in the modern world the English were sensitive to the distinction between power and authority. Their

[1] The varieties of English eccentricity are amply illustrated in literature; the subject is too vast to explore here, but the reader may gain some illumination from Edith Sitwell's *English Eccentrics*, London, 1933, and from Paul Fussell, *Class*, London, 1990.

[2] J.S. Mill, *On Liberty*, London, 1862.

remarkable constitution was an attempt to separate the two in reality, as they were separate in thought, and to set authority in judgement over power. This attempt was mirrored in their personal lives. The English did not believe that the mere fact of possessing power entitled a person to exert it. Confronted with power they would question its authority, and would resist it to the utmost if they thought that it had none. Hence they were constantly reaching for the institutions, the customs, the precedents that would justify them against their oppressors, and would stand up for their rights whenever a powerful person sought to disregard them. 'Rights', in this context, did not mean the kind of thing that modern people sue for in the courts, whenever they see a chance of gain; it meant the ancient prerogatives of the people, respect for which was a necessary condition of any legitimate exercise of power. Nineteenth-century historians like Macaulay saw this habit as the motor of English history, and even the modern debunkers, looking back over the great contests of English history, have conceded that the refusal to be governed without right has been a major factor in the evolution of English politics.

What they have not sufficiently seen, however, is the deep connection between this attitude to authority and English reserve. English society was a society of strangers, who kept each other at a distance, while acknowledging each other's right to belong. It is this which explains the peculiarly English habit of apologising. If an Englishman found himself knocked over by a stranger in the street, or short-changed by a shop assistant, or humiliated by an official, he would at once apologise. Anger establishes a relation: it is a bond between opponents which verges on intimacy. The English habit of apology was a way of bowing out of conflict, lest it breach the barriers which kept people comfortably apart.

Strangers do not live together by affection, by family sentiment, by swearing bonds of blood-brotherhood in the manner of the Arabian tribes. They live together by law, convention and a silent appeal to precedent. They settle disputes not by violent quarrels or vengeance, but by laying their grievance before an impartial judge, himself a stranger at one further remove. Two momentous facts congeal around this one – whether as cause or effect we need not yet try to discover. The first is the instinct for justice and fair play; the second is the institution of common law – law not invented but discovered, through the workings of impartial justice.

The instinct for fair play was so obvious a characteristic of the English that a whole intellectual industry has been devoted to proving its non-existence. It was not this, we are told, which led to the attempt to impose legal order on the colonies, but a desire to whitewash the gains of empire. It was not this which led to the abolition of the slave trade, but a desire to ruin the slave-dependent economies of rival colonial powers.[1] In any case, as is said to be proven by hundreds of episodes, from the internment camps of the Boer War to the massacre at Amritsar, from the Zulu War to the Boxer Rebellion, the English sense of fair play hardly extended beyond their own privileged tribe.

The Marxists go further, and dismiss the very idea of justice as 'bourgeois ideology', with arguments that were once refuted by Plato,[2] but which continue to appeal to those who recognise that justice remains a mere idea until someone has the power to apply it, and that power means submission. Suffice it to say that it has become, as it once was not, controversial to attribute the instinct for fair play to the English. Now that the principal ways in which that instinct was revealed have been effectively destroyed, it is hard to establish the case – certainly hard to establish it in the face of a one-sided anti-colonial literature which has effectively demonised the empire.[3] Only

[1] See for example the influential account by Eric Williams (subsequently Premier of Trinidad), *Capitalism and Slavery*, London, 1944, paperback edn, 1964, pp. 135–68 and 209–12. The accusation that it was the British, and not the Nazis or the Communists, who invented the concentration camp, has proved useful to propagandists for those disreputable causes: see the Nazi wartime film *Ohm Kruger*, 1941.

[2] See the refutation of Thrasymachus at the beginning of *The Republic*.

[3] Still, there are some fairly effective ripostes to this literature, of which Jan Morris's

those who caught glimpses of England will know for certain that this instinct existed, that it was fundamental to everything the English did, the cause of their commercial and political success, and also, some say, of their downfall.[1]

The English character was profoundly influenced by the common law. For English people the law was an objective reality; it did not depend upon the will of sovereigns or parliaments, but stood in judgement upon them. It was a version of the Holy Ghost – always present, always vigilant, always personal, always benign. The policeman on his beat was its real embodiment, kindly, impartial and the guardian of the community. When a felon transgressed it was not the state but the law which pursued him, and the essential goodness of the law was symbolised by the fact that policemen carried no arms. Policemen were chosen for their height, with hats that emphasised their superior stature. But they were representatives of authority, not power – the authority of a law that stood above all earthly powers and could never be reduced by them. In popular films the police confronted gun-toting criminals with the same phlegmatic confidence as radiated from those idealised schoolroom portraits of General Gordon of Khartoum, in which the General faced the spears of savages with a calm acceptance of his fate, as safe and unflustered in death as he would have been on the thickly carpeted stairwell of his London club, conscious that his authority was only enhanced by his lack of power and that one day, thanks to his quiet sacrifice, order would be reimposed.[2]

This image of the law was of fundamental importance to the English in their war effort, and was renewed after the Second World War in the films from Ealing Studios – notably Ted Willis's *The Blue Lamp* (1950), in which PC George Dixon meets the fate of General

finely written *Pax Britannica: the Climax of an Empire*, London, 1968, is of particular distinction.

[1] See Correlli Barnett, *The Collapse of British Power*, London, 1972.

[2] See R.W.K. Paterson, in *The New Patricians: an Essay on Values and Consciousness*, Basingstoke, 1988.

Gordon of Khartoum. So popular was this particular hero that Willis revived him in 1955 for the TV series, *Dixon of Dock Green*, in which Jack Warner, in the role of Dixon, won the hearts of millions with his simple goodness and unruffled calm. The American sociologist Geoffrey Gorer, exploring English character in 1955, found universal enthusiasm for the English police as role models, distinguished by their fairness, gentleness, decency and devotion to duty.[1]

'It would hardly be too much to say,' wrote W. Macneile Dixon, 'that into this one word, duty, the English have distilled the whole body of ethics.'[2] The merit of this notion, he argued, lies in its simplicity: it strikes no high-pitched or rhapsodical note; it applies as well to daily drudgery as to the heroism of war. It makes no claims at all for the person who obeys it, but on the contrary records his act as something expected, implying that anything else would be an aberration.

At the same time, the ethic of duty was an ethic of right. Built into the English view of law was the belief that individuals must take responsibility for their own lives and suffer the consequences of their actions. Staying on the right side of the law was not merely a duty therefore; it was also a liberation. For it guaranteed that you were safe, that no busybody could give you orders or force you to comply with a routine that you had not chosen. The law was there not to coerce you or to shape you into regiments obedient to the state. It was there to free you from the state and its officials, and to allow you to 'get on with your own life' in private. Those who minded their own business and attended to their duties were rewarded with inalienable rights. And the most important of these was the right to do what you ought.

The extraordinary result of this was that, while the English believed in law and authority, they despised officialdom and distrusted the state. English society was the creation of amateur

---

[1] Geoffrey Gorer, *Exploring English Character*, London, 1955.
[2] W. Macneile Dixon, *The Englishman*, London, 1938, p. 78.

initiatives; its most valuable institutions were the result either of private patronage, such as that exercised by William of Wykeham in founding Winchester College and New College in Oxford, or of people making common cause and clubbing together. Such networks of self-help are natural, and exist wherever the state has not extinguished them – as it extinguished them in Revolutionary France and later in Nazi and Communist Europe. In England, however, private foundations, amateur circles, clubs and friendly societies sprang up not merely from the normal superfluity of social energy, but in response to social problems, calling upon the resources and consciences of individuals to resolve them. It was not the state but friendly societies and building societies which provided industrial workers with housing. It was not the state but People's Dispensaries and volunteer hospitals which first brought the benefits of modern medicine to the poor. The real advances in health care in the nineteenth century were due on the one hand to the determination of Florence Nightingale to make nursing into a science and a profession, and on the other hand to the doctors and surgeons who founded the Provincial Medical and Surgical Association in 1832 – a body which was to become the British Medical Association in 1856, by which time it had already established its path-breaking journal and prompted Parliament to take an interest in the nation's health. Schools, universities and colleges began as private foundations and, when it came to leisure, every village was a centre of spontaneous institution-building, with its football club and cricket club, its Boy Scouts and Girl Guides, its Women's Institute and its circles of amateurs devoted to needlework, music, photography, theatricals, brass bands, jam-making and ballroom dancing.

Societies of amateurs existed elsewhere in Europe, and especially under the aegis of the Austro-Hungarian Empire. Nevertheless, the English case was exceptional. For the common law gave credibility to private initiatives and protected them from the jealousy of legislators. There therefore grew up in England a unique attitude to officialdom, and to the rules and regulations which modern governments impose.

While they loved ceremony and tradition, the English also knew them to be human inventions. Authority was intangible, removed from the human world and at the same time permanently and benevolently concerned with it. It could be identified with no real human being and certainly not with an official. The English love of ancient customs, precedents, uniforms and formalities was tempered by an irrepressible urge to laugh at them – not maliciously but gently and ironically, by way of recognising their merely human provenance. The empire reached its summit of pomp at the same time as Gilbert and Sullivan wrote the operas which affectionately satirised its ruling offices: the peerage, the judiciary, the army, the navy and even royalty itself.

Again, however, we touch on a deeper and more spiritual trait: the English love of nonsense. Language has something official about it: rules of grammar, etiquette, style and pertinence constrain everything we say, and in speaking we enter a public and official world where we cannot invent the rules. The English spontaneously rebelled against this state of affairs, and from the earliest times took delight in speaking nonsensically and out of turn.[1] Following quickly on the triumphs of Gilbert and Sullivan were the nonsense poems of Edward Lear and the two 'Alice' books of Lewis Carroll – books which for many readers capture the spirit of Victorian England far more effectively than the works by which the Victorians hoped to be remembered.

This love of nonsense was not truly subversive. A poem like 'Jabberwocky', which mocks the afflatus of Romantic verse and mimics its antiquarian rhythms, also reaffirms the Romantic ideal on the level of comedy. Its assault on language is at the same time a creation of language (adding words like 'slithy', 'beamish' and 'chortle' to the vocabulary of English). By means of such nonsense the English expressed their dual attitude to forms and dignities: the

---

[1] For the fascinating history, with telling examples, see Noel Malcolm, *The Origins of English Nonsense*, London, 1998; see also Paul Jennings, *A Book of Nonsense*, London, 1980.

desire to respect them, and the desire to send them up. They knew that grandiloquence and pomp were a social necessity; but they also recognised them as a human invention, consisting largely in theatrical disguises worn by people as shy and private as themselves.

This conflict was particularly vivid in their attitude to monarchy: for them the monarch was sacred and mysterious; but the sanctity and the mystery were attached to a mask, behind which another private Englishman had retired. The Queen was revered as an ordinary person, whose ordinariness was only increased by the gorgeous splendour of the Crown. The English approach to such conflicts of attitude was to make a game of them. Hence monarchs and their predicament formed a recurring theme of English nonsense. But the game was also serious. The paradigm of nonsense is the abracadabra of the magician; and the English recognised that by describing their country in nonsensical ways they also enchanted it.

Connected with the love of nonsense was a whimsical vision of children. Renaissance poets had represented children as closer to God than adults – witness Vaughan and Traherne. Blake's *Songs of Innocence* and Wordsworth's Immortality Ode both portray the child as possessing secret knowledge of religious truths which had been publicly eclipsed by science. But it was only later that childhood became central to English culture. At the very moment when the Arnoldian public school was teaching boys to be adult, addressing them as though they already were so and flogging them when they failed; when less fortunate boys and girls were working in mines or scrambling up chimneys and less fortunate children still were begging on the streets of London, the English discovered childhood – not as a stage on the way to adulthood, but as a distinct spiritual condition, and one to which they never ceased, thereafter, to aspire.[1] They were

---

[1] On the Victorian discovery of childhood see Peter Coveney, *The Image of Childhood* (originally *Poor Monkey: the Child in Literature*, London, 1957); the crucial literature, apart from Charles Kingsley's *The Water Babies*, 1863, includes the *Princess* books of George MacDonald, F.H. Burnett's *The Secret Garden*, 1911, and of course the waifs and strays of Dickens.

not alone in this, of course. The cult of Christmas and the Christ-child grew in continental Europe and America during the nineteenth century, and children's stories, nursery rhymes and carols were promoted everywhere to the rank of serious or semi-serious art. Children's literature was not an English but a German and Scandinavian invention, and the French, drawing on their native tradition of moral tales and fables, excelled at it.

Nevertheless, there was something especially poignant about childhood as the English described it. The English childhood in some way fulfilled the dream of England, and therefore compensated for the disappointing reality. Like the water babies in Charles Kingsley's story, the English entered this imaginary realm in order to be washed clean of their tainted routines. The child's England was an Arcadian countryside, cleared of its industrial accretions, peopled by English eccentrics like Winnie-the-Pooh and Eeyore, Rat and Toad, the White Queen and the White Rabbit, the mice and moles of Beatrix Potter – all of them human beings concealed in animal skins, just as the English were concealed within their clothes: safe, quiet and untouchable. In this enchanted realm you could do as you wanted, provided you were decent; and everything was held in place by unseen authorities who could be mocked with impunity if you didn't go too far. Often the search for this magical realm produced nauseating sentimentality – as in J.M. Barrie's *Peter Pan* (though Barrie, it should be noted, was a Scot). But it also provided children, and young children especially, with a unique moral education, offering them intelligible versions of the good and manageable images of evil.

In search of their lost childhood (which in truth had never really existed) the English would go to extraordinary lengths, not only in literature, but also in life. They played with toys into late middle age; they made model boats and cars and villages; they collected stamps and mats and cigarette cards; and they spent their happiest hours with animals – riding them, walking them, playing with them; 'fancying' pigeons, showing horses and puppies, or breeding rare types of goat. And when the animal was an antagonist – as in hunting, shooting and fishing – they described the encounter as a 'sport'. Nothing more accurately captures the permanent child in the Englishman than the art and literature devoted to this kind of activity – from the brilliant evocations of the chase in Fielding, Trollope and Surtees to the popular caricatures of hunters and fishermen which could be found on the wall of every country pub.

The Englishman carried this image of childhood within him for the simple reason that it was an idealised version of home – in other words, it was a vision of England, purified of guilt, as cool, unthreatening and redemptive as the water which baptised Kingsley's little chimney sweeps, and restored their angel nature. The English felt abnormally protected in the midst of danger, partly because they preserved a part of themselves that looked on the adult world as unreal, and which made deliberate nonsense of its most solemn prescriptions.

Through their love of nonsense the English threw in their lot with ordinariness. This too was an aspect of their reserve. They believed seriously in class distinctions (in so far as they believed seriously in anything), and in differences of station and degree. There was, for them, a great divide between the somebody and the nobody, and they both renewed and chafed at the boundaries which held the two apart. Despite this, however, they believed it to be permissible and desirable to be a nobody. Even while striving to ascend the social ladder, they looked with pity on those who had reached the top of it, and whose lives had been destroyed by the loss of the only thing which made an English life worthwhile – namely, doing your own thing in private.

Here too we find a bundle of contradictions, and the raw material of many a farce, from Wilde's *The Importance of Being Earnest* (subtitled 'a trivial comedy for serious people') to *The Diary of a Nobody* by the Grossmith brothers, in which the life of the nobody is vindicated in all its well-meant disastrousness, and in which the nobody wins through at last, as the proud possessor of a mortgage, and therefore a home.

This brings us to one of the most important and least understood manifestations of the English in their apartness: the sentiment of class. England was an aristocratic society, in the very real sense that it possessed a hereditary aristocracy, decorated with titles, privileges and political power, and endorsed by a political system which treated aristocracy as a genuine honour, to be bestowed upon those who had deserved well of the state. But it was also an aristocratic society in the more subtle sense. It esteemed breeding and believed in heredity, regarding the cads and criminals among the aristocracy as shameful traitors to their station. It distinguished well-bred from ill-bred behaviour, and believed in well-bred behaviour as the social and moral ideal. The patriotic films which were made during and just after the last war are replete with examples of this ideal, which mingles aristocratic graces with a superhuman patience and sang-froid. Such is the portrait of Commissioner Sanders – an idealised version of Mr Chapman – in the films made by Alexander Korda from the story by Edgar Wallace.

Hence there grew in England three quite distinct ideas of aristocracy. There was the aristocracy based in titles of nobility. There was also the aristocracy based in breeding and descent, which might have no title to its name, but which nevertheless occupied a place in the social hierarchy as high as that of the lords and dukes. Some of the oldest and noblest families of England were of this kind, more proud of their Anglo–Norman or even Saxon names than of the mere accident (as they saw it) of a title, bestowed or withheld by some latter-day upstart of a king. (It is significant that it fell to the commoner John Hampden, whose family had been lords of Hampden and its demesnes since Saxon times, to lead the revolt of Parliament against the Stuart Crown.)

Finally, there was the aristocracy of breeding in the looser sense, according to which breeding could be acquired by all who put their mind to it. The public schools furthered this third idea, as did, in their own way, the grammar schools. In its twilight years, England was a country in which anybody, whatever his origins, could acquire the reputation of a well-bred person, and enjoy the very real social advantages that came from this. A thousand-year-old name was one thing; an inherited title another; but more important than both were the little signs – accent, idiom, manners and social veneer – that you were or were not a lady or a gentleman.

The class system will occupy us in later chapters. Suffice it to say that, for the English, it was at the root of society, accepted or rebelled against as the primary social fact. Those who accepted it did so for two reasons: first, because they were either content with their own position or convinced that they could improve it; and second, because they saw the class system as part of the enchantment that lay over England. This enchantment was crystallised not merely in the fact of good breeding, but in the ideal of the gentleman which shone through it.

This ideal was so frequently proclaimed and acted upon that (unlike the ideal of the lady) it has attracted both commentary and emulation from foreigners, many of whom have adopted the word 'gentleman' into their language as an explicit acknowledgement that it names a peculiarly English condition and a peculiarly English virtue. When seen in the context of all the other characteristics that I have enunciated, the concept of the gentleman takes on a hue very different from that bestowed upon it by the detractors of the class system and the rebels against the English forms of snobbery. Readers of Proust will know that French snobbery was (and still is) more potent and more vigilant than the English variety; they will also recognise that snobbery of the French kind, while being in its extreme form a reprehensible weakness, involved in its day-to-day exercise a work of self-sacrificing labour. People like Proust's Mme Verdurin, who were permanently excluded from the upper regions of society, worked selflessly to keep those regions in place, bestowing their good will on grandees who never returned it.

The principal difference between French and English snobbery lies in the central place occupied by the idea of the gentleman in English social aspirations. In the figure of the gentleman social hierarchy and social mobility are reconciled. The gentleman is defined in terms of the manners, culture, virtue and aloofness of an old aristocracy; but defined independently of lineage and wealth. You can become a gentleman, therefore, without becoming an upstart. The gentleman rises to the upper regions of society without polluting them with anything from below. He overcomes the paradox so tellingly voiced by Groucho Marx: 'I don't want to belong to any club that will accept *me* as a member.' His rise leaves the social order unaffected, and he radiates the image of a society every single member of which can aspire to the upper class, a society of rigid hierarchical order, the lower echelons of which are entirely unoccupied.[1]

My grammar school devoted itself – with only partial success – to the production of gentlemen. The world into which I was born acknowledged that titles, ancestors, wealth and power were good things to have: but only if you were also a gentleman. Conversely, you could be a gentleman without any of those things, and be all the better for it – for you would possess the only social attribute that could never be tarnished, and which would be acknowledged and admired in the midst of adversity. The gentleman could be relied upon; he was the guardian of order because order reigned in his soul.

If we were to look for an adjective with which to summarise the English as they aspired to be, it would not be 'reserved' or 'law-abiding' or 'repressed', however apt those descriptions might be from this or that perspective; it would be 'gentle' – a word of Latin origin, to which the English gave their own peculiar and multi-faceted meaning. The gentleman emulated those of 'gentle' birth; and in doing so he became gentle in another sense. In the midst of social failure he retained the ability to deal kindly, distantly and humorously with others, and if he nonetheless insisted on his high social merits, he would only become ridiculous – in other words, not gentle,

---

[1] There are comparable examples from other traditions – notably Poland, where at one time more than 50% claimed to be 'nobility' or *szlachta*. But here the criterion, however loosely applied, was one of birth and blood.

but merely 'genteel'. This is the drama of Mr Pooter, the 'nobody' of the Grossmith novel: that he steers between the gentlemanly and the genteel, and saves himself by being both gentle and, when embarrassed, as he frequently is, jaunty (which is another adaptation of the same Latin root).

Of course, in emergencies, and in times when the fighting spirit must be called upon, the English would propagate another image of themselves – the stubborn, invincible John Bull of eighteenth-century caricature. In truth, however, this figure was always doubly mythical: it was always a myth that he embodied the myth of England. The real myth – the *muthos* that told the inner story of England, as *The Odyssey* and *The Iliad* told the inner story of Greece – was Mr Pooter, the nobody who was somebody, because he had made himself a home.

All the features that I have touched upon in this chapter I have also made out to be virtues; and to every virtue there corresponds a vice. Just as courage becomes rashness when prized free of the reasonable-ness, honesty and justice that subordinate it to the moral life, so does reserve become coldness, so does law-abidingness decline to fussy pedantry and gentleness to sentimental guff. But readers can perhaps follow this corollary through for themselves.

It will be said, nevertheless, that I have not described the English as they were, but at best only as they aspired to be. I have described an ideal, not a reality – although an ideal that was repeatedly affirmed by the culture of imperial England. This is true. But it is not the whole truth. When people are animated by an ideal, then, to whatever small degree, they endeavour to live up to it. It is not in the gross and material things that a national character is revealed, but in the superfluities, the places where people are at one with themselves and endeavour to be what they ought: the institutions of education, justice, religion and leisure. In these areas ideals make a difference. They do not become reality, but they strain constantly to incarnate themselves, and act as 'regulative ideas' in the day-to-day conduct that invokes them. When this ceases to happen – when people discard, ignore or mock the ideals which formed their national character – then they no longer exist as a people, but only as a crowd. That is what is happening now, in England.

Chapter Four

Community as Person

In our love of country (and also in our hatred of it) the first-person plural becomes, in some mysterious way, a first-person singular. 'England expects', just as you expect and I expect. Our country stands before us as another person, loved, hated, respected, despised as people are, magically re-formed as a moral unity.

What do we mean by 'person'? This question, first put into words by St Thomas Aquinas, has occupied some of the greatest modern intellects – which is fortunate, since it means that we can consult them for an answer.[1] The human person is an animal, a member of the species *Homo sapiens*, the word 'sapiens' referring to that capacity – reason – which makes personality possible. The animal is the raw material from which the person is built. To be a person it is not enough to have sensations and emotions; not enough even to have thoughts, beliefs and desires – although there is an ascending scale of complexity here, which implies that many animals approximate to persons, and stand just behind an impassable barrier, staring in helpless fascination at the human drama.[2]

Personality involves language, communication and the consciousness of self. Above all it involves the dialogue which is the foundation of moral life. Persons, unlike animals, have rights and duties; they lead their lives according to moral scruples and conscious goals. They

[1] The answer that I give draws on Aristotle, Locke, Kant, Hegel, Spinoza, Gierke, Pufendorf, Maitland and St Thomas. Even Sir Ernest Barker gets a look in.
[2] I have defended this view of animals in *Animal Rights and Wrongs*, 3rd edn, London, 2000.

justify and criticise their own and others' actions; and in everything they do they recognise a distinction between the permissible and the impermissible. They do not merely think and feel and do: they have the question *what* to think, *what* to feel and *what* to do. And that is why we call them rational.

The human person is not, however, an angel or a god, but a mortal creature, constrained by need, and preyed upon by fear and appetite. The conflict between his animal nature and his rational aspirations is real, ineradicable, both tragic and comic by turns. When we refer to the human character it is in part this conflict that we have in mind. People differ most of all in their ways of coming to terms with their mortal condition. In virtuous people, duty trumps desire; in vicious people, desire prevails. Personality is the place where this contest – between what we value and what we merely want – plays itself out. All that is loved and hated is here on display, and the significance of the human face lies in the fact that it embodies and reveals the individual attempt to be a person – to live the life of a moral being, in a world of temptation.

There is a distinction to be drawn between personhood – the fact of being a person, which you and I have in common – and personality – the thing that distinguishes you from me. Force of personality comes when great ambitions, or great moral strength, overcome the waywardness of appetite, so that the limitations of our animal nature sink from view. Sometimes this happens because a person is animated by an ideal – not merely paying lip-service to it, but consciously striving to emulate it. Sometimes it happens because he adheres to a code or a habit with a punctiliousness that ignores the adverse conditions that make it absurd. There is a nobility in these forms of conduct: the first is idealism, the second eccentricity. And the English were given to both.

Personhood is a kind of artefact: the product of a cooperative endeavour, whereby human beings mutually shape themselves as individuals. In another sense, however, we are *naturally* persons, since it is natural to us to *become* persons, and something in our nature remains unfulfilled if we do not do so. Hence it is legitimate to contrast natural persons, like you and me, with those artificial persons embodied in no human frame, and which are the product, or the by-product, of our mature decisions. The law recognises the 'corporate person', such as the firm, the church or the university, which can take decisions, assume responsibility, pursue goals and acquire rights and duties in the world of negotiation to which you and I belong. This legal construct gives judicial recognition to a social fact. Every form of human membership casts a personal shadow which marches behind us or in front of us, above us or below, and which takes on a moral reality of its own. It is the product of our decisions, but also gradually transcends them, becoming an object of loyalty, affection or resentment, just like you and me. Such 'artificial persons' are also in a sense natural, since it is in our nature to create them, to acknowledge them, and to relate to them in the way in which we relate to each other. But we might properly distinguish them from you and me, in that they are embodied in no particular organism, and are identified with no physical entity.

Some philosophers deny the independent existence of these corporate persons, describing them as mere 'abstractions' from the life of individuals, with no reality over and above the words, deeds and thoughts of their members. But this is false. Corporate persons do things which none of their members do: they enter into contracts, declare war, intercede with the Almighty, even though these things are done by no human being. They exist unchanged beyond the death of their present members – they may even exist with no members at all, like the English Crown during the interregnum. More importantly, they play an inescapable part in the development of the individual. It is through ties of membership that we become fully persons, deriving from these artificial persons the sense of identity without which the natural person remains incomplete and unfulfilled. We are essentially persons; and what is necessary to our completion and fulfilment as persons must therefore be as real as we are.

There is, of course, a crucial and relevant difference between the corporate and the incarnate person. The individual is an 'I', a centre of consciousness, who knows himself immediately and who looks out on the world from a point of view that is uniquely his. The corporate person is not, in that sense, a 'centre of consciousness', and although Louis XIV sent a frisson of recognition through his hearers when he said that '*L'état, c'est moi*', he was uttering a deliberate paradox. When a corporation speaks in the first person, it is with the first-person plural – the royal 'we' of the English sovereign. This 'we' distinguishes the Queen herself from the Crown, which in itself is selfless. The consciousness of a corporation is not a consciousness of self, but a collective consciousness, shared among its members, and embodied in the traditions and the culture that unite them. But although the corporate person has no self of its own, it may actively penetrate the self-identity of its members, so linking their conscious-ness to a larger tradition of thought and feeling, amplifying their projects and telling them who they are. In that sense it has a real mental history, and a mind of its own.

Such a view was defended by Hegel, Gierke and other German Romantics. And because their conclusions fed, by however devious a route, into the insane collectivism of the twentieth century, they have been regarded by English philosophers (not counting a few exceptions[1]) with suspicion. This does not alter the fact that England was a country of corporate persons, a country whose law encouraged their creation. The corporate person has this inestimable advantage over the natural variety – namely, that you cannot touch it, caress it or be embarrassed by its physical presence. You can entertain towards it every warm emotion, except those, like erotic love and sexual desire, which require an incarnate object. You can love it from a posture of chaste and inviolable remoteness. And that is the way the Englishman loved his old school, his regiment, his pub or club, his

---

[1] The exceptions include F.W. Maitland, J.N. Figgis, and R. Scruton, whose 'Corporate Persons', *Aristotelian Society, Supplementary Volume*, 1989, gives the philosophical argument in full, with a survey of the sources.

team and even his family. His habit of joining things, of working together as part of a committee, was of a piece with his reserve. The well-known charitableness of the English, their tendency to rush to the relief of people quite unconnected with themselves, was a way of emphasising their own existential position – as strangers in a world of strangers, for whom this relation of mutual support was the best that could be hoped for and all that should be desired. If love were to emerge from this, it was love first and foremost for the thing you joined – the institution, club or regiment that focused your common energies.

And that is the way the English loved their country. England, for them, was a place of clubs and teams and societies: it was a land saturated with the sense of membership. And the country itself was conceived in these terms: a personal entity, with rights, duties and claims, yet one both greater and more remote than any carnal representative. This was the real reason for the English attachment to monarchy as a form of government. The king or queen symbolised the personhood of England – its unchanging and vigilant claim on our affection.

The term 'person' comes to us from Roman law; its original meaning in Latin is mask – the *persona* worn by the actor in the theatre. And the monarch was the mask of England – the representation of something which lived longer and meant more than any individual. That was why the English regarded the monarch simultaneously as an ordinary human being, and as a manifestation of their own identity, the consecrated symbol of the land itself.[1] The Queen could be both these things only because her office was inherited, and because she was moulded from childhood to its shape. When the English toasted 'Queen and Country', therefore, they were commemorating not two things but one. And that one thing was England – the land construed as a person.

[1] For the English, therefore, the unsolicited touching of the monarch was an act of transgression, a presumptuous depleting of magical powers. It could cure you of illness – hence the myth of the 'King's evil' – but would also bring down holy retribution.

Legally speaking, there was such a person: the Crown, acknowledged in English law as a 'corporation sole', which is to say a corporation which had at most one member at a time, but which was distinct from any of its members, having rights, duties and claims which belonged to no individual. This extraordinary legal concept arose from the attempt to adjudicate powers which are not extraordinary at all – the powers of an hereditary monarch towards a people who regard her as neither more nor less than their representative.

The country itself was not strictly a corporate person. It had neither the legal nor the moral status of a church or a firm. Nevertheless, it grew in the same way and from the same moral need, and should be understood as clubs and teams are understood, in terms of an order that we know in ourselves: the order of moral life.

Like the human being, a country is composed of unalterable raw material which sets limits to what it can accomplish. And also like the human being, a country contains psychic layers and residues. If we are to know what is essential, and what accidental, to its life and identity, then we should approach it as we approach the individual: as a multi-layered product of the dialogue between persons.

The raw material of a country comprises the land, the people, the climate and the staple diet. Some countries have natural boundaries – rivers, seas and mountains – which make it easy to defend them against invaders. England is such a country, a fact which is of the first importance in understanding the psychology of the English. Only from the north could England be invaded by land; and the threat from the north was overcome through the fiction of 'Great Britain' as the body of which England was the soul. The situation of a people who can defend their territory is completely different from that of people who are forced to accept foreign control. The nations of central Europe, for example, have until recently been governed from Vienna or Moscow, compelled to treat their own languages as local eccentricities of no relevance to the bureaucratic machine, and to regard their local customs as having no legal authority and no guarantee of survival. In these circumstances people learn to keep their heads down, to ignore the public world of politics and to cultivate their allotments.[1] They do not easily acquire the taste for dangerous adventures, for noble causes or for large-scale and visible actions. On the contrary, they tend to look on such things with cynicism, believing that great intentions are sure to bring defeat. It goes without saying that the English did not take that view. Their adventurousness stemmed from an underlying sense of safety – the sense of being secure in their island home, amid congenial and unembarrassing strangers.

Furthermore, the island home was not remote in the manner of Iceland or the Hebrides. It was adjacent to the continent of Europe, separated by a narrow channel from a land mass teeming with opportunities for trade. It was as secure as a home could be, in the midst of a hundred markets.

The topography of this home also played its part in shaping the English character. England is a country of gentle gradients, slow-moving rivers, long and well-drained valleys; even the uplands are level and unsurprising. Almost every part of it can be crossed on foot or horseback, and to none of it is access barred by nature. When the forests had been tamed and cleared, and the land enclosed for agriculture, there emerged a web of gradual transitions, in which hills and valleys, plains and moorlands melted together imperceptibly as in a painting. The undulating surface of the land made visible the many settlements; village greeted village across a grey-green sea of trees. In whichever direction you looked, the countryside revealed its human meaning, and the English enhanced the effect by building tall steeples to their churches, and equipping them with bells that could fill the valleys with their jubilant changes, claiming the landscape as ours.[2]

---

[1] See the classic account by the Hungarian exile, Istvan Bíbo, *Les misères des nations de l'Europe Centrale*, Paris, 1964. Compare too the real adventures of English explorers of the eighteenth and nineteenth centuries with the wild fantasies of adventure in German Romantic literature, often written by people who would risk nothing more than a long country walk – the *Abentauer aus Geborgenheit*, that exists only in the imagination.

[2] Campanology is surely one of the most characteristic features of English popular

This easily domesticated landscape, where settlements displayed themselves to the traveller, abounded in short cuts. The English did not need roadways to beat a path to places they could see from afar; they took their own way across the meadows. English law found ways to reconcile this habit with the private ownership of land. Rights of way and byways, footpaths and bridlepaths were inscribed on the landscape. When common land was enclosed, it nevertheless remained partially open. The hedges and walls had to permit the long-established paths that breached them. The resulting landscape has, to my knowledge, no parallel elsewhere: it was entirely enclosed, with the most intricate pattern of walls and hedgerows, and also entirely open, with a way through to every point. In a very real sense, the landscape was both privately owned, and owned in common.[1]

When considering the human material from which English civilisation was made, our ancestors would refer to the English race, this 'happy breed of men', whose offshore island was the guarantee of their racial purity and apartness. Untenable now for reasons both scientific and moral, such beliefs were already lampooned by Defoe in his portrait of 'The True-Born Englishman', published in 1701:

> In between rapes and furious lust begot,
> Betwixt a painted *Briton* and a *Scot*:
> Whose gend'ring offspring quickly learnt to bow,
> And yoke their heifers to the *Roman* plough:
> From whence a mongrel half-bred race there came,
> With neither name nor nation, speech or fame,

culture – a mad defiance of the spirit of music, an eccentric cacophony of permutations, which nevertheless succeeds, from the distance at which it aims to be heard, in becoming a gentle lilting voice of the landscape itself. For the history of this peculiar art, see A.M. Samuel, 'The Bells', in *The Mancroft Essays*, London, 1937.

[1] How the English countryside came into being is a topic beyond the scope of this book. Suffice it to say that much of what we were told at school about enclosures, and about the recent and artificial nature of the contours that we now observe, was a myth. See Oliver Rackham, *The History of the Countryside*, London, 1988, and contrast W.G. Hoskins, *The Making of the English Landscape*, revised edn with notes by Christopher Taylor, London, 1988.

> In whose hot veins now mixtures quickly ran
> Infus'd betwixt a *Saxon* and a *Dane*.
> While their rank daughters, to their parents just,
> Receiv'd all nations with promiscuous lust . . .
> A True Born Englishman's a contradiction!
> In speech, an irony! In fact, a fiction!

Defoe exaggerates of course. At the time when he wrote there was as much, and as little, sense to the idea of a true-born Englishman as there was to the idea of a true-born anything. Nevertheless, his potted history is enough to remind us of the absurdity of racial ideas when invoked to explain national character. Instead, we should ponder what happens, when people live together on an island unconquered, as the English were unconquered during the centuries that made them. There occurs a gradual homogenisation in appearance, in deportment and in temperament. A bodily rhythm is acquired and passed on. This rhythm becomes established as an almost physiological trait, recognisable at a glance to the foreigner in England, and to the Englishman abroad. In such a case it is not surprising to find our Victorian ancestors referring to the English race, to 'kith and kin', to the 'island stock', and so invoking, through idioms that are now widely disapproved, a perfectly normal and natural human fact. England was associated, in the minds of those who claimed it as their homeland, with a recognisable physical type, with its own varieties of male and female beauty. Paintings, photographs, poems, novels and descriptions show that this type existed in large numbers, before immigration and emigration began to alter it.

As with the landscape, however, the human form is shaped by culture: what is identified as raw material – the 'racial' inheritance – may turn out on closer inspection to be a cultural acquisition. Not the blue eyes, but the cool glance; not the pale lips, but the shy smile; not the tall figure, but the erect carriage – these are the features that spoke to our ancestors of 'race' and 'breeding', and of course they belong to our cultural rather than our genetic endowment.

Much has been written about the English climate, which was, like the landscape, inclined to a gentle variety, an untroubling changeableness, an avoidance of extremes. The earth is now warming and the Gulf Stream, generator of the sodden, temperate flow of air that brushed the English hilltops, is moving south. Soon the English climate as it was celebrated in our art and literature may be a thing of the past. But there can be little doubt that it affected the national character and reinforced the sense of home. England was a moderate, gentle place, soothing and exasperating by turns. Coming home from abroad you were abruptly reminded of the madness of those southern regions with their burning suns and still afternoons, of the unnecessary violence of those snowbound winters far from the sea, of the sheer impudence of the tropics and the desert sands. To come home was to rediscover order, moderation and reality, to reassume the habits of a people who muddle along in private, taking things as they come.

The raw material of a country is shaped by consciousness and culture. The fundamental force – which is to a nation what consciousness is to the individual – is the common language. People form communities by talking; language will therefore always be at the root of the distinction between 'us' and 'them'. The English language is such a remarkable hybrid that many people have looked in it for the explanation of the English character. Formed from Anglo-Saxon by the seepage of Norman French, it includes all the roots of both Germanic and Latin vocabularies. Its lexicon is roughly twice as large as those of other European tongues and, by drawing on contrasting roots, it can distinguish two applications of the same idea. Thus *brotherhood, fatherly, heavenly, kingly, foxy, boyish* and *hellish* exist alongside *fraternity, paternal, celestial, royal, vulpine, puerile* and *infernal* – the difference being one of nuance and suggestion. Richness in vocabulary permits elasticity in grammar, which in the case of English has loosened at the seams and given way, relying on idiomatic constructions. This makes it both easy to adapt and hard to learn. The English language is not lawless; but it is decidedly individualistic, allowing the invention and adoption of new words and idioms without reference to any college of authorities like the Académie Française. It absorbs words easily from other languages, and sets them hospitably within its own easy-going syntax. Even so basic a terminology as the colour chart reads like a record of conquests: black and white are Anglo-Saxon, violet is French, purple Latin, red and green are German, while crimson is the Turkish *krímízí* and azure the Arabic for blue. The empire brought home rich pickings from India – bungalow, jodhpur, gymkhana, numnah, curry, wallah, jute, thug, pukka, juggernaut, and the soldier's word for home: 'blighty'[1] – while the English-speaking peoples of America, Africa and Australia continue to create idioms and words which are accepted into the language without question, since nobody exists with the authority to question them. The *Oxford English Dictionary*, begun in 1884 by James Murray as the *New English Dictionary*, was the work of amateurs. It has been expressly descriptive rather than prescriptive in intention, being designed to record private initiatives but not to control them.

As a result of this the English had an extraordinary *embarras de richesses* when it came to finding the right expression – and not having the right expression for this, they borrowed that phrase from French. To denounce a smell you can use downright Anglo-Saxon words like smell, stench or stink; you can describe what you sniff in neutral French, in which case it becomes an odour; or you can praise it with other words of Latin origin, like scent, fragrance and aroma. If you really dislike it you can try the French malodorous; but it is far more likely that you will call it hateful, horrible, odious, loathsome, repulsive, offensive, disgusting, distasteful, nauseating, sickening or

---

[1] See the famous and never-to-be-overpraised lexicon of Anglo-India, compiled by Henry Yule and A.C. Burnell, *Hobson-Jobson*, ed. by William Crooke with an introduction by Anthony Burgess, London, 1985. 'Blighty' is *bilayut*, corrupted to *bilaiti*, meaning a foreign place: not a native Indian word but a corruption of Arabic *wilayat*, meaning a province. It was applied to anywhere that was 'elsewhere', and by the Afghans to their own country. English soldiers in the Great War applied it to the welcome wound that took one home for the duration.

(in more old-fashioned vein) noisome. The Eskimos were once said to have twenty words for snow,[1] but the English had twenty words for everything (except snow). Whether this vocabulary is still in common use may be doubted: but in the days when the English talked expressively they drew upon a range of nuances that is probably without compare among the world's spoken languages. It is hardly necessary to offer Shakespeare as the supreme example; but it is useful to note that the power of this writer is inseparable from his lexical richness. Six thousand words appear in his writings, compared to the thousand or so in Racine (whose achievement, however, is inseparable from the economy with which he shapes his lines).

Language is the *sine qua non*, without which there cannot be a national identity or culture. It is the fundamental stratum of the collective consciousness, and its influence is reflected in all the institutions and customs of society. The openness of the English language, which stems from the historical compromise that gave birth to it, fed into the social habits of its users. They were ready to innovate, and also to adapt innovation to the existing customs. Rules were made in order to be broken by mutual consent; compromise and conciliation were preferred to absolute standards, and concrete realities were given precedence over abstract ideas. It would not be too great a stretch of the imagination to suggest that empiricist philosophy, common law reasoning and even the institutions of parliamentary government are all limned in the concrete vocabulary and compromising syntax of English.

Things were thrown into relief by the multiplicity of lexical sources. Thus an Englishman could approach the skeleton in three ways: as bony (Anglo-Saxon), osseous (Latin) or the subject matter of osteology (Greek). The move away from the Anglo-Saxon is a move towards abstraction, marked out by the artificial sound of the language; conversely the Anglo-Saxon idiom acquires a concreteness

---

[1] This claim was fraudulent: see G.K. Pullum, *The Great Eskimo Vocabulary Hoax*, Chicago, 1991, pp. 159–71.

and knobbliness which is framed and endorsed by the smoother and more other-worldly idioms that surround it. The real and threatening foe (Anglo-Saxon) can be confronted as an enemy (French) or an adversary (Latin), and so studied from perspectives which are progressively more scientific and disengaged.

The 'native thew and sinew' of the Anglo-Saxon tongue has therefore been exploited by our poets to convey the fullness and thinginess of the material world (though Hopkins was stuck for a Saxon equivalent of 'native'). Hopkins is, of course, a leading instance. Look at 'Pied Beauty' – Hopkins's celebration of the here and now as a revelation of eternal things – and you will find an abundance of Anglo-Saxon consonants, used to convey the inescapable thisness of the sensory world: couple, brinded, stipple, fallow, gear, tackle, freckled, cow. Hopkins uses the Saxon monosyllables to bring the most abstract of ideas down to earth, and to bind them to the stuff of human existence:

> Here I creep,
> Wretch, under a comfort serves in a whirlwind: *all*
> *Life and death does end and each day dies with sleep.*

Even more telling is Shakespeare, who played the Latinate and the Germanic lexicons against each other, so as to show the predicament of man, torn between time and eternity. When Horatio offers to join Hamlet by drinking the poison that has just killed Gertrude, Hamlet deflects him with these words:

> Absent thee from felicity awhile,
> And in this harsh world draw thy breath in pain
> To tell my story.

The Latinisms of the first line beautifully evoke the abstract and tranquil quality of the life to come, while the second line, with its panting Saxon monosyllables, conveys the concrete reality of suffering on earth. In no other language could this contrast be so vividly made – it is not just described, it is *enacted* in the verse. English, in Shakespeare's hands, opens like a fruit, to reveal two other languages still only half blended within. In this lexical dualism is foreshadowed all the other dualisms that were to emerge in the English character: peers and people, Whig and Tory, Church and Chapel, U and non-U, officers and other ranks, cavalier and roundhead, High Church and Low Church, and a hundred more.

When I was jolted into an awareness of literature, by that oblique encounter with a Leavisite schoolmaster, it was by the juxtaposition of two Anglo-Saxon words: 'felt life'. The phrase comes in fact from Henry James;[1] but it was prized free from its serene and rhythmical context by Leavis, and thrown down like two wrestling limbs, locked in some violent struggle that continued long after the death of the sentence that had joined them. The ugly clash of consonants, the stabbing monosyllables, the concrete impression of the thing described – these emphasised the message of the Leavisites, that culture was too important a thing to be merely beautiful, and that literature was fundamentally not an aesthetic but a moral exercise, in which we wrestled with our destiny and despised the world of charm.

It is not consciousness, Leavis taught, that makes humans into moral beings, but culture. The same is true of a country. It is not the English language that moralised the English and gave England its distinctive personality, but English culture. But here we enter an area of intense controversy which Leavis, with his secular outlook, did little to moderate. A culture cannot be sustained by literary criticism alone; it must be constantly renewed from its social and religious sources. English culture was first and foremost the English religion, which imbued people with the consciousness of guilt and gave concrete sense to moral precepts – even to those precepts so forcefully urged on us by the Leavisites. This religion grew with the language, which it profoundly influenced and by which it was influenced in turn. It determined the musical, architectural and

---

[1] See the preface to *The Portrait of a Lady*.

storytelling traditions of the country at large, and was the single most important source of the customs whereby English society renewed itself.

If you look on religions with the eye of an anthropologist, sympathising with all of them but believing none, then you are likely to be struck by the fact that, through each doctrine, there shines the fate of a community. Even the universal religions – Christianity, Islam and Buddhism – bear the marks of an original social experiment, and achieve longevity because they are taken up by this or that community and woven into the seams of membership. If religion were primarily a system of belief, then it would strike us as extraordinary that there should be reserved, for those who make some small error in their reasoning, the name of heretic, and the terrible punishments which that name invites. In religious belief and observance, however, it is not the large differences that count but the small ones. The nearer someone is to me in his religious convictions, the greater my revulsion at the 'errors' which divide us. This is because belief is being treated, not as an attempt at the truth, but as a criterion of membership. The heretic is the one who speaks against the community from a place within its territory. He is the enemy within. The heathen, by contrast, is safely beyond the walls, excluded by his own invincible ignorance.

Hence we find that there are almost as many variants of Christianity as there are enduring communities of Christians. At the same time, Christianity is a universal faith, addressed to all mankind; like Islam, it claims jurisdiction over all the faithful. The attempt to reconcile these two aspects of the Christian religion has been one of the motors of Western civilisation. The real universality achieved by the Church of Rome was made possible partly because the Church inherited an international language and a transnational system of law. It also made use of rituals and festivals that offered another form of community, higher and more durable than the friendships of this world – a community whose leading members were dead. But for this reason local churches were constantly breaking away from Rome, or falling under the spell of personalities and doctrines that redefined their allegiance against the distant demands of an antiquated jurisdiction.

In England, Christianity adapted itself to the language and the circumstances of the community in which it had taken root. Its vital function as a criterion of membership entailed that it had to reflect the sense of belonging which animated the social feelings of the English. Whenever the question of identity became urgent – with the conflict between the Crown and the papacy under Henry II, with the Tudor usurpation, with the muddled loyalties of the Stuarts and the armed insurrection of the tax-paying classes under Cromwell – it clothed itself in doctrine, as each contender for the future invoked upon his opponent the divine retribution meant for heretics. Even in its last years England experienced religious violence, as the Northen Irish strove to dignify their rival forms of membership with religious uniforms. Religion had already ceased to be a path to salvation or a humble duty to the Lord. 'Catholic' and 'Protestant' were defined by heredity, rather than faith. They had become labels for two historical experiences of membership, and retained little of religion besides the sacred permission to kill.

In the light of all that history we should understand the Anglican Church for what it truly was – a *settlement*, an attempt at peace, in which Christian belief was moulded according to the needs of an idiosyncratic community, binding people loosely together and enabling them to feel sure that the strangers with whom they lived could remain strangers without becoming foes. Once the precious synthesis has been achieved, which binds a community together under a shared religious observance, doctrine becomes the greatest social benefit: the means whereby an ethical inheritance can be clarified and taught, and new generations brought under the aegis of a common discipline. It is then that a people becomes a person, with a will that is something more than the 'invisible hand' of the market.

Without this religious dimension nations and countries do not emerge as clearly defined moral entities. Of course, there can be *states* without religion – the modern world is full of them, and they provide us, in the examples of Nazi Germany and the Soviet Union, with useful examples of collectivism, in which what might have been a person became instead a machine – no longer a people, but a crowd in chains. No student of English history can fail to see that religion was from the very first mingled with the sense of English identity, and that the history of English religion and the history of England are in many epochs inseparable.

Nevertheless, religion is only the foundation of a national culture and not the whole of it. We must consider also the law and institutions which form the decision-making part of the collective consciousness. And we must consider too the habits of association, of commercial enterprise and artistic expression, if we are fully to understand the corporate personality of a people. If we look at things this way – building the person by stages on the raw material of place and climate – we shall arrive at a conception of national identity free from the old racial myths. And we shall understand more nearly just which elements of the national character are essential to the personality, and which merely remarkable.

The human face is, in its outline, a physical object, a natural endowment which grows and changes in obedience to the laws of organic nature. But the growth of personality transforms this face, which becomes gradually transparent to the moral unity that speaks and sees from it. Hence in all relations of love and loyalty, the face of the other remains the focus of emotion – the sign and incarnation of the spiritual essence.

In a similar way, the culture of a people feeds back into the psychic and physical layers in which it grows. The English, refusing to be imposed upon by foreigners, began to demand that the scriptures and the liturgy be given to them in their own eclectic tongue. Long before Wycliffe the demand for an English Bible took root in the national consciousness. And the Reformation, when it came, was as much an answer to this demand as a repudiation of papal authority. English was not merely infected by the language of William

Tyndale's Bible and Cranmer's Prayer Book. It was entirely recast in a mould of Christian patriotism. It was a consecrated language, which seemed to invoke another and unearthly England, in which those feet really did walk upon England's mountains green.

The transformation of the language was matched by an equal transformation of the landscape, which, like the human face, became transparent to the moral entity that shone from it. Your love of your native landscape is quite different from the tourist's interest in scenery. The landscape and townscape of your native country are irradiated by the national character, as the face is irradiated by the soul. You do not consciously infer from their contours the history, laws and institutions that shaped them; you see these things directly, as you see the moral character of another when you look him in the eyes.

And that is what I mean when I describe England as an enchanted landscape: it was enchanted in just the way that a human face is enchanted, when a person lives in it not for himself but for others, and bends its contours so as to reveal his heart. To describe the attitude of the English to their landscape as Arcadian is to miss the real significance of what they did. They remade the landscape as the outward sign of their inner unity, as a place that was a fitting home for their collective act of dwelling. And all that they most loved in their society – the permeable boundaries that kept them apart, the negotiations and compromises that healed the wounds of conflict, the overarching law-abidingness and the sense of belonging and owner-ship which redeemed the accidents of nature – they unconsciously imprinted on the face of England, to produce that inimitable patchwork which was one of the few things, besides the clouds and the climate, that their painters knew how to furnish with a soul.

England was a place, a climate and a language, which had been welded together and endowed with personality by an experience which was fundamentally religious in its meaning. The institutions and culture which grew with the English religion were not accidental additions but organic outgrowths, and expressions of a collective soul. In surveying the institutions of the English we are surveying the essence of England – the *genius loci* which enchanted the land.

Chapter Five

The English Religion

'It hath been the wisdom of the Church of England, ever since the first compiling of her Publick Liturgy, to keep the mean between two extremes, of too much stiffness in refusing, and of too much easiness in admitting any variation from it.' So begins the preface to the Book of Common Prayer, the liturgical authority of the old Anglican Church, and the greatest gift of that Church to the English people. As those words suggest, the prayerbook was a compromise, designed to secure harmonious relations among people for whom the English liturgy was a symbol of their common home, and of the Providence that had placed them there.

The English Church, like the English law, Parliament and Crown, was a *settlement* – a solution to long-standing quarrels and discontents, in which rival beliefs, rival masters and rival liturgies finally congealed around an acceptable common practice. The eccentricity – indeed, the downright weirdness – of the Anglican Church and its Nonconformist offshoots were hardly noticed by the resulting community of half-believers. What mattered to them was less the clarity and certainty of a religious faith, than the shared experience of sanctity, which blessed in familiar but elevated tones the country and society that were theirs. Their ruling thought was, in Santayana's words, that 'nothing can be obligatory for a Christian that is unpalatable to an Englishman'.[1] And behind the orderly

---

[1] *Soliloquies in England and Later Soliloquies*, London, 1932, p. 45.

offices of their Church, stood a long tradition of apologists, from Richard Hooker to Archbishop Temple, offering a theology of imperfection in which orthodoxy went hand in hand with lenience.

My first encounters with the religion of the English were at school. In both primary school and secondary school the day would begin with an assembly, in which lessons were read, prayers offered and hymns sung, to the accompaniment of a piano played by a member of staff. The words used were invariably those of the King James Bible and the Book of Common Prayer, and when we said the Lord's Prayer it was to Our Father *which* art in heaven, with a promise to forgive *them that* trespass against us.[1] These peculiar idioms seemed to have no other explanation than the unfathomable holiness of the being to whom they were addressed, and this effect was only enhanced by the fact that God spoke and was spoken to in a language that was both richer, more ceremonial and in a strange way more intimate than any used among ourselves. The rudiments of theology were conveyed by the readings and the hymns, and the invocation of the main items of Christian faith in all public ceremonies ensured that none of us was ignorant of God the Father, God the Son and God the Holy Ghost – though the word 'ghost' would send a shiver down the spine, reminding us of another Christian doctrine, that God should be not only loved but feared.

Real religion came later. My parents were sensible people who had lived through the war and come to the conclusion that no God could possibly have permitted it. As far as my mother was concerned, that was the end of the matter. But it was not the end of the matter for my father, who had been brought up among Nonconformists, saved from starvation by the Salvation Army, and constantly offended by the Anglican Church, which his mother had forced him to attend, and which for him was one arm of the ruling conspiracy that cast a shadow over England. He wished his children to graduate to atheism

---

[1] The grammar of the old Lord's Prayer (which dates from Cranmer's liturgy of 1549) was already antiquated in 1662, when the Book of Common Prayer as we know it was finally imposed.

from a heritage of Nonconformist gloom. That way they would acquire a healthy contempt for robes and chasubles and rood screens, for toffee-nosed vicars and the gentry in their private pews. My sisters and I were sent first to a Methodist chapel, where we encountered the hymns, lessons and prayers that were already familiar from school, and then, when this experience seemed not to improve us, to a Baptist chapel, a place so cold and bleak and forlorn that my parents never set foot there.

The Baptist chapel offered services of a confused and mysterious kind. We knew that they were preparations for the terrible ordeal in which, it was rumoured, we would be forced to plunge naked into a tank of water, before a crowd of onlookers so purified by their own immersion, as to be able to stare at a naked body without sin (a feat of which we, by contrast, would be for ever incapable). The thought of this ordeal gave a peculiar urgency to the biblical instruction, conducted by a slow-spoken old man who was a carpenter by trade, and whose horny fingers with their blackened nails conveyed, as they traced the verses on those India-paper pages, such a weight of simple trust and piety that I was touched in spite of myself, and would often put all my pocket money into the velvet collection pouch that came round at the end of the class. At the first sign that the regime of parental vigilance was slackening, however, we escaped from the Baptist yoke and joined the company of unbelievers. My father did not insist, assuming that we had acquired the rudiments of proletarian religion and would now be safe from the encroachment of a forbidden holiness.

He was wrong. All over the neighbouring countryside were those sleepy hamlets and half-vacant villages, each with its Norman or Early English church of flint and stone. And in these churches a peculiar silence had been stored, along with the sweet damp smell of plaster, the mouldering prayer books, the embroidered kneelers and the Victorian altar cloths with their gold and emerald fabrics, like robes left behind by some visiting angel. You could not ignore these places. My father too was drawn to them, for he was a country lover, a disciple of H.J. Massingham. He delighted in country lanes and shady churchyards, where you could contemplate the beauty of a landscape made in the image of the Anglican God, who in turn had been made in the image of the landscape. When we moved to Marlow it was partly to escape from the ever-expanding exurbia which had turned High Wycombe from a country town to a place of office blocks and motor-mad vandals. And it was in Marlow that I discovered the English religion.

I had adopted my father's habit of country walks; and like him I would make a point of entering the churches. Some years before, in 1955, Philip Larkin had published *The Less Deceived*, with its beautiful elegy entitled 'Church Going'. Its last stanza spoke to a whole generation of people who were seeing the last of England:

> A serious house on serious earth it is,
> In whose blent air all our compulsions meet,
> Are recognised, and robed as destinies.
> And that much never can be obsolete,
> Since someone will forever be surprising
> A hunger in himself to be more serious,
> And gravitating with it to this ground,
> Which, he once heard, was proper to grow wise in,
> If only that so many dead lie round.

On first reading, those are the thoughts of an archaeologist – the uncommitted visitor, unearthing the trinkets of a vanished piety. On second reading, however, you recognise that the lines don't merely *describe* the Anglican faith; they *express* it. Just this is what the English once believed.

English churches tell of a people who preferred seriousness to doctrine, and routine to enthusiasm – people who hoped for immortality but did not really expect it, except as a piece of English earth. The walls are covered with discreet memorials, placing the dead at the same convenient distance that they occupied when living.

The pews are hard, uncomfortable, designed not for lingering and listening but for moments of penitence and doubt. The architecture is noble but bare and quiet, without the lofty aspiration of the French Gothic, or the devotional intimacy of an Italian chapel. More prominent than the altar are the lectern, the pulpit, the choir stalls and the organ. For this is a place of singing and speaking, in which biblical English passes the lips of people who believe that holy thoughts need holy words, words somehow removed from the business of the world, like gems lifted from a jewel box and then quickly returned to the dark.

Christianity inherited from Judaism a hatred of idolatry and from Greek polytheism a love of idols. Each Christian sect has had to resolve this paradox in its own way; the Anglican way being forged over centuries of conflict. The English Church recognised that, in the last analysis, God is not distinct from the way of representing Him, yet identical with no physical thing. The earthly phenomenon through which He can be most accurately viewed is language – which has both a temporal reality and a timeless sense. It is through language, therefore, that the Anglican Church defined its God. It drew on the full resources of English to present a God who is dignified yet down-to-earth, at home in the world yet inscrutably withheld from it. God, as represented in the sacred text and liturgy of the Anglican Church, was an Englishman, uncomfortable in the presence of enthusiasm, reluctant to make a fuss, but trapped into making public speeches. Like His fellow countrymen, God hid His discomfiture behind a solemn screen of words, using old-fashioned idioms which somehow excused the severity of what He was bound by His office to say. In His presence you used the same antique language and, although both of you knew that this was in some measure a pretence, it suited you to rehearse your relationship in words that distanced it from the world outside. More than in any country I have visited, the English country church was a home – God's house, the private space which was both here and elsewhere, a part of England, and an immortal projection of England in a realm beyond space and time.[1]

That was why the village churches of England made such a deep impression on those who entered them. God had been in residence here, among much-polished things, had moved with stiff English decorum around these light-filled spaces, had played the part of host to generations of people whose shyness He respected and shared. You came away with a sense that here and now were once as sacred as eternity and the grace of God on offer twice a week.

That this had not come about without a painful history was evident from the very appearance of those quiet interiors. Iconoclasm and puritan vandalism had swept through these arches like a boiling tide through seashore caverns and, retreating, had left them bare. But you sensed too that the storms had passed, that the architecture was the purer and the cleaner for the brutal torrent that had washed away its ornaments, and that the stunned tranquillity of those pitted walls would remain everlastingly.

I began, aged fifteen, to attend Marlow church. My father believed that I went each Sunday morning to the Baptist chapel, having inexplicably rediscovered a desire to inspect my sins. I excused the lie, since it was told on God's behalf. But it was also a fitting apprenticeship in the English religion, that I should begin my devotions from a posture of pretence. Marlow church is itself a pretence: a large, Gothic revival structure in flint and stone, designed to look as though it had stood for ever at the end of a high street where it was in fact the newest building.

Until Pevsner came on the scene, and intimidated the English with censorious German scholarship, the Gothic revival had been accepted as an integral part of the English settlement, a good-natured attempt to ensure that God found suitable accommodation in the country that was His. Of course, the revival made an impact on the continent –

[1] It has been argued that the idea of a privileged relation between the English and their God precedes the Reformation by centuries. See J.W. McKenna, 'How God became an Englishman', in D.J. Guth and J.W. McKenna, eds, *Tudor Rule and Revolution*, London, 1982, pp. 25–43.

but it was with isolated and showy monuments like the Hungarian Parliament. Only in England and its colonies did neo-Gothic architecture fulfil its spiritual mission, as an unassuming vernacular idiom which remade the landscape as something ancient and immune to change. It was a deeply moral architecture, composed in a syntax that deliberately denied the manufactures which made it possible, just as biblical English denied the everyday speech of those who used it in their worship. And, having established its legitimacy in ecclesiastical use, the neo-Gothic style rapidly spread through the culture, encrusting factories, law courts, schools, colleges, waterworks, railway stations and houses with fairy-tale pinnacles and dreaming towers. To the visiting architectural historian it had turned the English towns and cities into vast arenas of pretence, as hypocritical in their appearance as in the religious manners which the buildings signified. To the English, however, the Gothic revival was simply a new way to reaffirm their ownership of England, and to restore their country to its true condition of enchantment.

And this charge of hypocrisy – so often made by foreigners, and endorsed from time to time by the English themselves – should be viewed from the Gothic perspective. The hypocrite is someone who pretends to believe something, or to feel something, in order to score some advantage by deception. English religion was not, in that sense, hypocritical, any more than good manners are hypocritical, even though they involve conventional expressions of goodwill which could not possibly stand up to interrogation. The intention was not to deceive, still less to score an advantage, but to collaborate in the work of re-enchantment. For the English had long since accepted what Wilde meant when he said that in matters of the greatest importance, it is style and not sincerity that counts.

For this reason 'we have in England,' as Addison put it,[1] 'a particular bashfulness in everything that regards religion'. The very topic of religion was embarrassing, as unmentionable as sex or love or hygiene. Like patriotism, of which it was a part, the English religion

[1] *Spectator*, no. 458, 15th August 1712.

had been placed beyond question. This was not because people did not question it – on the contrary. It was because it was common knowledge that there was nothing to be gained from doing so. The English knew in their hearts that religion is a human invention – the whole history of their Church reminded them of this. The census of 1851 showed that already only 50 per cent of them were regular worshippers – a figure which dropped to 25 per cent in some city areas. Yet they automatically put 'C of E' on any form inquiring after their religion, and acknowledged the necessity of religion in every ceremony in which their loyalties as Englishmen were rehearsed. Their religion was a conscious artefact. Like good manners, it did not bear too close an interrogation. It was a collective polishing of the world, and veneered the ordinary life of England in the way that a smile veneers a face.

The Gothic revival captured this aspect of English religion perfectly. And Ruskin, its greatest advocate after Pugin, made architecture and religion into matters of syntax. All that he wrote on this great theme is in the tone of voice of the English Church, moving from penitential cries to iron exhortations with the rapidity of liturgical speech. His writings are an attempt to sanctify and sacramentalise the things that he found beautiful – to find in them the inspiration and the focus of prayer. His writings combine down-to-earthness with hieratic dignity, in the manner of the Book of Common Prayer, and he made the search for beauty in architecture coterminous with the search for salvation. 'When we build,' he wrote in *Seven Lamps of Architecture*, 'let us think that we build for ever.' And he meant this 'for ever' as much, and as little, as it is meant by those who pray in church, rounding off their words with 'for ever and ever, amen'. All buildings perish; and the Gothic revival both accepts and denies this fact, raising symbols of forever which may be as improvised and transient as a chapel in corrugated iron, or as rooted and immovable as Liverpool Cathedral – that last great creation of English architecture, by the man who also gave us the cast-iron telephone box.

Marlow church had a 'High Church' vicar, with a double-barrelled name (Vaughan-Wilkes) and an upper-class voice, who lived in the old rectory beside the churchyard. His services were conducted to the letter of the Book of Common Prayer, and his sermons were elaborations of its poetry. His wife was daughter of the Very Reverend Cyril Argentine Alington, Anglican divine, headmaster of Eton, and author of many famous hymns, including 'Good Christian men, rejoice and sing!' The Rev. Vaughan-Wilkes had himself been a master at Eton, and then headmaster at Radley, before entering the Church. I later learned that he was a holy and humble man, who had for many years practised his vocation among miners, who had always refused ecclesiastical preferment, and who spent his energies in charitable work. At the time, however, he was for me a symbol of the Anglican Establishment and a representative of its peculiar charm. Marlow was a church which prided itself on doing things properly, where robed choir boys sang in procession, leading the Rev. Vaughan-Wilkes to the altar in his flowing chasuble like cherubs drawing some airborne god. The mystery of the Catholic faith wafted around the altar, while the old Protestant call to duty resounded through the hymns. The psalms were chanted by the choir in that peculiar tuneless and metreless idiom, by means of which the Anglican Church retained the mesmerism of plainsong while carefully removing all traces of its monastic appeal. The organist began and ended with voluntaries, drawing extensively on the French repertoire (Franck, Widor and Vierne), which released an ineffable loneliness – the loneliness of the organ loft itself – into the space of the church, muffling every soul that knelt there. And during communion the organist would improvise on muted pipes, whimsical watery sequences, full of fifths and fourths in the manner of Vaughan Williams and Herbert Howells. It was as though the Holy Ghost himself were present, humming quietly to himself in an English accent.

Sexual intercourse, Larkin tells us, began in 1963. Certainly it had

not begun in 1959 – not in Marlow at least. All our encounters with
the other sex were veiled in hesitation, and the imagined ecstasies of
love were projected into a remote and inaccessible realm which could
be entered only after long ordeals of separation, and only by means of
rituals and charms whose secrets were yet to be discovered. To put it
in another and more anthropological way: sex was a rite of passage,
which could be accomplished only through the ceremonial assent of
the tribe. And the same was true of the old religion. The Anglican
Church stood at a distance; its secrets were offered only after careful
preparation, and only by virtue of a ceremony of confirmation, in
which His Lordship the bishop came to lay on hands. And the two
rites of passage were easily confused.

The spotless girl in white whom I had glimpsed at my first
morning prayer turned up at the confirmation classes in the rectory.
Each Sunday she was in church, her demure pale cheeks bandaged in
a scarf, her eyes downturned and unobtainable. I never spoke to her,
knew nothing about her, not even her name, except that she lived in
Marlow Bottom. But thanks to this girl confirmation classes were, for
me, a coming to light of the loveliest mystery, whose meaning could
be captured in no theological doctrine since it was a matter too deep
for belief. Religion, like sex, was an unfolding flower, which released
its perfume into the morning air and lingered thereafter as a memory.
After confirmation I never saw the object of my passion in church,
and I too ceased to go there.

That first full sighting of the English religion made a lasting
impression, nonetheless. All the elements of the faith had already
been conveyed to me: the language, the stories, the hymns, the
liturgical response to the world and its misdoings. And now it had
crystallised around the Anglican rite. The meaning of all this, I dimly
sensed, was not detachable from the spiritual reality of England. The
Christian faith had been melted down by history and recast in this
peculiar ornamental form. The result was a revelation, not of God
only, but of God's chosen people, as the English with shy but
implacable determination assumed themselves to be. This assumption

was not peculiar to the High Church tradition of Marlow; indeed, it was never more explicitly stated than by the puritan Milton, who wrote that 'God reveals himself to his servants, and as his manner is, first to his Englishmen'. Still, Milton's state of mind belongs with Bishop Jewel's *Apology*, with John Foxe's *Actes and Monuments*, which told the story of the protestant martyrs under Mary Tudor, and with Bunyan's *The Pilgrim's Progress*. Like them, it is part of the archaeology of English religion, which had yet to undergo the decisive transformations of Wesley, Methodism and the Nonconformist churches. And it had yet to encounter the Oxford Movement, which divided High Church from Low Church within the Anglican rite itself. Looking back now, on that first full glimpse of this spiritual achievement, my impression is one of wonder that this subtle artefact had been able to sustain itself for so long, to adapt itself to so much and to flow through so many coexisting, contending and yet in the end mutually accommodating channels.

The contest between Church and State, which divided all the peoples of Europe throughout the Middle Ages, was experienced in England as a conflict between papal jurisdiction and the 'ancient customs of the realm': so the matter was put by King Henry II at Westminster in 1163, when the bishops one by one climbed down and acknowledged the jursidiction of the civil courts – all save Thomas à Becket, Archbishop of Canterbury. Thus came to a head the conflict which ended with the murder and canonisation of Thomas, the penitence of the King, and a lasting settlement in which it was left undecided whether the Church of England was the sovereign's or the pontiff's fiefdom.[1] In fact it was neither, and had already taken on a life of its own. The Church *in* England had already become the Church *of* England, an autonomous institution persisting, in English fashion, by compromises, volte-faces and delays, until the time of Henry VIII, who was raised to the title of 'defender of the faith' by Pope Leo X on account of his defence of the seven

---

[1] Here as elsewhere I am skating over matters that remain highly controversial among historians. See G.R. Elton, *The English*, London, 1992, p. 61, and the references therein.

sacraments against the sarcasm of Martin Luther. Having secured the goodwill of the pontiff, Henry VIII declared himself to be in law what he already was in fact, namely, the titular head of the Church of England, neglecting to specify, however, whether the Church remained part of, or apart from, the 'apostolic succession' which supposedly gave precedence to Rome. Henceforth the Church was to be subject to, and expressive of, 'the law of the land'. The Athanasian creed remained in the liturgy, so that English congregations declared their belief in 'the holy Catholick Church; the Communion of Saints and the Forgiveness of sins'. Moreover, the Anglican Church continued to dispense the sacraments, and to perpetuate the offices, hierarchies and functions that were previously the exclusive property of Rome.

The Reformation was a seismic force, and precipitated the iconoclastic tides that stripped the glorious churches of England. Nevertheless, it owed much of its lasting influence to the fact that it coincided in its intent with the existing interpretation of the Catholic faith. The English refused to recognise the authority of a power so foreign to their language and customs as the Roman papacy, and found nothing peculiar in the fact that the Crown – which was, after all, only a legal personification of England – should be the titular head of their Church. Such had already been implied in 1164, when Henry II forced the Constitutions of Clarendon on Archbishop Thomas. Hostility to Rome was more an expression of national identity than of doctrinal dissidence; it led twice to the rejection of the Stuarts, largely because their Catholic connections seemed to threaten the safety of the realm. For the English, sovereignty and the national religion were ultimately identical. Hence the Reformation was imposed on them through Parliament – something that did not happen elsewhere, and which testified both to the worldliness of English religion, and to the other-worldliness of English laws. This sequence from the Prayer Book of 1662, heard with utter astonishment by visitors to England, was therefore, for the worshippers in Marlow, merely an acknowledgement of the obvious:

Priest. O Lord, shew they mercy upon us.
Answer. And grant us thy salvation.
Priest. O Lord, save the Queen.
Answer. And mercifully hear us when we call upon thee.

Many critics find the spirit of the Reformation in Chaucer and Langland, in the medieval passion plays and mystery plays, and in the long-standing and irrepressible desire for an English Bible. The Reformation is certainly present in Wycliffe (*c.* 1320–1384) and his followers (the 'Lollards'), and is both cause and effect of the most important social achievement of the English Church, which is the sanctifying of the English language. Despite ecclesiastical censure, translations of biblical and liturgical texts (some attributed to Wycliffe) proliferated in the fourteenth and fifteenth centuries. By the time Henry VIII declared himself the head of it, the English Church had acquired an English Bible, ostensibly the work of Miles Coverdale, and published under his name in 1535, but largely pillaged from William Tyndale, who was burned as a heretic near Brussels in the following year. Versions continued to proliferate both before and after Mary Tudor's rejection of the whole idea and combustion of its advocates. By the time King James I commissioned fifty-four divines to produce what is now known as the Authorised Version (1611), it had become clear that the English Church and the English Bible were inseparable. Henceforth both those who accepted the Anglican supremacy and those who dissented from it expressed their beliefs in the sanctified idiom of Tyndale. God had found a voice, and the voice was English.

The English Prayer Book was imposed in its final form by the Act of Uniformity of 1662, but, like the English Bible, came into being over a century of experiment, initiated by the genius of a single man, in this case Archbishop Thomas Cranmer, whose liturgy was first enforced in 1549. Between them Tyndale and Cranmer created that extraordinary idiom which enabled the English to express complex moral sentiments in direct and simple terms, and to endow the objects and institutions of their world with a nimbus of home-grown sanctity. Some of this language has passed into everyday speech: 'the fat of the land', 'men of renown', 'in the land of Nod', 'a fool's Paradise', 'scapegoat', and so on from Tyndale; 'miserable sinners', 'the world, the flesh and the devil', 'the time of our tribulation', and similar from Cranmer. But much of biblical and liturgical English remained apart from the common tongue – influencing it and influenced by it, but discreetly haloed, nevertheless, as it worked its miracles in the everyday world. Words like 'almighty' and 'everlasting'; phrases like 'the author of peace and the lover of concord'; images like those of the general Confession: 'We have erred and strayed from thy ways like lost sheep. We have followed too much the desires and devices of our own hearts' – all these transfigured the things and situations to which they were applied. They were familiar, dignified words, which lost nothing from repetition. Armed with their sound and syntax, the congregation at Marlow was never at a loss for prayer. And liturgical English endowed them with a mysterious key to God's presence – the archaic 'thou' which made the most binding intimacy into another and holier form of remoteness.

It was this language that the English Church held in trust, and which formed the real essence of its religion. Historians continue to argue over the causes of the Cromwellian Rebellion and of the Puritan rage against the Church and the government of England. But the literature of the time makes abundantly clear that the sound and syntax of the Bible gave shape to the prevailing bellicosity. It was an age when truth seemed more important than compromise, and when the settlement envisaged in the thirty-nine articles (which date from the realm of Elizabeth) was suddenly under threat. Englishmen could now shout at one another in God's tone of voice, and this lent exultation to their anger. But the very fact that the language was a common possession led at last to a renewed attempt at compromise. And in the event it was compromise that won. True, the imposition of the Act of Uniformity led to the departure of some nine hundred ministers from the Church of England. But within six decades the Nonconforming congregations had won the right to build their own churches, and the language heard in them was the old liturgical idiom of Tyndale and Cranmer.

Thus we find the evangelical John Wesley addressing his followers in the same idiolect as the popish Edward Pusey. Both were Anglicans; each defended a faith that he called 'catholic'. Wesley, advocating scriptural worship and union with a God-fearing congregation, describes the true catholic as 'one who, retaining these blessings with the strictest care, keeping them as the apple of his eye, at the same time loves – as friends, as brethren in the Lord, as members of Christ and children of God, as joint-partakers now of the present kingdom of God, and fellow-heirs of his eternal kingdom – all, of whatever opinion, or worship, or congregation, who believe in the Lord Jesus Christ'.[1] And this magnanimous gesture of toleration is so shaped by the English Bible as scarcely to be told apart from it. The words ('brethren', 'partakers', 'kingdom') are biblical; the idioms and allusions too are biblical or liturgical ('apple of his eye', for example, is from Deuteronomy 32, 10; 'members of Christ' is from the catechism in the Book of Common Prayer, and ultimately from St Paul), and the whole is presented in the same spirit of compromise as is declared in the opening sentence of the Prayer Book. (Wesley owed his following partly to his advocacy of human freedom; he was not a Calvinist but a believer in free will, who saw the Anglican Church as a congenial society in which the bid for personal salvation could be politely made.)

The evangelical emphasis on the scriptures was possible only because the Bible and liturgy had been translated into a sacramental language. Religion without sacrament decays first into dogma and then into doubt. The Victorians knew this in their hearts, and therefore set out to reconsecrate the language, the customs and the

---

[1] John Wesley, 'Catholic Spirit', in *The English Sermon*, vol. III, 1750–1850, ed. Robert Nye, Manchester, 1976, p. 55.

physical reality of their Church. The Oxford Movement arose because Newman, Keble and Pusey feared that the scriptures were being detached by the Wesleyans from the sacraments that were their real – because mysterious – meaning. Yet even the Tractarians, drawing on the same tradition as the evangelicals, use the conciliatory language of the Prayer Book to imply and create a unity of purpose that will allow all sorts of Englishmen to remain beneath a common ecclesiastical roof. 'So,' wrote Pusey, 'while we each think all good of the other, may we all together, strengthened by the Same Bread, washed by the Same Blood, be led, in the unity of the Spirit and the bond of peace and holiness of life, to that ineffable Feast, where not, as now, in Mysteries, but, face to face, we shall ever see God, and be ever filled with His Goodness and Love.'[1] The words, taken from St Paul and from the Prayer Book, are again saturated with the common store of religious utterance, a reminder that the English Church will be always one and whole, so long as its words remain unaltered.

Where in all this was the conflict between Protestant and Catholic? This is a question too complex and contentious for such a book as this, but I shall nevertheless venture a suggestion. Those historians, such as Linda Colley, who argue that the 'British' identity of the English kingdom emerged from a common Protestant culture, seem to me to have got things the wrong way round. It was much more that the English understood Protestantism in terms of their expanding idea of nationality, than that they understood their nationality in terms of the Protestant faith. They *called* themselves Protestants, certainly, but not so loudly as to deny that they were also members of the Catholic Church. And they abhorred the Pope – though, as Defoe remarked, the streets of London were, at the time of the 'no Popery' riots, full of 'stout fellows willing to fight to the death against Popery without knowing whether it be a man or a horse'. The contest with Rome remained what it had always been – a dispute over jurisdiction and sovereignty, and a tenacious adherence

---

[1] Edward Bouverie Pusey, 'The Holy Eucharist a Comfort to the Penitent', in *ibid.*, p. 232.

to local custom and historic compromise as the true sources of legitimacy. Mary Tudor's brief return to Rome alarmed the English because it also threatened a catastrophic surrender to Spain. The burning of Cranmer, and the subsequent publication of Foxe's *Actes and Monuments* (popularly known as the Book of Martyrs), were taken by the English as warnings of what might happen, were they to surrender their Church and their country to the rule of Mediterranean despots. The dispute concerned sovereignty rather than doctrine, and survives to this day in Northern Ireland, where two communities of pagans cling to the labels 'Protestant' and 'Catholic' by way of defining conflicting political loyalties.

That, surely, is how we should see the Protestant succession. The law stipulates that the Crown of England must be conferred on or inherited by a Protestant: the reason being that, for a century or more before the law was passed, Roman Catholicism had meant allegiance to Rome, to Spain or to France, in conflicts which were critical for the future of England. The English have cared less about the origins, titles or sanity of their kings and queens than about their commitment to upholding the law of England – the very law by which they hold office, and which can be used if necessary to eject them. The true interpretation of the law of succession is not that the monarch should be a Protestant in any real sense of the term, but that he or she should be wholly and exclusively committed to upholding the law, customs and sovereignty of the English people. This deeply rooted attitude to the law is precisely what makes so many English people antagonistic to the European Union, the European Courts and the 'directives' of the European Commission, which are orders dictated from on high, rather than laws discovered within.

It is true that the genuinely Protestant Churches of Calvin, Luther and Zwingli influenced the Anglican faith. In matters of liturgy and doctrine, however, the English Church remained obstinately attached to the ancient mysteries, preferring unexplained and inexplicable tradition to rational systems of theology, and inventing for itself a sacred language that retained the ancestral tone of Latin, while being the voice of the English people as they dialogued with God. Only in two particulars did it depart from the Roman Catholic tradition, and this was in its repudiation of the monastic ideal, and its admission of a married priesthood. Through the cathedral chapters and the Oxford and Cambridge colleges, the Anglican Church retained another and more domesticated version of the monastic orders. And by allowing priests to marry it integrated them more firmly into the society of England, enabling them to compete on equal terms with the rural squirearchy among whom they lived. (This led to the odd result that, until late in the nineteenth century, the fellows of Oxford and Cambridge colleges could not marry, while their college chaplains could!)

The first full flowering of Protestantism in England preceded the invention of the 'British' people, and very quickly dwindled into a form that could be digested by the English Church. The seventeenth-century Puritans, like the nineteenth-century Nonconformists, were defined by their opposition from within to the gorgeous trappings of the Anglican ceremony. And, with the Toleration Act of 1720, which permitted dissenters to build churches of their own, the English Church recuperated its dissident offspring, offering new forms of worship in which the only thing that mattered – the sacred language and the sacred texts – remained unaltered. As I prepared in my confirmation classes to take part in the ritual which in many Anglican churches was still known as 'Mass', I studied *The Pilgrim's Progress*, and found nothing incongruous between this Puritan exhortation and the mystery for which I was being groomed.

The principal influence of continental Protestantism was in fact not verbal but musical. Much as we should be grateful for the language and liturgy of the Anglican Church, we must deplore the weird interdiction which killed off polyphony at the very moment when Tallis and Byrd (successive masters of the Chapel Royal, and both of them Catholics) had learned to rival Palestrina and Victoria in this supremely religious art form. By way of compensation, the Anglican Church embarked on the musical experiments which were eventually to lead to one of the most fertile forms of popular music that has ever existed: the vernacular hymn. The Geneva Psalter of Calvin, and the choral hymns of Martin Luther, gradually seeped into the Anglican service – even though, when this began to happen in the early eighteenth century, it was strictly speaking illegal. John Wesley could be more visionary in his hymns than ever he was in his sermons, and if the English became Protestant under his influence it was not because of any change to the liturgy, but because his verses drew on the Bible rather than the Book of Common Prayer, and made the daily dedication of life more important than the weekly commemoration of the Eucharist. Here is an example:

> Jesus, the first and last,
> On thee my soul is cast:
> Thou didst the work begin
> By blotting out my sin;
> Thou wilt the root remove,
> And perfect me in love.

> Yet when the work is done
> The work is but begun:
> Partaker of thy grace,
> I long to see thy face;
> The first I prove below,
> The last I die to know.

Erik Routley has detected no less than eleven biblical references in these lines, to Old Testament, Gospel and Epistle, all achieved by evoking words and phrases from the Authorized Version.[1] Wesley could also be magnificently doctrinal, as in this famous condensation of the doctrine of the Incarnation:

> Veiled in flesh the Godhead see,
> Hail the incarnate Deity!

[1] Erik Routley, *Hymns and Human Life*, London, 1952, p. 70.

Pleased as man with man to dwell,
Jesus, our Immanuel . . .

Mild he lays his glory by,
Born that man no more may die;
Born to raise the sons of earth,
Born to give them second birth.

But this intrusion of abstract theology into English worship was accommodated and neutralised by singing. At Marlow we belted out this famous hymn ('Hark, the herald angels sing') to the music of Mendelssohn, that gentle fellow-traveller of the Christian faith whom Queen Victoria, then head of the Anglican Church, took to her heart, as the Church did also, despite the fact, and also because of the fact, that he was a Jew.

The hymnal shows us the extent to which the English Church was not merely a religious institution, but the foundation of a genuine popular culture. Legal uncertainty meant that the official Anglican Church did not admit hymn singing into its services until the practice had become a thriving means of recruitment to the evangelical missions and therefore a threat to the Anglican supremacy. The first church hymn book for general use was published in 1769. John Wesley's brother Charles wrote verses which were repeatedly set to music, and his two sons – Charles and Samuel – were among the foremost composers of their day, though Samuel's conversion to Roman Catholicism led him to write masses, motets and glees rather than straightforward hymn tunes. Samuel's illegitimate son and namesake, however, was a leading force in the choral movement which made the cathedral choir into one of the glories of Victorian England. His anthems and services, with their Romantic harmonies and poignant English melodies, epitomise the nostalgic vision of our country which lies at the heart of the Anglican faith, while his hymn tunes remain among the most memorable in the hymnal.

Hymns passed freely from the Nonconformist to the official

church and back again, so that, by the middle of the nineteenth century, the hymn was the living symbol of the English churches, and of the unity-in-diversity which made these churches into a single and singular social force. The Oxford Movement brought back many of the old Latin hymns, while the evangelicals explored the more dignified products of the German Reformation. Operatic dross was discarded in favour of solid, psalm-like, pilgrim-pushing melodies, and these were again the common property of the English churches.

Thus the hymnal, like the Bible, has helped to unite the Anglican and Nonconformist churches. The hymns have been shaped by the liturgy; but they in turn have shaped the service of the Anglican Church. They have provided the important moments of participation, in which God is praised and worshipped in song, and the drama of the service is momentarily interrupted by the chorus. They have replaced the psalms as vehicles of collective sentiment, and the psalms in their turn have become part of the liturgy.

The hymns emancipated themselves from orthodoxy by virtue of their musical power, becoming the foundation of a popular musical culture centred on Nonconformist worship. The Labour movement would not have been the peaceful thing it was, without the repertoire of hymns which gathered people in congregations, rather than in armies, behind the brass bands of the collieries.

The hymns rely on memorable and popular tunes; but they are in no sense a low-grade art form. Hymns are among the masterpieces of medieval monody, of Renaissance polyphony, and of German Renaissance and Baroque counterpoint. Few strophic songs achieve the melodic sublimity and harmonic intensity of the Passion Chorale, harmonised by Bach for the *St Matthew Passion*, and for a long time one of the most popular of Easter hymns. Fragments of plainsong have survived in the hymnal – 'Pange Lingua', 'Veni Emmanuel'[1] – and several of Palestrina's hymns are still with us. So too are the

---

[1] Evidently of plainsong origin, though transcribed 'from a French missal' by Thomas Helmore (1811–1890).

favourites from the Geneva Psalter, such as the 'Old Hundredth' ('All people that on earth do dwell'). Bach, Handel, Mendelssohn and Haydn are all represented in the hymnal. But the most important input has undeniably come from English composers themselves, and especially from the Romantics and proto-moderns. A whole school of Victorian composers arose from the cathedral choir and its musical context, and the church choir, which was the foundation of musical education in England, helped to spread their music far and wide across the country. The very language of English Romanticism, from Parry and Stanford through Elgar, Holst and Vaughan Williams (editor of the *Anglican Hymnal* of 1906), to Ireland and Bax, is saturated with the idiom of the hymnal. Song and collective worship form the background to their music; and it is hardly surprising to discover that some of our most memorable hymns come from their pens.

There is a feature of the hymnals which deserves our notice, since it shows the connection between English religion and the sense of England as a dwelling place. Hymn tunes composed since Victorian times have almost always been named from the place of composition, and their titles form a lexicon of unadvertised shrines: Luckington, Down Ampney, Cotham, Lower Marlwood, Wareham, Heathlands, Limpsfield and Ballard's Lane.

The hymnals do not contain tunes with accompaniments. They contain four-part chorales, in which popular tunes are provided with matching bass and inner parts, for the most part impeccably combined, so that each voice follows its own internal logic. It is not only church choirs that would sing all four parts of a hymn: congregations too prided themselves on their ability to divide into voices. Voice-leading determines not only the harmonies but also the melodies of our greatest hymns, even of such florid products of the brass-band tradition as John Hughes's 'Cwm Rhonnda' and Jessie Irvine's 'Crimond' ('The Lord is my Shepherd'). Those brought up on the Anglican hymnal acquired an instinctive feel for the principles of classical harmony, and a knowledge of the multidimensional character of musical expression. In Marlow too it was not uncommon for the congregation to divide into parts – two at least, and sometimes three. And the trebles of the choir would have a descant in the concluding hymn, so completing their temporary transformation from urchins to angels.

The choir was a crucible of the religious alchemy. The boys in their lace collars and surplices, standing before their booming guardians, evoked all those distinctively English feelings about the cycle of human life: the innocence of childhood, the impassable distance from the other sex, the repressed homosexuality, the pastoral idyll evoked in verse and melody, and the whole mixture stirred together by a priest who may or may not have believed the words he uttered, but who recognised in any case the saving grace of a collective self-deception. This was the English enchantment at its most accessible and guiltless. And in all its details it verged on guilt.

Marlow afforded a glimpse, too, of the social reality of the old English Church. Like so many English institutions, the Church was decentralised in structure, and rural in its roots. It had not one but two primates, the chief of whom was located not in London or any other place of commerce, manufacture or trade, but in an insignificant market town in Kent. Its great cathedrals had sprung up in towns and villages where farmers came, and each was surrounded by a 'close' in which rural air was sequestered and shielded from the surrounding industry. It was an Arcadian institution, which fostered the high culture and learning that seek naturally to plant themselves in country retreats.

Its priests were often appointed to their 'livings' by private patrons, whether aristocratic or collegiate, and its wealth and standing enabled it to recruit from the most educated section of the community. Hence a learned naturalist like Gilbert White could find himself vicar in the village of Selborne, where he composed the book that brought poetry and science together in celebration of the English landscape. And hence the Church became identified with the national mind – a web of knowledge, culture and social aspiration, laid like a net over the countryside, trapping and uniting the forms of local life. Trollope was able to perceive in this web of influence the inner workings of the human lust for power. But from Trollope too we come away with the same softened perspective on the religion of the English – a religion in which compromise, tolerance and a lack of inner conviction were combined with a concerted effort to bring God down among the English, so as to nod His approval at the land.

And this returns us, in conclusion, to the vexed question whether England was a Catholic or a Protestant country. Here is one way of seeing the matter. The Protestant movement that led to the Reformation was fundamentally a protest against the sacramental character of the Roman Catholic Church. It was a rejection of mystery, magic and ritual in favour of the human conscience and its reasoning powers. In other words, it was a rehearsal for the Enlightenment. Like all protests, it depended for its identity on the thing that it fought; hence the dwindling of the sacramental character of Roman Catholicism in the twentieth century has brought about the effective collapse of the Protestant Churches in continental Europe. Protestantism displayed itself in England as an ongoing protest of the 'common people', with their stubborn Anglo-Saxon attitudes, against clerics and friars educated in foreign ways. It was, like most English protests, non-violent and domestic, shared equally by Langland, the poet of the people, and Chaucer, the poet of the court. Wycliffe gave it doctrinal credibility, and the Lollards strove to give it social and political power. But for the most part it lived side by side with the official rites and ceremonies, grudgingly accepting them as ancient customs which had been perverted by the Roman hierarchy into manipulative superstitions.

Henry VIII defended the sacraments against Luther, and the Anglican Church has never rejected them. When the frenzy and fanaticism of the seventeenth century had dwindled to a murmur, the English Church re-emerged as *Anglo-Catholic*, justified by tradition and succession, conveying unfathomable mysteries through immemorial rites. But these rites and mysteries were by now bound up with England and its history, rather than with the history and ambitions of Rome. The Anglican Church had, in effect, purloined the sacraments, and used them to define local rites of passage, a local experience of membership and a national identity coterminous with 'the law of the land'.

During the nineteenth century England experienced its own version of the conflict between Catholic and Protestant. But by now the contest was mild and eirenic. It occurred between the Anglican Church, with its sacraments and rituals, and the Churches which would not 'conform' to these rites, believing that scripture, instruction and the individual conscience were higher authorities than the Book of Common Prayer. The hold of the Anglican Church was weaker in those parts of the kingdom where people did not identify themselves as English – the Scots lent towards Calvinism and Presbyterianism, the Welsh towards the 'chapel' religions of the Baptists, Methodists, Congregationalists and Unitarians. And in the industrial cities too Chapel won against Church. Nonconformism was not merely a religious protest. It was a protest against the Anglican vision of England, as an Arcadian landscape enchanted by its law and institutions, and made holy by ritual and prayer. For what relevance did this vision have, to those who had fled the countryside where they had been threatened with starvation, to the great, bleak, smoke-filled cities where nothing was promised except a wage? But when the Anglican Church lost sight of its sacramental character, began to play with 'Alternative Services' and camp-fire hymns, permitting divorce and remarriage and trivialising its communion, the Nonconformist churches vanished overnight, and now stand bleak and abandoned in all the towns and villages of England.

Chapter Six

The English Law

As we discover from their literature, the Anglo-Saxon and Nordic tribes were litigious people.[1] This fact testifies not to their quarrelsomeness so much as their desire to settle quarrels peacefully, by laying them before a court. From the beginning, therefore, courts, customs and past decisions took precedence over royal decrees. The Anglo-Saxon codes were summaries of custom, which the king declared as law. When, in the Middle Ages, the English Parliament began to emerge as a law-making body, it was conceived, and described, as a court of law – a final arbiter of questions which could not be settled by local magistrates. Its authority was never greater than that of the courts which applied its decisions, and only little by little did the executive arm of government begin to resent the fact that the mass of English law had not been decided by Parliament but discovered by the subordinate courts.

The 'common law' of England denotes the law common to the whole land, as opposed to the local customs and variations (such as the system of land tenure called 'gavelkind' which persisted until 1925 in Kent). It arose from local judgements, and not from decrees issued by the sovereign, whose tenure was regarded by the English as conditional on his undertaking to uphold and adhere to the 'law of the land'. The vast body of this law was, and remains, unwritten, except in the form of reports and commentaries. It is known as 'case

---

[1] See, for example, *Njál's Saga*, tr. M. Magnusson and H. Pálsson, London, 1960.

law', since it derives from the judgements delivered in individual cases. Some describe it, therefore, as 'judge-made' law, on the assumption that law is always made by someone, and if not by the sovereign body, then by the person who decides the leading case. But this description is also a misdescription. The common law is no more *made* by the judge, than the moral law is *made* by the casuist. Kant argued that the moral law is known to all rational beings, and that they acknowledge it even when they cannot put it into words. Whether or not Kant was right in this, it is certainly true that the common law of England developed in the manner that he described. As in the Kantian morality, those who obeyed the law were not necessarily those best able to explain it, and in all difficult cases an effort of impartial reflection was needed, if the rights and wrongs of the matter were to be known. It was to this task of reasoned reflection that the courts were devoted.

The process that led from the Anglo-Saxon moot to the procedures described by Blackstone, in his incomparable *Commentaries on the Laws of England* (1765–70), is intricate and obscure.[1] But the resulting system is of an admirable simplicity, embodying a vision of law that did not merely distinguish England and its colonies from almost all other countries in the world (except those, like the Scandinavian kingdoms, which had arisen from the same mysterious beginnings), but provided a paradigm of natural justice. It has begun to sink at last, under the weight of centralised legislation, the bureaucratic 'law' of the European Commission and the politicised judgements of the European courts. But it has retained until our day the noble aspiration which had always guided it, namely, to do justice in the individual case, regardless of the interests of power. Even more

---

[1] See J.H. Baker, *An Introduction to English Legal History*, 2nd edn, London, 1979. The Common Law was effectively established by 1150, but survived into modern times partly because of the prerogative courts of the sovereign, which issued royal writs, enforced judgements, and protected judges and juries from intimidation. It was not until the Tudors that the system had the strength to stand on its own feet against those who resented its judgements.

than the English Church, it fed the root conception of the English body politic, that power is one thing and authority another. And it furthered the determination of the English to stand up to power, whenever justice was opposed to it.

The common law rests on the doctrine of *stare decisis* – that particular decisions should stand unaltered. These decisions have the status of 'precedents', which must be followed wherever they apply. In general, the English courts have adopted the principle that decisions of higher courts are binding on the courts beneath them (otherwise, what could be meant by distinguishing 'higher' from 'lower' courts?). This principle naturally poses problems for the highest court of all, the House of Lords, which in 1966 arrived at the typically English conclusion that it could disregard its own decisions, so that no judgement, in the end, is eternally binding on anyone, since the judgement of any court may be overruled by the House of Lords. To discover whether a precedent applies, a judge must ascertain its *ratio decidendi* – the reason for the decision. This may not have been explicitly stated by the original court, but merely implied in the reasoning of the judge. Those brought up on Roman law or the *code napoléon* find this amazing, since they see law as a deductive system, beginning from first principles, and working downwards to the particular case. But we need only recall the close connection between common law and moral judgement to see that it is not amazing at all. The important thing in moral life is to do what is right, not to expound the principle which makes it so; and often the principle eludes us, even when the rightness of the act is clear. Readers of Jane Austen will not need to be reminded of this. Like morality, the common law builds upwards from the particular to the general. The abstract rigour of civilian (i.e. Roman law) systems is no guarantee of their justice. For justice is done in the particular case, and until tried in the courts abstract principles have no more authority than the people who declare them.

This is particularly obvious if we attend to civil law – the area in which the English legal system has excelled. When one person has a complaint against his neighbour and applies to the judgement of a court, he is seeking a *remedy*. The facts of the case may never have been considered before, and the judge may have no explicit rule of law, no precedent and no Act of Parliament to guide him. But still there is a difference, the common law says, between a right and a wrong decision. Thus it was, for example, in the leading case of *Rylands* v. *Fletcher* (1865) in the law of tort. The defendant was a mill-owner who had constructed a reservoir on his land. The water burst through old mine shafts into the mines of the plaintiff, which were thereby flooded and put out of use. No similar case had come before the courts, yet clearly there were questions of right and liability to be decided. The Court of Exchequer Chamber (one of the antique courts which then existed, signalling its history in an exquisite name) gave judgement in the following words of Mr Justice Blackburn: 'We think that the true rule of law is, that the person who for his own purposes brings on his lands and collects and keeps there anything likely to do mischief if it escapes, must keep it in at his peril, and, if he does not do so, is prima facie answerable for all the damage which is the natural consequence of its escape.' This rule, the judge added, 'seems on principle just'.

Until *Rylands* v. *Fletcher*, however, no such rule had ever been formulated. The facts of the case arose in the context of new industrial activities, generating conflicts that had not been tried at law. Therefore, did Mr Justice Blackburn merely invent the rule? If he did, then Mr Fletcher was penalised by an act of retroactive legislation – in other words, by the invention of a law of which he could have had no prior knowledge. Surely that would be a flagrant injustice. But notice the judge's words: 'We think that the true rule of law is . . .' In other words, in Blackburn's own eyes, he was not inventing the rule, but discovering it. And such was the opinion of the House of Lords, in upholding his judgement. The common law was based on the assumption that there *is* a law governing each judiciable conflict, and that its right application will provide a remedy to the person who is wronged, and a penalty to the person who has wronged him. The business of the judge is to discover that law and apply it in the given case. He may do this as Mr Justice Blackburn did, by explicitly formulating the law and then bringing it to bear on the particular facts. Or he may merely apply the law, without saying what it is, in which case those judges who are bound by his decision must search for the *ratio decidendi* of the case. A higher court may decide that a case was rightly decided, while disapproving the *ratio decidendi* – implying therefore that the law has been wrongly described. A lower court may refuse to follow a precedent by arguing that the facts of the case before it are sufficiently distinct to imply that the law which decided the precedent cannot safely be applied. And so on. All these legal manoeuvres assume that the common law is a process of discovery, not invention, and that what is discovered is not merely the 'law of the land' but the just solution to the conflict.

This beautiful idea stands in need of a philosophical defence. But to the English it was obvious, and was at the root of their respect for law, and their willingness to abide by its judgements. Moreover, it made the law into a far more flexible instrument of social reform than Parliament. The case of *Rylands* v. *Fletcher* is itself a telling instance. The English did not have to wait for politicians to consider the environmental consequences of the new forms of heavy industry. As soon as an individual was able to prove that he had been damaged, the law stepped in with a binding remedy. Study that branch of the law of tort known as 'occupier's liability' and you will see the common law running constantly ahead of legislation, to defend the innocent victim from the misuse of land.

But there is, from the spiritual perspective, a more important aspect of the common law. The final authority in English law was the particular case, which had to be studied with all its facts, in order to extract the law which was its *ratio decidendi*. Hence English legal thinking remained concrete, close to human life and bound up with the realities of human conflict. The cases show an acute awareness of this, with judges going out of their way to give the psychological and dramatic context that compels their verdict. Many of the leading judgements – Lord Denning's, for example – are also celebrations of the ordinary individual in his attempt to live by the law. And no student of the English law can fail to absorb a concrete sense of English history – not just of the wars and parliaments and kings of former times, but of *what it was like* to live in them. The individual emerged from this unfolding narrative as the hero of English law, and the law itself as a form of consecration – a lifting of daily life into a realm where rights were acknowledged and duties obeyed.

Another device of English law furthered this development. The civil law in England was conceived as an instrument to provide relief to the injured subject. Its concern was to offer remedies to perceived wrongs, and so to moderate human conflict with the offer of a peaceful solution. Where the common law was slow to find a remedy, statute supplied the need – though statute interpreted by common law judges, who did their best to harmonise the two sources of law. Even so, it was not possible to provide relief to every sufferer: statutes were too rigid and common law confined to specific forms of action, leaving areas of grievance for which no action was available. Because the sovereign was guardian of the law, and answerable for its good reputation, subjects began to petition him directly, whenever the law could provide no remedy for their grievance. Such petitions were addressed to the sovereign through the Lord Chancellor, who, by the sixteenth century, was presiding over a 'court of chancery' established in order to hear petitions to the Crown. The concern of this court was to provide relief to the petitioner, by doing justice in the individual case.

The law that emerged from the court of chancery was called 'equity', from the Latin *aequitas* or fairness, as opposed to *strictum jus*, the strict and literal application of the law. It was, in effect, an application of philosophical principles of natural justice (the 'maxims of equity') in order to soften the strictness and supply the deficiencies of the law. These maxims include the following: Equity will not suffer a wrong without a remedy; He who seeks equity must do equity; He who comes to equity must come with clean hands. It was established, following a bitter wrangle between King James I and Chief Justice Coke, that, in any conflict between them, equity takes precedence over law. And the effect of this has been to grant to the judges of chancery the power to override both statutes and the common law.

The most important device that emerged from equitable jurisdiction was that of the trust – a concept peculiar to Anglo-American systems of law, and one of immense social and political significance. Suppose John dies, having left his property to Harold, on condition that Harold use the property to care for John's children. And suppose that Harold keeps the property for himself. What remedy do John's children have? None in law, since the property was transferred legally to Harold who is now the absolute owner. But equity will protect the interests of the children, by holding Harold liable to fulfil the terms of his agreement with John. It will say that Harold is *legal* owner of the property, but that he holds it in trust for John's children, who are the *beneficial* owners. Should Harold be in breach of trust, then the children have a cause of action, and equity will compel him to make good their loss – provided they are innocent in the matter and come 'with clean hands'.

The concept of trust has been used by the courts to protect the most intricate property rights, to rectify the most surreptitious forms of injustice, and to give legal form to the most spontaneous and informal of social practices. F.W. Maitland assessed the matter correctly: 'If we were asked what is the greatest and most distinctive achievement performed by Englishmen in the field of jurisprudence I cannot think that we should have any better answer than this, namely, the development from century to century of the trust idea.'[1] And nothing better illustrates the purpose of law as the English conceived it, which was not to exercise power over people, but to grant them *relief* when power was abused. Whether or not the parties had declared a trust of property, it was for the court to determine

---

[1] F.W. Maitland, *Selected Essays*, London, 1911, p. 129.

whether a trust existed, and it would so determine, if by doing so it could thwart an injustice. Thus arose the concept of the 'constructive trust', used, for example, by Lord Denning to confer property rights on a discarded mistress, whose lover had profited from her cooperation in acquiring and restoring a house.

Trusteeship in English law is the strangest form of ownership: for it consists entirely of duties, with no personal rights. The idea of ownership as a duty seeped into the national consciousness, and provided a model for the relation between the English and their country. Throughout the nineteenth century we find writers and statesmen explaining patriotism in such terms. The English were to see themselves as trustees of an endowment, which they could not squander or abuse without violating the rights of the beneficiaries – the future generations who would in turn enjoy their inheritance only by becoming trustees of it. The English thereby gave moral form to the vision of society made canonical by Burke. Their society was not a contract among the living, but a partnership between generations, with the living as trustees of an inheritance bequeathed by those who had died to those who had not yet been born. In other words, England was a partnership most of whose owners came always before or after, and were never here and now. And this was another reason for identifying England not through the people who lived there, since they were only the brief stewards of the landscape, but through the land itself.

The idea of the 'law of the land' gained credibility from two procedural features of the English system: the dispersed network of courts, and the right, in the more serious criminal cases, to trial by jury. Criminal cases were brought in the first instance before the 'justices of the peace'. This unpaid office first appears in 1252; the Justice of the Peace was a local notable, nominated by other local notables or by royal writ, charged with trying summary offences and committing more serious offences for trial by jury. These more serious offences were passed up to the county courts, while civil cases were dealt with by local assizes. The county courts were organised into 'circuits', to be visited in turn by one or more superior (usually High Court) judge. Justice was in this way dispersed across the land, while being maintained to a single central standard, set down by the High Court in London.

The jury is an ancient institution, with both Saxon and Norman elements. It took something like its modern form following the Assize of Clarendon (1166), but was not yet what it came to be, as a result of the rule in Bushell's case (1670), which held that an honest verdict was to be accepted by the court, and that no juror could be punished for delivering it. Despite abuses (and no human institution is immune from abuse), the jury system ensured that questions of fact were clearly distinguished from questions of law, that the accused had a fair hearing, and that the assumption of innocence was maintained, with the onus on the prosecutor to establish beyond reasonable doubt that the accused was guilty of the crime. It also ensured that the law remained responsive to the ordinary conscience, since juries would not convict if the penalty seemed to be too severe or the crime a mere formality. Most important of all, it ensured the involvement of all citizens in the administration of justice: jury service was (and remains) a duty. The law of England was therefore perceived as a common property of all, which each had a duty to uphold and which reached impartially into every household. The law was, to that extent, domesticated, and the general assumption was that only wrongdoers need be afraid of it.

This friendly presence of the law was symbolised by its most visible incarnation – the local constable. The English policeman, descended from the Bow Street runners of the early nineteenth century, bore all the distinctive marks of a law-abiding country, in which law stood above power and politics. The police force was not an arm of central government, but a local organisation, responsive to the county councils. The 'bobby' himself was trained as a friend of the community he served, and the sign of this was that he was armed only with a notebook and a comic tin whistle. He knew the people on his beat, and took a benign and paternal interest in their welfare.

Children went to him when they were lost; strangers asked him directions, and everybody greeted him with a smile. Idealised, but not caricatured, as PC Dixon of Dock Green, his role was to rectify wrong, to restore equilibrium, and to guide his own community along its peaceful path to nowhere. PC Dixon cultivated begonias, sang in the police choir, was a member of the police darts team and was in general as worthy a participant in the 'little platoons' of Dock Green as any of those who might be called upon to serve on the jury.

The English law existed not to control the individual but to free him. It was on the side of the subject against those – whether usurping politicians or common criminals – who wished to bend him unconsenting to their will. All the great constitutional crises of the English, therefore, were experienced as violations of the law. They would characteristically end with a reaffirmation of the law and a charter guaranteeing the rights of the individual against the usurpers. The first of these charters – Magna Carta of 1215 – expressly affirmed ancient rights and freedoms, and demanded that the king be subject to the law. It was entirely in the English conception of monarchy that, when King John tried to evade the charter which he had signed at Runnymede, the barons renounced their allegiance and offered the crown to Louis, heir to the throne of France.

The last true constitutional crisis was likewise resolved with a reaffirmation of ancient rights and freedoms, in the Bill of Rights of 1689. This endorsed the ancient writ of 'habeas corpus', guaranteeing that no subject could be imprisoned without due process of law, and re-established English law as the common property of the subject, rather than the private possession of the sovereign power. The greatest benefit that the English conferred on the world, was to propagate this conception to its colonies – thereby arming the colonists in America against the Crown, and providing the foundation both for the Pax Britannica of the nineteenth century, and for the Pax Americana of today.

Still, it should not be thought that English law was built solely on the conception of individual rights. Equity ensured that this would not be so, by placing the concept of duty at the centre of its rulings. The dutifulness of the English stemmed in part from the nature of their law. At every point it was made apparent that the individual possesses rights only because he is also burdened by duties, and that to attempt to have the one without the other is to threaten the possibility of both.[1] The English law of tort was built not upon the idea of individual rights, but upon that of the 'duty of care' which each person owes to the innocent stranger. And it was thanks largely to the law of tort, and to the equitable concept of the trust, that social conflicts in England resolved themselves through the peaceful operation of the courts and not, as so often on the continent of Europe, through civil unrest and revolution.

The English law was regarded as having an authority greater than any temporary sovereign or legislator. Hence it was able to grow, like the topsoil of a forest, by slow accumulation over centuries. This was especially manifest in land law, a field rich in deposits from previous times. The common law does not allow an individual subject to own land, but only to possess a 'tenure' from the Crown. This tenure grants an 'estate', which lasts for a certain time, and may be qualified by rights and easements in favour of others. The doctrines of 'tenures' and 'estates' are not legal fictions, but foundational principles, creating a web of rights and duties that clings to England like the walls and hedgerows that are its physical by-product. Rights of way, sporting rights, restrictive covenants; leases, sub-leases, tied tenancies; byways, bridle paths, footpaths; the residues of feudal tenures, with their hierarchical rights and duties, their scutage and knight service and sub-infeudation – all these compose the face of England, which reveals in its every contour a long history of peaceful settlement.

Furthermore, until the Land Registration Acts of 1925 and 1926, there had been no obligatory system for the registration of titles. The

---

[1] The assumption of the English law that there are no rights without duties goes back to feudal times and beyond. See G.M. Trevelyan, *English Social History*, London, 1944, p. 30f.

sovereign and his advisers literally did not know who owned what land or under what terms. This greatly enhanced the autonomy of the individual, whose property could not be confiscated without a long process of discovery. Where titles to land were unregistered, sale and purchase would require elaborate proof of title, involving title deeds, leases, conveyances and grants, all written in copperplate and embellished with seals. Every small transaction placed in the lawyer's hands a packet of English history. To complete a sale or purchase it was necessary to sift through a pile of old parchment, and discover how land had been parcelled out and mutual uses determined between generations of people who had been answerable in the matter not to the sovereign but only to themselves.

The offices of the English law were also determined by its nature as a final authority, rather than an instrument of social control. The English barrister was a servant of the law, a forensic agent, concerned to test the case to its utmost and to force the law to declare itself before the facts. The barrister's client was not his master, but the occasion of his brief. The prime duties of the barrister were to the court: to deceive no one, to question everything and to make the best possible case on the facts. Mere knowledge of the law was not enough. Intellect, imagination and culture were also required, and the best advocates often came to the law from some other discipline. Lord Denning, for example, began life as a mathematician, and owed much to a deep familiarity with English literature which gave power and concreteness to his words. And because the profession was an autonomous body, which set its own exams and its own rules for membership, such people were admitted in large numbers to the Bar.

England was one of the few places where the profession of barrister retained the collegial character that it had acquired in the Middle Ages. The Inns of Court – such as the Middle and Inner Temples, both situated in a maze of old buildings enclosing the Round Church of the Knights Templar, built during the first crusade – were the only authorities that the profession acknowledged, and they were private societies, outside the control of the state. As part of your preparation for the Bar you were required to dine in hall each week, and to linger over port with your fellow students, while the 'benchers' – distinguished judges and jurists – sipped their claret on the bench at the end. There was a library, debating clubs, 'moots' at which the students practised their adversarial skills. There were concerts, a drama group and a midsummer ball. Those reading for the Bar were required to wear gowns in hall, and meals began and ended with a Latin grace. Moreover, many of those who practised from the Temple also lived there, at the top of creaking staircases which bore their name in classical lettering on the board below. The Inns of Court were, and to some extent remain, pure examples of the autonomous institutions which were the foundation of English society, and whose corporate personality shaped the personality of those who joined them. Their autonomy endowed them with an important constitutional role, since it enabled them to provide support and refuge to their judges. Hence the Inns of Court helped to make judicial independence into an enduring feature of English government.[1]

Although the solicitors had tried, through the Law Society, to instil an ethic into their profession, the solicitor could not be, as the barrister was, an uncorrupted servant of the law. He was the servant of his client, and his career depended upon obtaining the best deal for the client, however crooked that client might be. Hence the English law separated the barrister from the solicitor by as great a distance as possible, and allowed only the former to argue a case in court. In this way the barrister became not merely the servant of the law, but also its guardian. He shielded the court from the interests that pollute it, and provided a kind of filter, by which human motives were purified of their partiality and presented as in a theatre, objects of sympathy but also of judgement.

As a student of the English law, I learned that human beings are capable of creating and sustaining real authority, and of making

---

[1] See John Bowle, *England, a Portrait*, London, 1966, p. 35.

judgements that are objectively binding and intrinsically just. I also came to see that the English law is only one instance of this, and that the spirit expressed in it – the spirit of peaceful coexistence in a common home – will find as many outlets as are permitted, in its desire to inhabit and transform the material world.

One instance of this should be mentioned, since it returns me to a central topic of this book. In 1980, together with various academic friends, I became involved in the 'underground university' in Communist Czechoslovakia. Our desire was to help our Czech and Slovak colleagues to continue teaching and learning in private after losing their university positions and being reduced to menial jobs. I had, during my studies, admired the English law of charity – a unique creation of the common law and equity, which protects property put aside for charitable uses both from maladministration and from taxation by the state, and which makes a distinction between charitable and political activity.

Charity heals communities, whereas politics divides them. Such, at least, was the English view, and three centuries of case law had given it concreteness. Here, before us, was a wonderful illustration. The Communists regarded all gatherings which they had not authorised and did not control as subversive. In Communist thinking, there was no such thing as an apolitical meeting, an autonomous institution, or a corporate person other than the party and the state, both of which arrogated the rights of persons, while despising and rejecting the duties. Society had been conscripted to the ruling purpose, which was the extension and perpetuation of Communist power. Private charities were illegal and no citizen could initiate them without running the risk of gaol.

Under English law, however, our association, being for educational purposes and not for profit, was a charity. The fact that the Communist regime of Czechoslovakia would regard it as a political (and criminal) organisation was of no relevance. It was for the courts to decide which purposes are charitable and which are not. And the courts could take no notice of the Czechoslovak government's implacable hostility to private initiatives, only of its own official pronouncements, which committed it, under the Helsinki Accords, to the free flow of information, learning and research. It therefore seemed to me that we could work as a charity under English law, and the Charity Commissioners agreed. (Note, however, that the Commissioners had no authority in the matter, since it was a matter of law, to be determined by the courts. Although a state-appointed body, the Commissioners were reduced to offering a mere opinion, about a question which the state itself could never decide. This too shows something of the power of law in the English imagination.)

English society grew from the private initiatives and public spirit of its members. The protection afforded by the law of charity made it possible for Englishmen to come to the relief of their fellows without asking official permission and without losing control of their funds. The Jan Hus Educational Foundation comprised a group of colleagues who differed in virtually all their opinions, while agreeing on the intrinsic value of intellectual freedom. The shared burden of trusteeship, the shared risks of arrest when travelling to Czechoslovakia, the shared concern for our beneficiaries and the shared belief that what we did was not merely permissible but morally right – all these worked the peculiar magic so familiar in England, transforming individual initiative into corporate personality. The Jan Hus Educational Foundation soon had a mind, a will, a destiny and a face of its own. It was an object of respect, even love, and its beneficiaries were astonished by its concern for them. Autonomous institutions had been wiped out by the Communists in 1948; the idea of charity had been eliminated from official discourse, and the appearance in those fear-haunted streets of a person who had no other business to be there, besides that of helping his fellow human beings, was regarded with a kind of awe.[1]

And there is no doubt that, just as we collectively formed the

[1] The history of the Jan Hus Educational Foundation is told by Barbara Day, *The Velvet Philosophers*, London, 1999.

character of our trust, so did the trust reform the character of each of us. Membership, which consecrates human action, transfigures those who share in it. We led each other on, gave each other purpose and were accountable to each other for what we did on the trust's behalf. This work of institution-building is what we ought to mean by 'civil society', and it was the genius of the English law to permit it, to protect it and to turn it to the best account. The law of charity existed not to control private initiatives, but to *protect* them. It told the state and its functionaries to stop at the threshold of charitable work, and neither to appropriate the funds nor manipulate the actions of those who took a part in it.

We encouraged our French and German colleagues to set up similar institutions. And we noticed that they needed permission from the state – permission which was so long in coming in the German case that the project had to be abandoned. Only with the official seal of approval could our French colleagues form an association for the relief of the Czechs and Slovaks; and once the seal was granted it was to the government that they looked for funds. We, however, needed permission from no one, and raised our funds from private donors. We witnessed, in this, the contrasting social consequences of a law built upwards from the individual case, and a law built downwards from the decrees of a central power.

The ease with which we could form our association was a gift of the law of trusts. Clubs, schools, colleges, universities, professional bodies, churches, the City Guilds, the Inns of Court – all began life as private foundations, and each developed a mind, an ethos and a conviviality of its own. England was a society of corporate persons, objects of loyalty and duty which held people together while keeping them just sufficiently apart. English eccentricity flourished by virtue of the club, which protected the habits of its members, and reassured them that their oddness would go unremarked. English dutifulness was at heart the 'team spirit' of the natural joiner, who knows what to do just as soon as someone else has joined with him in doing it.

The law of trusts enabled charities to exist for generations on the strength of a single donation. In 1610 the merchant Thomas Sutton endowed a public school, Charterhouse, together with an almshouse, and both survive to this day on the strength of his original gift. Nor was the gesture insignificant in the annals of English history. Pupils of Charterhouse include Crashaw, Lovelace, Addison, Steele and Thackeray, as well as Blackstone the lawyer and John Wesley the preacher. They also include Mr Chapman, who spoke of his old school in tones of subdued reverence, as though it were Charterhouse and not England that he had served for long years in the tropics.

Although the law of trusts facilitated charity, however, it was not the cause of it. The English were well known for their disposition to provide help in emergencies. This disposition went to the heart of their conception of society, as a duty-bound relation between strangers. Their charitable behaviour was a way of emphasising that strangers are just as important as friends – because all of us, in the end, are nobodies. By devoting yourself to the distressed stranger you make it clear that you too are a stranger in this world. You reaffirm the distance between yourself and others, by showing that the motive that binds you to society is one of impartial justice and objective duty. The charitable relief of strangers was simply another aspect of English reserve.

Czechoslovakia was important to my understanding of law for another reason. Although the Communist states were governed by some local version of the 'socialist legality' introduced by Stalin, it was in every way apparent that socialist legality was not really a form of law. Crimes were arbitrarily invented; verdicts were dictated by the party; and in all cases that the party regarded as important, prosecution, defence and judge acted under party instructions. I was astonished to discover that in the important trial of Charter 77 activists which landed Václav Havel in jail, the defence counsel stood up in court to denounce his clients: the reason being that, had he actually defended them, he would have gone with them to jail. I discovered that there was no authoritative record of cases and no institution for establishing the meaning of statutes. I also discovered that the vague and menacing legal code, which forbad everything that it did not explicitly permit, was provided with a commentary that made every disputable term yet more vague than it was. The criminal code was not a collection of rules specifying acts to be avoided, but a set of ritual formulae, to be pronounced whenever it was required to punish someone.

A rule of law depends upon conditions which had been destroyed in Czechoslovakia, but which were intrinsic to the common law of England. The most important of these were judicial independence and the right to redress. Both were so deeply woven into the English jurisdiction as to be impossible to eradicate without doing violence to the whole system. They ensured that a legal solution could be found for every human conflict, and that the law would heal far more wounds than it inflicted. The creativity of common law, and the inherent fairness of its judgements, made law into England's largest invisible export, with a majority of international traders choosing to submit their disputes to English courts. And no sooner did some new area of conflict arise than the common law would rush into the midst of it, engaged like a knight errant on its ancient task of rescuing the individual from the wrongful use of power.

Often, when the English tried to put into words the enchantment that lay over their country, they would describe England as 'the land of the free'. And there was truth in the description. But the particular kind of freedom that the English enjoyed was a creature of the common law. English freedom existed because it was protected; the common law stood like a shield between the individual and the sovereign power. And although the law guaranteed the rights of the subject, it also enumerated his duties – duties which arose not because some powerful person demanded them, but from the nature of just dealings between beings who are free.

There is a philosophical question that arises when someone praises an arrangement for its goodness, beauty or charm. People have a rooted disposition to think that these qualities are fictions, products of our own emotions, rather than real and objective features of the world. Nothing, they say, is *really* good, or just or beautiful or enchanted. The only fact of the matter is that we *think* in this way. And the reasoning is backed up with a 'distinction' between 'fact' and 'value', or between 'is' and 'ought'. 'Facts' are 'objective', 'values' 'subjective'. And, as likely as not, the argument is left there.

The popularity of this way of thinking should not lead us to endorse it, but on the contrary to question it. Because people no longer live by ideas, they prefer convenient conclusions to the reasoning that impedes them. By believing that all 'values' are 'subjective' people imagine that they escape judgement, that they are free to do as they please without anyone having the authority to question them. And when someone undertakes what I have undertaken in this book, which is to spell out an idea through which people lived and understood themselves, to show its intrinsic merits and its deep-down truthfulness, the motive is all the stronger, in those who have broken free from that idea and found nothing whatsoever to replace it, to think that, after all, it was no more than a human invention, which described nothing real, nothing 'objective', nothing that might give grounds for judgement.

The business of philosophy is uncomfortable truth. Those who take refuge in a distinction between the 'objective' and the 'subjective' do not, as a rule, have the faintest idea what they mean by it. Consider a painted portrait. Here, before you, is a face; turn your eyes in this direction and you cannot help but see it. Moreover, you learn much about this face – more perhaps (supposing it is the work of a master) than you could ever learn from staring at the man himself. But is this face 'objective'? Does it belong with the 'facts'? Is it part of an independent 'reality'? Clearly these terms are beside the point. The face is a work of the imagination; but it is also there to be seen. Someone who fails to see it is not seeing rightly. It is no more up to us to invent the face that lies before us than it is up to us to invent the man himself.

Equally instructive is the case of the common law, as I have considered it. When Mr Justice Blackburn decided the case of *Rylands* v. *Fletcher* he did not invent the law: he was not improvising; nor was his judgement in any way 'subjective' – whatever that might mean. He ventured an opinion as to the way things are: 'We think that the true rule of law is . . .' And when the Court of Appeal upheld his judgement it did not merely add one opinion to another: it said, in effect, that Mr Justice Blackburn was *right*, that this *really is* the rule of law.

To those who protest that, nevertheless, the law is a human artefact, that it exists only because we are disposed to regulate our lives in legal terms, and that it has no 'independent reality' I would again question their terms. The Cathedral of St Paul's is a human artefact: does that imply that it has no 'independent reality'? Look again at the reasoning of the courts: it is not a process of 'invention', but a process of discovery. And even if, in some broad sense, the legal system is a work of the human imagination, this is at best a proof that the imagination is sometimes needed if the world is to be seen as it is. The English law was an attempt to understand the human world; it both uncovered and endorsed the impartial justice whereby the English people ordered their lives. And by measuring the world against an ideal it showed the world as it is.

Those thoughts require more philosophy than I can here provide for them. But they should be borne in mind when considering what I have said about the enchantment which lay over England, and which formed the bond between those who lived here. It is no more plausible to dismiss this enchantment as a 'fiction', or a 'value' or something 'subjective' or 'invented' than it is plausible to say the same of the face in the picture, or the rule of law in *Rylands* v. *Fletcher*. True, there comes a time when people cease to believe in such things and therefore cease to perceive them. And then, to be sure, they are dead. But ideas of the imagination transfigure the world and make it habitable. They are the creators of human communities as much as the creatures of them. And those who live by these ideas see everything – themselves included – in another way. They too are changed and – in the case that I am considering – changed for the better.

Chapter Seven

English Society

The most baneful legacy of Marxism has been the theory that law, politics, culture and religion have one primary function, which is to secure the economic foundation on which societies rest. Some version of this theory was taught by philosophers, sociologists and political scientists throughout my days as a student; and it influenced the doctrines, the aims and the language of socialism, in those days when socialism was assumed to be the answer to whatever was the question. The Marxist theory simplified human society, made politics coherent, gave a clear sense of purpose and a ready instrument of contempt towards 'things by law established'. Its only defect was that it was false – though with the kind of wily and evasive falsehood that distinguishes religious heresy from scientific error, and which endlessly shields itself from refutation.

According to the Marxist theory economic forces are the motor of history: laws and institutions are merely the effect of them. All politicians act as though the theory were true, placing economic facts at the centre of their business, not in order to alter them, but in order to capitulate before their 'historical inevitability'. But the Marxist theory becomes true only when people believe in it. Law becomes the slave of economics because politicians make it so. Until that happens, it is not economics which makes the law but law which shapes and engenders commercial life.

The expansion of English trade in the seventeenth and eighteenth centuries, and the ensuing Industrial Revolution, were caused by the institutions of the English, which had encouraged free enterprise, private property and self-help from the earliest Middle Ages.[1] The common law of contract and the concept of equitable ownership generated from their inner logic the rights and remedies necessary to a modern economy. The conception of law as the subject's defence rather than the sovereign's command liberated the English from the customary restraints on trade and the power of royal monopolies. The unique blend of dissent and compromise that had created the English religion shaped the aims and emotions of those who accepted it, endowing them with the two most precious virtues of the tradesman: obstinacy in everything that concerns oneself and toleration towards the obstinacies of others. The decentralised nature of English administration ensured that wealth ended up as much in the countryside as in the city – a fact which in turn fed the growth of English law, by sustaining local magistrates and local juries. The safe havens of the consecrated homeland gave zest to foreign adventure, and the biblical culture removed all moral doubt from those who went abroad in search of their fortune. They travelled as missionaries, carrying God's message in God's language to people who paid for this spiritual benefit with material goods. So successful were they in transplanting their eccentric faith that the spirituality of the Anglican Church now depends upon its legacy in Africa. Throughout the empire, from the industrial cities of Victorian England to the slums of Calcutta, was manifest the same indomitable belief in wealth as the reward of duty, and the same faith in the religious validity of enterprise. Even after the loss of empire and the disappearance of the moral vocation that had grown from it, London remained the financial centre of the world. True, many of its initiatives had been originally inspired by Holland, in the years of fierce competition between the Dutch and English merchant adventurers. But the City of London owed the dominant position that it was to achieve to

---

[1] See, for example, Alan Macfarlane, *The Origins of English Individualism*, Oxford, 1986. Macfarlane is anticipated in much of his argument by G.M. Trevelyan, *English Social History*, London, 1944.

English attitudes, English institutions and the peculiar history of England.

Indeed, perhaps nothing illustrates the falsehood of the Marxist theory more eloquently than the City of London, whose economic success is a product of common-law jurisdiction and a moral culture conducive to trade. The City of London had grown during the Middle Ages as a unique self-governing venture, with its own rules and customs, under the protection of the trade guilds (or livery companies), and administered by its own mayor and aldermen. Its independence from the state and the court was symbolised by its geographical separation from the city of Westminster, and it has had a continuous history of resistance to the high-handedness of sovereigns and their favourites, being the first to side with Parliament against King Charles I. Its most important financial institutions – such as the Bank of England, Lloyd's, the merchant banks and the Baltic Exchange – began life as private ventures, outside the control of the state, and subject only to the law of the land. But they were not founded simply with a view to short-term gain. They were seen as contributions to a collective experiment, necessary components in the apparatus of free trade, which demanded new forms of property, new responsibilities, new ways of including strangers as accountable partners in a common enterprise.

Certain factors made it possible for the City to develop in the ways required. The first was probity. The motto of the Baltic Exchange – 'My Word is my Bond' – was the unspoken motto of the City. There were cheats and scoundrels; but until recent times these were the exception, and their activities were systematically marginalised by the honest houses which formed the central conduit of the City's affairs. English commerce in general, and the City in particular, were vivid illustrations of the thesis defended in recent years by Francis Fukuyama, that trust is an integral component of economic success.[1] All long-term enterprise and all creative risk-taking depend upon an

---

[1] Francis Fukuyama, *Trust: the Social Virtues and the Creation of Prosperity*, London, 1995.

element of trust; and as the network of mutually trusting businesses expands, so does the wealth of each of them.

Trust grew among City businesses because they began life as small family ventures or partnerships, and maintained towards one another a posture of impeccable respectability, honouring obligations and neither demanding nor giving any ostentatious proof of friendship. The reserved and unflappable character of the English was the bedrock of City life. Business proceeded on the assumption that if anyone went out of his way to show you favours, this was sure proof that his aim was not long-term social standing but short-term profit. In other words, his frame of mind was not that of the English gentleman but that of the Italian godfather, who would find nothing insuperably wrong in bribery or dishonest conduct. Of course, it went without saying that you were in the City to make money; but precisely because it went without saying, it was vulgar to mention it. Much more important than money was reputation: one entered the City to become known and respected, to accumulate a list of discreet but distinguished clients, and to be received at last with frosty acquiescence into one of the City Guilds – calm backwaters of collegiate life amid the oceanic turmoil of international finance.

Equally important to the success of the City, therefore, was the clubbable character of the English businessman. Lloyd's began in 1668, among the club of gentlemen merchants who were in the habit of meeting at the Edward Lloyd Coffee House, and who decided to establish an institution with which to protect each other from bankruptcy. The English banking system was founded by the City Goldsmiths, whose deposit receipts were already circulating as currency in the seventeenth century, while the Bank of England, although established in 1694 by Royal Charter, was the invention and the property of a club of City traders. The Stock Exchange began as a private club among brokers who met at Jonathan's Coffee House in Change Alley in 1762, and established itself as a self-governing institution subject to a common code of probity. The Baltic Exchange had already come into existence around 1740, in the same general way. And just as the English law developed in response to the odd social ventures of the English people, producing constructs like the law of equity which protected associations of strangers, so did the City institutions develop in response to the far-reaching bonds of trust that sprang up between English gentlemen. English reserve, which saw favouritism as a kind of personal assault, facilitated the growth of trust. For it relied upon bonds of honour that fell critically short of intimacy, and which could therefore be extended far and wide through the world of strangers.

To take account of the increasing risks involved in international trade, Lloyd's appealed for capital from outside the community of City traders, so founding the extraordinary system which was to bring first triumph, and then, in our day, disaster. The 'names' who provided the capital to the underwriters at Lloyd's were people of wealth and standing, who implicitly trusted this institution run by gentlemen, and who thought nothing of placing their entire possessions in the hands of a discreet and well-spoken stranger. Thanks to this extended relation of trust, Lloyd's became another of those corporate persons through which the English enchantment spread across the country. Its solid well-furnished buildings were treated as clubhouses; its routines were shrouded in mystery like the rituals of a church; and the old bell of the *Lutine* frigate, captured from the French in 1793, sounded eerily through its hallway to announce the loss or arrival of a strategic merchant vessel. It was the very image of the safety which the English associated with their homeland, and its well-bred clientele somnolently assumed that such an institution would last for ever, an unsinkable rock amid the tides of misfortune that afflicted lesser men. Not even the demolition of the Victorian clubhouse, and the erection in its place of a grotesque piece of modernist kitsch by Richard Rogers, awoke them to the fact that the City had been penetrated by a new generation of spivs with a wholly new agenda, and that goods held for centuries in trust could at any moment be converted to ready money in pockets for which they were never intended.

This brings us to the most important fact about the City, which is that it expressed and depended upon relations of class. All newcomers to the City mystique were reminded that the important thing is not what one knows but whom one knows. The old City banks – Flemings, Barings, Smiths – were family businesses whose members had made their way in society, attracting clients from an aristocracy to which they also, in time, were promoted. Typical were the Barings, descendants of an immigrant from Hamburg who started a cloth business in Exeter in 1717. Wealth brought political office, knighthoods, baronetcies and four separate titles of nobility. As earls of Cromer, the Barings provided a famous Governor of Egypt, a Lord Chamberlain and, most recently, a Governor of the Bank of England. Their story illustrates not only the importance of class in English society, but also the ease with which lowly, and even foreign, origins could be overcome by adroit social climbing. It also illustrates the tragically unguarded nature of the old City institutions, which were protected only by the honour of their participants, and could be destroyed overnight by one corrupted member of staff – as happened in our time to Barings.

The City represented, in other words, the spirit of the gentleman, incarnate in the world of commerce. Its institutions were eccentric clubs – corporate persons animated by a code of fair play, and enjoying the unique protection of the common law. It had its own sovereignty, with the Lord Mayor presiding from Mansion House over a society of little platoons. It had its ceremonies, banquets, guilds and churches devoted to the image of the City as a place apart. It even had its uniform – the dark suit, stiff collar, Bombay shirt, bowler hat and umbrella, which were still required when I first arrived in London in the early sixties, though not required of me, since I was only a washer-up in a City restaurant. In continental terms the City of London was not a city at all – for as time went on it rid itself of its population, expelling them to territories beyond its boundaries, purchased as part of the post-war programme of 'slum-clearance', but effectively ensuring that non-members should not be seen in the club. By night it was a ghostly precinct in which no mortal slept; by day it was a hive of industry, but one which dealt in spectral products. The City traded invisibly in weightless goods, among which English law and English honour were the staple ingredients. It was a corporate person, existing above and beyond its temporary streets and buildings; and when these were flattened by the German bombers, the City itself was not damaged at all, and walked among the ruins in starched collar and bowler hat, glad to be rid of its stone integument, like a spirit emerged from the tomb.

The City's greatest church – Wren's Cathedral of St Paul's – miraculously survived the devastation. But the famous inscription on the tomb of its architect – *si monumentum requiris, circumspice* – must now be read with a certain irony. The City survived the Blitz because it was a moral and spiritual idea, which could not be touched by bombs. But ideas have their architectural expression, and while the Victorian and Edwardian banks, with their classical orders and rusticated façades, conveyed the ethic of trust on which the City was founded, their successors in glass and steel and concrete belong to another world – the world of fast bucks, informal manners and cheerful offers of unmeant friendship; the world of takeovers, asset-stripping, insider trading and multinational capital. Honour, trust and even law can still be found in this altered world; but they are at a disadvantage. The noble commercial buildings that survived the war have been flattened one by one; and the Baltic Exchange itself, proudly announcing that 'My Word is my Bond' even as the bonds were being loosened, was finally blown to pieces by an IRA bomb.

Finance and manufacture were roughly divided between south and north, and no contrast in English society was more impressive than that between the life of the Surrey stockbroker, travelling each day to the City from the leafy lanes of his quasi-rural suburb, and that of the industrial worker in a northern town, living in a street of slums beneath the factory that employed him. Ever since Engels made him into the central figure of modern politics, the English industrial labourer has been used to exemplify all that is wrong in capitalism, in free enterprise, in the class system, in the division of labour and in England itself. Study the portrait of this character in literature, however – in Gissing and Arnold Bennett, in Orwell, D.H. Lawrence, J.B. Priestley and Arthur Morrison – and you confront a new but rooted type of modern Englishman, as much shaped by the image and ideal of his homeland as the City gent, and by no means implacably hostile to the surrounding social order.

From my father, who had been born in the slums of Ancoats into a family of eight children, two of whom died in infancy of scarlet fever, I learned something of the northern working class. Jack Scruton himself had left that class, thanks to the social mobility which was the ubiquitous gift of English institutions. But he retained towards his social origins an intense nostalgia, a memory of belonging which was all the stronger in that it was focused not on his family – which had been destroyed by a tyrannical father – but on the towns, the work, the religion and the customs which had been 'the making of the English working class'.[1] It became clear to me that the working class, as my father had known it, was a creation of the moral imagination. Old English virtues and old English customs had been consciously transplanted from their rural setting to the alleyways of the industrial towns, where they grew in straggling and light-hungry versions, seeking to rise higher than the dismal streets that harboured them and to regain a distant view of England.

My great-grandmother's surname was Lowe, and that was the name given to my grandfather by his birth certificate, which mentioned no father to the child. Just why my great-grandmother called her son 'Scruton' nobody knows. Attempts were made, later in her life, to discover her secret. But, even supposing you could find her in the gutters of Manchester where she habitually lay, she would never be sober enough to answer such a question. One popular

---

[1] Needless to say, my remarks in this chapter are only ironically related to E.P. Thompson's *The Making of the English Working Class*, a book which is nevertheless conceived in a spirit of nostalgia not unlike my father's. See the review of E.P. Thompson's book by Geoffrey Best, in *Historical Journal*, vol. 8 (1985), pp. 271–81.

hypothesis is that Margaret Lowe had been in service at Scruton Hall, in the Yorkshire dales, and had named her child after the place of her seduction. The squires of Scruton Hall were the Gales, to whose direct descendant, the journalist George Gale, I bear a striking resemblance.

Whatever the truth of the matter, Margaret Lowe endured the lot of many poor Victorian girls, and brought up her bastard child alone, working spasmodically at menial tasks in order to cover the costs of the child's food and the mother's gin. Matthew Scruton grew up strong, healthy and ignorant. His only school was the streets of Manchester, where he went barefoot selling newspapers. Later, on account of his strength, he obtained work as a carter in the vegetable market, handling the great dray horses that hauled the produce from port to market place. He was belligerent, good-looking and tall, and all men were afraid of him. He was also a lively raconteur, whose love of the spoken word was amplified by his ignorance of the written. Women were instinctively attracted to him, and one of them, Janie, whose father was in charge of the steam engines at the local cotton mill, caught his fancy. Their marriage followed the pattern laid down for the lower orders by D.H. Lawrence: powerful sexual attraction momentarily concealing the durable conflict of class. Janie was happy enough at first to come down to Matthew's level, despite her father's superior position in the cotton mill, and despite the education she had acquired at a Church of England school before herself 'half-timing' at the mill from the age of eleven. Matthew, however, had no intention of rising to Janie's level, and bitterly resented her attempts to provide their six surviving children with an education. He inherited his mother's vice and would blacken the household late at night with drunken violence. He died unforgiven by his children, whom he had mysteriously failed to attach to the street life that was good enough for him and therefore, in his thinking, good enough for them.

It was Janie, therefore, not Matthew, who was the picture of working-class virtue in the children's eyes. Neither she nor her husband had acquired any religious belief. Nevertheless, in true English fashion, she believed in religion. Her sister had married a Methodist lay preacher, by whose teetotal habits the family were both appalled and impressed. She insisted that the children attend the local Anglican church, in order to acquire another and higher sense of belonging than the one that prevailed in Upper Cyrus Street. She believed in charity, but not in receiving it, and admired the Salvation Army, which brought music, discipline and cheerfulness into the dreary channels of Ancoats. She belonged to a travelling library run by the Corporation and read everything she could lay her hands on. Had her husband permitted it, she would even have attended evening classes. And she spent her savings on an upright piano, which became the centre of family life and the symbol of her children's upward mobility. Her youngest child Bessy graduated as an LRAM before dying, aged eighteen, of tuberculosis. Janie sent the boys to night school, while my father won a scholarship at the age of eleven to Manchester High School, a grammar school which catered for the aspiring middle classes. This provided him with free books and uniform, and the opportunity to take the matriculation examination which would launch him on a career as a non-commissioned officer in the RAF. In everything she planned, Janie thought of one thing first of all, which was the social betterment of her offspring; and she worked until the age of seventy in the cotton mill that had taken the best years of her father's life, in order to put by money for their future.

Upper Cyrus Street ran back-to-back with the next street along, from which it was divided by a narrow alleyway. The back door of the Scruton household opened on to a tiny courtyard, where the earth closet was built against the house. Beyond the outbuilding was a door into the alley, from which another door opened from the house behind. In this house lived Mr Dickson, a fifty-year-old widower, and his spinster daughter Mabel. My father visited Mr Dickson whenever he could, since Mr Dickson was a self-educated man, who subscribed to the *Manchester Guardian*. Together they would listen to the crackling broadcasts of 2LO on the 'cat's whisker' wireless which Mr Dickson (alone in the neighbourhood) possessed. It told them of a world beyond Ancoats, where people helped themselves to the good things in life, and where style and wit and culture were widely distributed and universally admired. How to reach that world was my father's every thought, and it was because of this that he looked back with such nostalgia on a life that, in his heart, he believed he had betrayed.

Mr Dickson read socialist tracts; but he was not a radical. His vision had been shaped by Morris and Ruskin, and centred on the ideal of the craftsman and his honest work. His daughter moped in the house like a Pre-Raphaelite princess, and between them father and daughter created a kind of chapel to high culture in the midst of the overcast slums. They typified what was perhaps the most remarkable feature of working-class life in England, namely that it was not a prison but a maze, and that at any moment you might find yourself standing before an open door, with a vista beyond it of green fields and open skies. For some, like Janie, this door was the library. For others it was the church, the Salvation Army or the Mechanics' Institute. And Victorian moralists like Ruskin were everywhere hard at work, to remind the middle classes that the virtues which they most admired – honesty, fidelity and gentleness – were to be found more in the class beneath them than in the class above.

Certainly in Upper Cyrus Street honesty was the rule. Often the men had no money; but what money they earned was placed each Friday night on the kitchen table, in a wage packet whose seal it was the woman's right and duty to break. A shilling was handed back for beer; the rest was for the family. Even my grandfather, wastrel though he was, observed this custom punctiliously. When times were hard, people helped each other, though nobody liked to be 'beholden', since this tended to destroy the distance between neighbours without which neighbours were intolerable. The aim was to be 'respectable', and this meant not merely scrupulous in matters of sexual morality, but also properly dressed, well-mannered and able to redeem your valuables from the pawnshop before they were sold. Holidays were rare, except for 'Wakes' Week', an institution designed for factory workers, weavers and spinners by Victorian philanthropists. Each factory would shut down for a different week of the year, so that all the workers could be accommodated, factory by factory, in the seaside boarding houses at Blackpool. Janie could afford to take only the two youngest children – my father and his doomed sister Bessy – and she would bring her own food to Blackpool, the landlady cooking it for them and adding a few pence to the bill for her labour.

No efforts had been made to beautify Ancoats, though the millocrats who had built the place had sprinkled it with idyllic names. Flower Street was particularly dismal, while Angel Meadows was inhabited by the very poorest of the poor, who stuffed their windows with newspapers against the cold, and haunted the nearby gasworks with their wheelbarrows, begging for pieces of coke. Yet we know from the paintings of Lowry that these places too had their enchantment; and for my father, who learned in these alleyways the rhymes and games that were later recorded by the Opies,[1] who had walked here with his beloved sister and shared her excitement for the future and her hopes of a musical career, who had found, in Mr Dickson's back gate, his own private exit sign, who had fought in the epic street battles which divided Holley Street from Lind Street and Lind from Upper Cyrus, who had suffered the privations and the joys of a community which lived for small increases and knew how to bear far greater loss – for my father it was a place full of meaning, whose grim contours told a tale of puritan virtue as it struggled against drunkenness and prostitution, a place where life, assailed from above by every form of privation, nevertheless strove to be orderly, self-sacrificing and respectable, and to proceed along recognised English lines.

And Jack Scruton's romantic feelings were only augmented when he left the place at last and settled in the Chilterns, far from the

---

[1] Peter and Iona Opie, *The Lore and Language of Schoolchildren*, London, 1959.

industrial darkness which had nurtured him, pursuing a middle-class career, and married, like his father, to a woman from a class just higher than his own. His story is typical: it took three generations for the average English family to emerge from the slums. On every side existed the people, the institutions and the opportunities that would help men and women into the property-owning classes. From the beginning of the Industrial Revolution English clubbability had acted to mitigate the worst effects of it. Building societies were first established in Birmingham, at the moment when it began to grow into the industrial heart of England, in 1775. Thanks to these initiatives the respectable poor could fortify themselves with property, and pass on to their children an asset that was the emblem of English freedom. Janie Scruton did not pay rent; her weekly shillings went to the local friendly society, which, after twenty years, handed over the deeds of her house.

The plight of the industrial poor engaged the attentions of philanthropists, politicians and novelists from the beginning of the nineteenth century. The National Society was founded in 1811, with the purpose of establishing schools that would spread literacy and numeracy to the poorest people of England; it was followed shortly afterwards by the British and Foreign Schools Society. By 1870 they and the churches had made it possible for the government to introduce compulsory education to the age of fourteen, so that, by 1899, education had become the largest item in the government budget. The Factory Act of 1833 protected children from the worst abuses, and successive Factory Acts effectively abolished, at the moment when he was recording them, the privations noted by Marx in the footnotes to *Das Kapital*. Popular unrest was minimal in England, and the most famous episodes – the Peterloo massacre in Manchester in 1819, and the agitation surrounding the Tolpuddle martyrs in 1834 – bore no comparison with events on the continent of Europe. The panic at St Peter's Field, in which eleven people died, resulted more from clumsiness than malice, and the trade unionists of Tolpuddle served only two years of transportation before

Lord Melbourne granted a remission of their sentences. Even the worst of the urban riots – that which occurred at Bristol in 1831 – cost only twelve dead. In comparison with the civil unrest in Europe between 1789 and 1848 such figures testify to the remarkable peacefulness of England, even in times of unprecedented and painful change. For every radical Chartist there were eight or nine boys from the slums who were keen to be soldiers, sailors or policemen, and the industrial towns retained their village atmosphere and their loyalist sentiments, even in the worst days of the millocrats.[1]

Far be it from me to disparage the work of labour historians like E.P. Thompson and Eric Hobsbawm. By creating the myth of 'class solidarity' and sentimentalising the 'class consciousness' of people like my grandfather, they helped the intellectuals to feel good about the destruction of working-class life. My father, revisiting Ancoats, found no trace of Upper Cyrus Street, or of Mr Dickson's back door through which he had made his spiritual departure. All that exists of Ancoats is a waste of asphalt roads and trodden mud, from which blocks of concrete rise twelve storeys high. My father wept with indignation at a community destroyed, and a piece of English earth now disenchanted. But those post-war planners and ideologues who plotted this outrage believed that it was they who had finally freed the working classes from their chains, and not the churches, chapels, schools, institutes, friendly societies, youth clubs, cadets, brass bands and temperance societies which did the job without the condescending help of intellectuals. Nothing more vividly illustrates the creative spirit of the English, and their ability to domesticate even the most radical of changes in their way of life and economic circumstances, than these autonomous societies, through which they came together as strangers with a view to lightening their common lot.

This spirit of self-help and spontaneous association can be witnessed in the moots and witenagemots of the Anglo-Saxons. It

---

[1] See A.D. Harvey, *Collision of Empires: Britain in Three World Wars, 1793–1945,* London, 1992, pp. 178–9.

flowered in the medieval guilds, which played a decisive role in the destruction of serfdom and the emergence of a yeoman class. The trade unions revived some of the ceremonial and self-dignifying character of the guilds, and, in the Manchester of my father's youth, would march with proud banners and hats to mark the civic ceremonies. Although infiltrated by people with other purposes, they were, for most of their members, spheres of solidarity and mutual support, the aim of which was as much the joining in as what might be achieved by it. They were only one among many initiatives, which helped to lift the slums into the sunlight of spontaneous society.

Consider the brass band movement. This is as old as the trade union movement and indeed, at the outset, hardly distinguishable from it. The Besses o'th' Barn Band, for example, was already active in 1821, and acquired its present fame after 1880, when the great Alexander Owen came to it from the equally old and equally famous Black Dyke Mills Band. Most of the bands originated in works and collieries, and the instruments were purchased with money contributed by the players themselves. They were associations of musical amateurs, with all the catholicity of taste and variety of achievement that that implies. But they were also more than associations, gathering to themselves an extraordinary social ambience which was unmistakably English in its subdued pageantry and phlegmatic togetherness.

The brass band movement, like the Labour movement, was associated with Nonconformist religion (and with the Salvation Army in particular), with temperance, self-help and the campaign for an extended franchise. But it was not a protest movement, still less an exclusively working-class phenomenon. The bands often included owners and managers of factories, and were constantly recruiting from neighbouring trades and professions. Their purpose was harmony – musical, social and spiritual. Their repertoire illustrated this: a medley of favourites, associated with all classes and with none; hymn tunes, marches and popular songs, and also arrangements of serious music. The brass bands were also a vehicle of musical education in the industrial towns. Alexander Owen, when leader of the Besses o'th' Barn, arranged some of the most advanced music of his time for the instruction of his instrumentalists and audience – including the Prelude to *Tristan* together with a further twenty minutes of music from what was, to contemporary ears, the most difficult of all modern scores. The brass band movement acquired its own school of composers, whose legacy can be heard in much of the serious music written in the twentieth century. And through all of its activities it displayed a quiet but fervent patriotism that has nothing in common with the 'class consciousness' invented by intellectuals on behalf of their imagined constituents.

The National Brass Band Festival still takes place each year at the Royal Albert Hall in London. The audience, which comes in coachloads from the towns and valleys of industrial England, each coachload celebrating its local identity with banners and ensigns, is bound by a consuming common interest. The object of this interest is not material but cultural. It is also competitive – competitions having been an essential part of the movement from its beginnings, just as they were essential to the street life of Ancoats in my father's day.

This element of rivalry both unifies the crowd and lends tone and gravity to the impresario who addresses it. The event transcends all narrow class identity, to make contact with a tradition of worship and song which aims to be the common property of Englishmen. And the whole occasion is imbued with a quiet, serious patriotism, which finds culminating expression when the audience finally rises to sing the hymn which conveys the meaning of their movement: Parry's setting of 'Jerusalem'.

What I have described is a small fragment of the English response to collective hardship: a response in which 'joining in', corporate identity and singing along are the principal ingredients. The 'class conflict' observed by the social historians of the fifties and sixties may very well have existed; but it existed within the framework of shared institutions, shared expectations and a shared allegiance to the country. The conflict between the haves and the have-nots was

domesticated by the English. Each potential source of antagonism
was institutionalised, made normal, adapted to the moral and spiritual
needs of the English people. Class antagonism was experienced by
my father as something internal to himself – a contest between the
Anglican and Nonconformist forms of the English religion, both of
which had been implanted in him by his surroundings, and in neither
of which he believed. Like Mr Dickson, Jack Scruton was a socialist.
His socialism was not a creed of rebellion but an appeal for the
Englishman's birthright – which was the land itself. The true
literature of English socialism is not that of Marx and Engels, even if
they wrote in England. It is the work of Blake, Cobbett, Morris and
Ruskin (who called himself a Tory) – writers firmly rooted in the
pastoral tradition, whose desire was not to equalise the English, but
to reconnect them to their history, and to reconsecrate their blighted
townscape. English socialism went hand in hand with the medieval-
ism of the Pre-Raphaelite Brotherhood, with the Gothic revival, and
with the Ruskinian belief that piety and craftsmanship are the
foundations of order in both public and private life. For my father
this English socialism was inseparable from H.J. Massingham's
attempt to restore the simple ways of country living, and to rebuild
communities torn asunder by the machine.[1] It was the nearest he had
to a religion, and its language was in both senses of the word pastoral,
like the language of the English Bible.

This is not to say that English society was not divided – it was. But
the divisions were many, and each of those divisions was, as it were,
internal to the English settlement. Instead of the open war between
Catholic and Protestant, the English had an 'agreement to differ'
which bound Anglican to Nonconformist within the shared language,
beliefs and customs of the English Church. Their political division
was less a division of parties than a division of character – 'Whig' and
'Tory' denoting two complementary English types, each of which

---

[1] See H.J. Massingham, *The Faith of a Fieldsman*, London, 1951: a collection of
Massingham's articles from *The Field*.

could belong to the party led by the other. Instead of the murderous confrontation between people and aristocracy, the English had a shared belief in respectability, which the meanest workman could possess or the wealthiest duke fall short of. Instead of the conflict described by Marx – between capitalist and proletarian – or that described by Weber – between creditors and debtors – the English had a continuous gradation, between those who had inherited some vast estate, and those who were paying off the mortgage on a tiny one.

Even the division between north and south was moderated by the peculiar position of Birmingham, for a long time the industrial heart of England, where the suburbs were opulent but more grimy than those of Kent, and the factories modest but more leafy than those of Manchester, and where the drifting tide of labourers went sometimes north to earn, and sometimes south to spend. Birmingham had its own economic institutions, and its own banks like Lloyds and Barclays, the creations of eighteenth-century Quakers and puritans. It confronted the City of London, not as an equal, but as one freeborn Englishman confronts another – hoping to come quickly to terms, but not willing to abandon its apartness.

In all of this we see the mysterious workings of the social process for which the English are most famous – the process known as 'class'. Class comes about because we divide people up, and we do this in three distinct but interlocking ways. First, like all social animals, we recognise hierarchies. Second, we divide society into upper, middle and lower classes – with the middle area usually elaborately subdivided. Third, we have a tendency to adopt, in any emergency, a dichotomous vision of our kind – an 'us' and 'them' through which to focus our resentments and prepare ourselves for war. The Marxist theory, borrowed from Adam Smith, makes a tripartite division between rent, capital and labour, corresponding to aristocracy, bourgeoisie and proletariat. But its appeal lies in the fact that it inspires a dichotomous vision of 'us' and 'them', and so mobilises old and fertile resentments. The peculiarity of the English class system is that this dichotomising impulse was largely resisted. The middle class was 'invented' precisely to present a fluid and resilient barrier – a buffer zone – at the centre of social conflicts. It is in that buffer zone that my parents existed.

According to David Cannadine, the existence of this elastic middle region explains the stability and peaceableness of class feeling in England.[1] The recognition of a vast and mobile middle class neutralises class antagonism. Old theories of class – and especially those inspired by Marx – saw people as possessing a class identity. Hierarchical classifications, however, assume that you gain your social identity by occupying a particular position in a meticulously ordered procession. Your 'station' in life is defined not only by its rights but by its duties, and there is no reason in principle why it should not be changed, provided that you are willing to assume the duties as well as the privileges of the station to which you aspire.[2]

Hierarchy was much more important in Ancoats than any shared class identity, and this was one reason why day-to-day life was so stable. You might be low down the scale when it comes to money, influence or creative skill, but high up in the darts club. Incorrigible drunk and layabout though he was, my grandfather was esteemed for his strength, for his anecdotes and for his amazing achievement in the Great War, which he endured at the front for four years, unnoticed, uninjured, undecorated and unthanked. For those achievements he was honoured in the local pub, where it was customary to acknowledge his presence with a deferential greeting and a pint of bitter.

A wise person is one who attaches the most importance to those hierarchies in which he occupies a high position. The competitions between streets, localities, brass bands, schools and sports teams kept the people of Ancoats buoyant. And everywhere, encountered sometimes by seeking but more often by chance, was the exit sign

---

[1] David Cannadine, *Class in Britain*, Yale UP, 1998.
[2] For a profound philosophical examination of what this means, see F.H. Bradley, 'My Station and its Duties', in *Ethical Studies*, Oxford, 1876.

that stood, for my father, above the backdoor of Mr Dickson's, and which opened into the fields and flowers of England.

This love of hierarchy does not capture the full idea of class as the English experienced it. The social and political prominence given to the hereditary aristocracy gave credibility to the idea of a 'middle' class. Because the fixed stars glowed always in the social firmament, the rise and fall of the individual made sense, and it was in terms of this rise and fall that the middle class was defined. The middle zone was precisely the zone of perpetual movement. The nobility, by contrast, had the stillness of eternity. They occupied the unshifting edge of things and illuminated it with titles, ceremonies and historic rights and duties.

For this system to work, it was necessary for the nobility both to keep out the impostors and the adventurers, and to welcome those whose power made it dangerous to exclude them. There thus arose that remarkable class of people, whose role was defined both socially and politically, and which represented the summit of social aspiration – the ceiling beyond which you neither desired nor were able to travel. You could resent this class with impunity, since it occupied so small a region of the social scale. But it was hard to escape the soft supple radiance of its charm. And it conformed to three unspoken principles of English life: it was attached to the land; it possessed a corporate identity; and it had more authority than power.

Englishmen, when raised to the peerage, would rarely take their title from their family name, but subordinate their family for ever to a piece of English territory. In this way the land achieved another grade of man-made enchantment, with place-names being absorbed into the pyramid of dignities whose apex was the crown. A piece of the landscape, by becoming the 'seat' of a noble family, was itself ennobled.

The peerage had acquired an institutional and corporate identity through the House of Lords and its ceremonial offices, so that the nobility was perceived as a collective person, bound together by rights and duties that endowed it with a common face. A peer was not merely a person with a title, he was a member of the House of Lords, whose rights and duties were determined by his membership.

Finally, peerage symbolised the separation that existed in English life between power and authority. The social and political privileges of the aristocracy were once very great, and even in the nineteenth century the House of Lords could function as a powerful obstacle to legislation – often blocking important and necessary reforms, and opposing home rule for Ireland to the bitter end, so guaranteeing the bitterness. But from 1688 onwards this power was constantly diminishing, so that Bagehot, writing in 1867, identified the House of Lords as belonging to the 'dignified' rather than the 'effective' part of the Constitution. Its influence was marginal, ceremonial, a matter of style. Where the Commons had power, the Lords had authority, and the eventual powerlessness of the Upper House served only to increase its prestige. And even in its heyday, the English nobility was not, like the French *ancien régime*, a bastion of privilege and wealth, but an embellishment which rescued political power from its crude imperatives and endowed it with a halo of legitimacy.

This effect was enhanced by the fact that titles were limited by primogeniture. On the continent of Europe all sons and daughters of a count were also counts or countesses; in England only the heir could sport a title, and even that was allowed to him only as a 'courtesy' and only if his father were an earl or higher. Furthermore, the oldest families in the land, even those who bore the name of some significant part of it, had never been formally ennobled, and belonged to an aristocracy whose status was all the more secure in that few people were aware of it. A family like the Hampdens of Hampden or the Eastcourts of Eastcourt had some of the magic of King Arthur's knights. They were mystically identified with a place and resided there like a corporate *genius loci*. But for generation after generation the head of the family would be known merely as Mr Hampden or Mr Eastcourt.

The system could not protect itself, therefore, by distinguishing those with titles from those without them. Instead, it multiplied the signs and symbols of the upper class, and made clear that wealth and power were not among them. The instruments of social exclusion were principally three: land, education and accent. Ownership of land nourished the lifestyle of the gentry, with the country house as a kind of royal residence, employing servants, farmers and labourers in the maintenance of a 'seat', whether or not the squire was sitting in it. The public schools, in which trial by ordeal ensured that all boys, whatever their social origins, submitted to a common discipline, created a uniform élite from the mixed intake of old, new and aspiring aristocracy. And because country life and the public school were insulated from social and economic change, they preserved the peculiar intonation and accent which defined the English 'toff'.

It was not only titles that were subject to primogeniture: land, property and expectations were also passed from father to the eldest son. Hence English society abounded in younger sons who entered life as Mr, who enjoyed no great wealth or landed property, and whose sole marks of distinction from the surrounding middle classes lay in accent and style. Since these last two could be copied, and were copied, by those with social aspirations, the boundary between the upper and the middle classes was almost impossible to discern. The two classes could be told apart only by those like the Antiquary of Scott's novel of that title, whose recondite knowledge of genealogies and heraldic quarterings was also a sign of lunacy.

The English class system provoked widespread resentment. But most people learned to live with it, and also to be amused by the sparkle of absurdity which it scattered over everyday life. From Restoration theatre to Noël Coward, it provided the background to the comedy of manners, in which a collusive effort to *appear* distinguished was set against the inevitable failure to *be* so. In the writings of Oscar Wilde and P.G. Wodehouse there emerged a new kind of class ideal, not known elsewhere in the civilised world, in which upper-class manners were also a comic disguise. This ideal was nurtured in the fluid sphere between upper and middle class, where the younger sons of nobles and the elder sons of businessmen jostled each other in friendly competitiveness. By imitating this class, you entered it, since it was in itself a work of the theatrical imagination. And because theatre is also a form of distancing, which creates an impassable barrier between the actor and his audience, the English were especially good at it. In the character of Lady Bracknell Wilde gave us the theatrical representation of a theatrical representation. He showed us how to pretend to class and so obtain it.

This histrionic ideal spread across middle England. Everywhere the middle classes strove to ape the manners of their 'betters', adopting the customs, vocabulary and accent that seemed to them to be proper to the gentry. Hence the appearance of that peculiar style of bourgeois living which its detractors called 'genteel'. The cunning of the upper class was to tempt the lower orders into refinements which they could not manage, and then, with brutal frankness, to drop them in the soup. For a long time the old English napkin was called 'serviette' by the aspiring middle class, who believed this to be far more refined and picturesque a description, only to learn from Nancy Mitford, who revealed (and also mischievously invented) the secrets of her class, that it was decidedly 'non-U'.[1] Trapped by their social aspirations into saying 'pardon?' whenever they had misunderstood, the lower classes would be astonished to discover that their betters said 'what?' And not one of those dainty customs, which, for people like my mother, were the sign of social distinction would have been greeted by the true aristocrat with anything but laughter. The habits and language of the genteel class are exposed to mockery by John Betjeman, for whom they were, nevertheless, a symbol of belonging and of the blessedness of home:

> Phone for the fish-knives, Norman
> As Cook is a little unnerved;
> You kiddies have crumpled the serviettes
> And I must have things daintily served.

---

[1] Nancy Mitford, *Noblesse Oblige*, London, 1956, which also contains the essay by Alan S.C. Ross, 'U and Non-U: an essay in sociological linguistics'.

Are the requisites all in the toilet?
The frills round the cutlets can wait
Till the girl has replenished the cruets
And switched on the logs in the grate . . .[1]

In this language and in the routines to which it testifies we find a new form of enchantment, that of the suburbs, to which, in the twentieth century, the majority of English people began to gravitate. Vast tracts of the country were eventually settled in this way, inspired by the 'garden city' of Ebeneezer Howard, where tree-lined streets wound like country lanes between the hedged-in gardens. In this new environment, the refuge from the slums and the gateway to the middle class, people like my parents made their first stab at life. They brought with them their English shyness and reserve, and this was reflected in the architecture, each house standing apart, defended by its stretch of garden and sharing with its neighbour just one impassable wall. They brought with them too the ineradicable love of England, as the island home marked out by history. The houses were encrusted with 'historical' details: Tudor half-timbers stuck on like matchwood; panes of leaded glass, in bay windows that mimicked the windows of some Jacobean castle; stained glass above the doorway, casting a chancel light into the hall, and in the streets no sign of anything urban or dismal or productive – just a vaguely Gothic church and chapel, a shop selling newspapers and a pub with an Olde English name. Here the new middle classes lived out their blameless lives in full acceptance of the routine of ordinary things. Their heroic determination to leave the world unnoticed was recorded by the brothers Grossmith, in *The Diary of a Nobody*, and later by Noël Coward in *This Happy Breed*. No reader of those works can fail to be both amused and moved by the characters described in them – unassuming, punctilious and unclassifiable as they are.

The snobbery of this mobile middle class should be seen as what it

[1] John Betjeman, 'How to Get On in Society', in *Collected Poems*, London, 1958, p. 243.

was: a determination that hierarchies and rituals should remain in place. You cannot rise in society if there is no distinction between the bottom and the top of it. The middle classes were therefore vigilant in ensuring that the upper classes adhered to their God-given role. The purpose of lords and ladies was to maintain senseless rituals and idyllic customs, so inspiring the rest of us with a sense of the distance and the mystery of the illuminated regions where they moved.

This feeling of class was transmitted to everything that the English thought and did. When they ate fish and chips, it was with the consciousness that they were eating a working-class dish; when they bet on the horses, it was in full knowledge that spivs and wide boys were their current companions; when they attended the races in their frocks and hats it was in order to enter a higher and more entrancing social realm. Their snobbery was a form of social generosity, a way of dividing the social realm into distinct and self-justifying spheres, and of enjoying them all in imagination, while drifting between them in fact. The classes set each other off, and gazed into each other's spheres with a theatre-goer's exhilaration.

Even when the aristocracy began to crumble, therefore, the middle classes did their best to shore it up. A remarkable private society was formed – the National Trust – in order to safeguard the landscape of England. Its first concern was to save the seashore from bungalows. For the ordinary Englishman the seashore was sacred – the boundary of his island home, the place where it was kissed by its mother element, and which had therefore to be pure and undefiled. The religious feeling that prompted the Trust to protect the shore soon extended inland, to the Arcadian haunts of an aristocracy which, thanks to death duties and other forms of punitive taxation, could no longer fend for itself. One by one the great houses, with their treasures and parks and dependencies, fell destitute. Through the National Trust they were rescued by the middle classes, for whom the country house was the source of the magic which lay over the parks and meadows all around. So important did the National Trust become, that its powers and privileges were later confirmed by statute: it became – like the schools, universities, hospitals and asylums – another of those private institutions which were destined, with the decline of England, to be gathered up and ossified by the bureaucratic state.

That is only one instance of a general phenomenon. Class was ubiquitous in English life, but only in a certain measure was it a social barrier. The model was established by Chaucer in *The Canterbury Tales*: all occupations could travel together, taking it in turns to dominate the conversation, and showing off the distinctive qualities of their social milieu. And all deferred to that first and leading figure – the knight, archetype of the English gentleman, whose tale of courtesy, nobility and chivalry represented a common and class-based ideal. The effect of this class ideal was to maintain an element of feudal obligation at the heart of English society. When England entered the First World War it was understood by everyone that its armies would be led by officers recruited from the upper class. These gentlemen officers unfailingly exposed themselves to risks which they did not expect of the men beneath them, justifying the enormous privileges which they still enjoyed at the battle-front, by the brevity of their stay there, before leaving in a coffin.[1]

The ideals of lady and gentleman were class-based, but nevertheless in some measure available to everyone. It was part of the genius of the English class system, that it enabled everyone to become an honorary member of the upper class. You were not born but taught to be a gentleman, and there were manuals for achieving this status, such as the extremely successful book by Henry Peacham, *The Compleat Gentleman*, which first appeared in 1622. By behaving as a gentleman you became one. The test of virtue was to be found precisely in those moments when day-to-day considerations fell away, and you were face to face with temptation, difficulty or danger. It was to their ability to recognise and respond to such moments that the English owed what Ruskin called their 'constitutional serenity in

---

[1] See the account given by David Cannadine in *The Decline and Fall of the British Aristocracy*, Yale, 1990.

danger';[1] and it was this that the English cultivated through their sports and clubs and teams. Above and beyond every difference of class or occupation was the common code of conduct, shaped for emergencies, which brought the English instantly together in the face of any threat.

How should we define the gentleman? Cardinal Newman, in a famous passage, described him as a paragon of sympathy, fair-mindedness and cultivated ease.[2] But Newman's ideal was set too high for us, who were taught to be gentlemen in an age of doubt. More to the point is Čapek:

> What an English gentleman is cannot be stated concisely; you would have to be acquainted, firstly, with an English club-waiter, or with a booking-clerk at a railway station, or, above all, with a policeman. A gentleman, that is a measured combination of silence, courtesy, dignity, sport, newspapers and honesty. The man sitting opposite you in the train will anger you for two hours by not regarding you as worthy of a glance; suddenly he gets up and hands you your bag which you are unable to reach . . .[3]

Čapek's is a view from outside; but all that I have written suggests its inner meaning. He is describing the ideal member of the society of strangers, the one whom you can trust without reducing the distance between you.

The gentleman was a sportsman, which meant not someone who always won, but someone who was a 'good loser'. He 'played cricket', after that leisurely, interminable sport of gentlemen which offered opportunities to lose with dignity, while maintaining a seemly distance from both friend and foe and wearing a uniform of unsullied white like an angel. The gentleman was a 'brick', a 'sport', and

---

[1] *Praeterita*, I, xi, p. 206.

[2] 'It is almost a definition of a gentleman to say that he is one who never inflicts pain', J.H. Newman, 'Knowledge and Religious Duty' in *The Idea of a University*, London, 1852.

[3] *Letters from England*, p. 172.

showed 'pluck' and coolness under fire. He had 'grit' and was able to lead. But he was also willing to serve, and was guided in every emergency by public spirit and selfless concern for the cause. His virtues were precisely those which enabled people to stand together in the face of enemies, and to weather the severest storms. For Joseph Conrad, the virtues of the gentleman were exemplified by the English merchant seamen, and by the English colonists between whose ports they plied. His tribute to England is contained in the portraits of Gould and his wife in *Nostromo* – the sole points of moral order in a world that has succumbed to power and appetite. They are the archetypes of the English gentleman and his lady, inexhaustible sources of calm in the midst of danger, of grace in the midst of decay and of authority in the midst of lawlessness. They were fictions, but I knew people who were like them in fact.

One such was Kathleen Vaughan-Wilkes, daughter of the High Church vicar of Marlow, whom I had first glimpsed during my confirmation lessons, and who was more interested in horses than in the puny proletarian boy who stood each Saturday tea-time in the rectory hall, smelling of mothballs and clutching his Scripture Union Bible. I met her again twenty years later, when we were both visitors at Princeton University. She was now Kathy Wilkes, having revolted against the upper-class associations of her double-barrelled surname, and discovered a compensating *kudos* in her descent from the notorious eighteenth-century radical, John Wilkes. She, like me, was a philosophy don and she, like me, was a class traitor. The difference between us lay in our class. I had discarded my proletarian coarseness and socialist beliefs, and become a sceptical conservative; she had discarded her upper-class disdain and blinkered conservatism, and become a socialist. But none of this changed what Kathy really was and is – the type of the English gentleman, and a proof that the ideal has nothing especially to do with sex.

It was Kathy who began the adventure in Czechoslovakia that I touched on in Chapter Five. It so happened that Dr Julius Tomin, a Czech dissident who conducted philosophy seminars at his home in

Prague, had written to Western universities, asking if anyone would care to come as a visiting speaker. All universities chose to ignore the letter, save Oxford, where Kathy Wilkes, sitting on the sub-faculty board, drew attention to the request and volunteered to act on it. She was sent as an emissary from Wycliffe's university to the town of his disciple, Jan Hus. And the situation that she encountered awoke in her a quiet but intrepid indignation that would not be stilled until justice had been done. Deprived of all except the most menial employment, constantly arrested, harassed, beaten and abused, Dr Tomin and his students nevertheless continued, week after week, to read and translate from Plato, speaking in whispers while awaiting the fatal knock on the door. Kathy visited them, confronted the police with cool composure, strode unflustered through the streets of Prague, overweight secret policemen panting behind her in their leather jackets, organised what relief she could command, and eventually brought Tomin and his family to England as her protegés. Meanwhile, she called upon her friends and colleagues to join her in establishing a web of support that would protect those left behind – the students and teachers of the 'underground university' – from official persecution. All this she did because it had to be done, and because she was there to do it.

Later, when she had lost her right to travel to Czechoslovakia, she turned her attention to other and equally unfortunate places. She was present in Croatia throughout the troubles, stayed in Dubrovnik as the city was shelled by the Serbs, and conveyed to the people who sheltered around her in the battered watchtower that they, like her, were invulnerable. She made radio contact with all the influential people that she could summon, and brought relief to the wounded and comfort to the bereaved, in a situation as difficult and dangerous as any that we have seen in Europe since the war. In everything she remained calm, collected and innocent, believing that the rightness of her cause would guarantee its victory. And she took her collegiate personality and expectations with her, responding to those who sought her protection with the impartiality of a tutor. Because she sought no glory for herself, none but her closest friends were aware of what she was doing, and none of her good works are known to the world. She could truly say of herself what Donne once wrote, were she minded, as he was, to reveal it:

> I have done one braver thing
> Than all the worthies did,
> And yet a braver thence doth spring
> Which is, to keep that hid.

In Kathy I witnessed the virtue which distinguished English courage from every kind of boldness and bravado, namely, its quiet innocence. In her works of charity there appeared, limned as in a background picture show, the spectral society of strangers, in which trust was the ruling principle and people played by the rules. That there is no such society left in the modern world made no difference to Kathy; for it was, for her, a matter of breeding, the unquestioned premise of her thought and feeling, and she spontaneously obeyed its imperatives, since they had never been countermanded.

It was not only in emergencies that the English moral virtues were displayed. The English were linked together far more by moral ties than by ties of kinship, and this was visible in every aspect of their collective behaviour. The Mediterranean community is compact, warm, bound by honour and kinship. Offend one of its members and you risk vengeance from another; marry one of its members and you secure the protection of the rest. It survives by making space for itself among competing family groups, lives by the rule of honour and in contempt of universal justice, and is at war on all its borders. It is a society of intimates and blood brothers, who have little to say to each other since everything important goes unsaid.

The English community was wholly different: it was dispersed, cold, aloof, bound not by honour and kinship but by honesty, fair play and the rule of law. It took no vengeance for crimes, but punished them with impartial justice. It was open and borderless, surviving by negotiation and compromise. It was premised not on kinship but on manners – in which a sometimes exasperating habit of politeness replaced the hugs, kisses and handshakes of more agglutinative people. Its members were individuals, accountable to themselves, whose social feelings were of an abstract and public-spirited kind. It recognised the virtue of sharing, and its laws and institutions gave special place to the pooling and distribution of resources – witness equitable ownership and the concept of trust.

A vivid symbol of this last trait was the English money. The coins were large, solid, symbols of the stability of the Crown. Yet the denominations derived not from accumulation and addition, but from division and sharing. Instead of counting ten pence to the shilling, the English insisted that there must be twelve. For twelve divides by two, three, four and six, whereas ten divides only by five and two. This way of counting goes back to King Alfred the Great, in whose day there were already 240 pence to the pound. (240 has 16 factors, besides itself and 1; 100 has only 7 and 200 only 9.) In my youth there still existed threepenny pieces – those curious hexagonal coins of brass – as well as sixpences. The penny itself was divided, into the halfpenny, the farthing (or quarter penny) and (although this coin was extinct) the mite (which was half a farthing). The pound was divided not into ten but into twenty shillings, and although the crown (the quarter of a pound) had only a ceremonial existence, the half-crown was still very much alive. This led to the fertile coexistence of the half-crown and the two-shilling piece, differing in value by only a sixpence. In addition to the pound there was the guinea – worth twenty-one shillings, and therefore divisible by both three and seven. Even today, horses are sold at auction in guineas.

To the outside observer the English monetary system lacked all logic. To the English themselves, however, it was of a piece with their weights and measures, which were constructed by division rather than addition, and which therefore presented strange angularities of arithmetic: eight pints to the gallon, fourteen pounds to the stone, eight stone to the hundredweight; twelve inches to the foot, three feet to the yard and 1760 yards, amazingly, to the mile – not to speak of rods and perches, gills and tuns.

Weights and measures mediate our day-to-day transactions; hence they are imprinted with our sense of membership. They are symbols of the social order and distillations of our daily habits. The old English measures once had their equivalents on the Continent. But, the French revolutionaries believed, they were symbols of a hierarchical, backward-looking society, a society that paid more respect to custom and precedent than to progress and the future. They were muddled, improvised and full of compromises, in just the way that human life is full of compromises when insufficiently controlled. What was needed, the revolutionaries thought, was a system of measures expressive of the new social order, based on Reason, progress, discipline and the future. Since the decimal system is the basis of arithmetic, and since mathematics is the symbol of Reason and its cold imperatives, the decimal system must be imposed by force, in order to shake people free of their old attachments.

The distinction between the imperial and the metric systems corresponds to the distinction between the reasonable and the rational, between solutions achieved through custom and compromise and those imposed by a plan. Muddled though the imperial measures may appear to those obsessed by mathematics, they are – unlike the metric system – self-evidently the product of life. In the ordinary, cheerful and yielding transactions between people, measurement proceeds by dividing and multiplying, not by adding. The French revolutionaries believed that by changing weights and measures, calendars and festivals, street names and landmarks, they could more effectively undermine the old and local attachments of the French people, so as to conscript them behind their international purpose. The survival of the old weights and measures in England testified to the underlying principle of English society – the principle that society should be governed not from above but from within, by custom, tradition and compromise, and by a habit of reasonableness of which the single most important enemy is Reason. The English measures were designed for the promotion of comfortable deals and just shares, and not for the convenience of the state accountant. They were of a piece with those great inventions of English law – joint ownership (conceived as a 'trust for sale') and limited liability – inventions which instead of retarding enterprise, as those with rational minds imagine, put England a hundred years ahead of continental Europe in the search for industrial prosperity.

Much of the commercial success of the English, however, should be attributed to the ease with which trust was established between strangers. The English lived in families, and had evolved their own version of the Christian sexual ethic; but their social emotions were more collegiate than domestic. They were most comfortable in teams, clubs, regiments, schools and colleges, where intimacy was avoided, and an *esprit de corps* established in its stead. This aspect of English social life was enhanced by the public schools, and by the educational ethos which filtered down from these schools to the lowest reaches of society. Places like Eton and Harrow were paradigm corporate persons – objects of affection, resentment, veneration and lifelong dutifulness, which dominated the emotions of their pupils throughout their adult lives. The grammar schools emulated this corporate ethos, as mine did, and, through teams, competitions and school events, some of it rubbed off even on our local secondary modern, which vied with us in sporting, musical and theatrical events and often proved itself superior.

Of course, we only emulated the public schools; to reproduce their ineffable charm you would have to copy the two features which few grammar schools could match: their inner domesticity and their quaint architectural beauty. The public schools were single-sex boarding schools, in which young people were immersed in a quotidian social order. This order was cool, objective and often brutal in its antagonism to personal weaknesses and needs. It was the perfect apprenticeship for English society, and the real reason why people educated in public schools could advance so quickly in the world outside. As for the beauty, this arose neither by accident nor by design, but from the unconscious need for atmosphere, for a sheltering and quasi-maternal presence, in a place which banished the warm human mother and replaced her with a cold stone effigy. The gardens and quadrangles, the chapel and hall, the drafty oak staircases leading to poky rooms with windows of leaded glass; the Gothic-revival classrooms and solemn cloisters – all these made an indelible impression on those who spent the deliciously unhappy years of adolescence under their aegis, and their sorrowful image stayed in the mind thereafter, a symbol of mourning and of loss.

Two instances of the collegiate way of life made an especial mark on English society, and helped to shape its distinctive social élite: the collegiate universities of Oxford and Cambridge, and the gentleman's club. The original Oxford or Cambridge college was a medieval institution, contemporaneous with the Inns of Court, which owed its achievements to a medieval conception of the scholarly life. It had its own architectural blueprint in New College, Oxford, the foundation established by William of Wykeham, Bishop of Winchester, and completed in 1386. Hall, chapel, cloisters, library, staircases, lodgings and bell tower: all were symbols and tools of a new kind of domesticity, in which scholarship was the end and fellowship the means.

An updated version of Chaucer's Clerk of Oxenford still existed in my undergraduate days: a quiet bachelor don, who lived in college and dined each evening at high table, who, despite a phlegmatic Victorian scepticism, attended the college chapel and took an interest in its music, and whose days were spent in panelled rooms, poring Faust-like over texts to which he alone had mental access. Until the late nineteenth century dons were forbidden to marry, it being assumed (rightly, as it turned out) that the marital and the collegiate ways of life are incompatible, and that true scholarship involves a measure of monastic routine. Colleges, like the major public schools and grammar schools, were single-sex institutions, and the under-graduates were subject to a strict household regime, which required them to return before eleven each evening, to dine in hall, to wear gowns when in the town after six and to seek permission for any absence. Each undergraduate had a tutor *in loco parentis*, whose duties were pastoral rather than academic, but who was also charged with enforcing the discipline of college life. A good tutor would invite his pupils to dinner, instruct them in the matter of wine, and display the value of learning and the charm of high culture. He would also advise them in all matters relating to university life, and ensure that they did not waste their years under his jurisdiction.

One far-reaching effect of the collegiate way of life was the 'tutorial system'. Each undergraduate was assigned a director of studies, usually a fellow of the college, whose responsibility was to appoint one or more 'supervisors', as they were known in Cambridge, to whom the undergraduate would take his weekly essays. The supervisor might be a don, or a research student. His duty was to read the weekly essay and then to sit down face to face with its perpetrator for an hour, doing his best to compel the student to defend what he had written. This incomparable discipline was responsible for all that was best in higher education in England: the independence of judgement, seriousness of attitude and ability to make a case and defend it, which were the marks of the educated English mind. Nothing else was required of the student in the humanities apart from the weekly (or sometimes twice weekly) essay. Lectures, which were arranged by the university and not by the college, were optional. It was up to the lecturer to interest the students; should he fail to do so, then he would find himself talking to an empty hall. The advice often given to the new undergraduate was to attend the best lectures, in whatever subject they happened to be. Although reading philosophy at Cambridge, many of the lectures I attended were given by the departments of English, Modern Greek and German. It was not unknown for an undergraduate to be awarded a first-class degree without ever having attended a lecture. The important thing was to read, to write and to defend what you had written during that crucial hour of advocacy and interrogation.

There was another and equally important consequence of collegiate organisation, which was the unprecedented academic freedom that the fellows enjoyed. In modern universities, academic posts are available only to those who are working in some recognised subject, with a faculty and curriculum of its own. In the Cambridge that I knew many of the fellows were attached to no university faculty, and pursued researches that no university bureaucracy would endorse with a grant or a stipend. This freedom extended to undergraduates too. Since undergraduates were admitted by the college and not by the university, they were free to fashion their own career. I went up to Cambridge with a scholarship in natural sciences, my intention having been, when entering the sixth form at school, to study biochemistry. During my year of wandering prior to university, I had acquired an interest in literature, and a distinct aversion to the natural sciences. My first discussion with my tutor, Dr Laurence Picken – a bachelor don of the old school, an established scholar in the fields of biochemistry, cytology, musicology, Chinese, Slavonic studies and ethnomusicology, world expert on Turkish musical instruments, Bach cantatas, ancient Chinese science and the reproduction of cells – concerned my course of study. Under Dr Picken's influence I opted for philosophy (then called 'moral sciences'). And so I discovered my vocation.

Dr Picken typified the osmotic process whereby a cultural and intellectual inheritance was transmitted within college walls. You could pick up from him any amount of knowledge on any number of subjects – from baroque keyboard ornamentation to the vinification of burgundy, from the wave structure of the benzene ring to the translation of the Confucian Odes, from Frazer's theory of magic to the chronology of Cavalcanti – and the very irrelevance to the surrounding world of everything he knew made the learning of it all the more rewarding.

This irrelevance characterised the curriculum as it developed in England during the great years of the public school. Although the natural sciences gradually came into their own as subjects of study, they were taught not for their practical but for their theoretical content. Pure mathematics was expressly separated from 'applied mathematics', and given the higher standing proper to a true intellectual pursuit. Latin, Greek and ancient history were at the heart of the old curriculum, literature was studied through classical texts and national history was assumed to have stopped some hundred years earlier than the time of study. You learned poetry by rote, and even at the lowest level of study you were taught to read Chaucer in the original. The further the subject seemed from the day-to-day concerns of the student, the more worthy of study was it held to be.

This resolute devotion to the pure and impractical curriculum went with a belief in the unseen examination as the true test of a student's competence and knowledge. Many of the founders of grammar schools had recognised the value of examinations, in setting a standard independent of wealth and power, and thereby offering the opportunity for advancement that the poorer classes required. In the England that I knew there was no attempt to guarantee a standard of attainment through a national curriculum; it was enough that people had been tried and tested, so as to be in possession of whatever they had been taught. The result was a particular kind of intellect – the English intellect, as idiomatic and eccentric in its attainments as the French intellect was rational and standardised. It was an intellect through and through steeped in the collegiate idea of scholarship, which saw knowledge as a way of life detached from the arena of action. And for that reason its detractors saw it as increasingly irrelevant to the modern world, and one cause of England's eventual collapse under the pressure of modern politics and the modern economy.

In a series of brilliant books Correlli Barnett has made the case against the English élite and its education, telling us that the ethos, curriculum and lifestyle of the public schools and the collegiate universities did little or nothing to prepare the English for the great conflicts of our time.[1] The ideal of the gentleman, with its emphasis on fair play and honesty, left the English at a disadvantage in the struggle against calculating and cynical forces. The classical curriculum put the modern world at too remote a distance from the scholar who had absorbed it; the downgrading of science and technology meant that the English were beset by a crippling nostalgia, which caused them to gothicise their industry and surround it with feudal prohibitions. The education instilled by the public schools and the old colleges was, in Barnett's words, not a preparation for the world but an inoculation against it.[2]

All such criticisms are based on a mistaken view of education. Relevance in education is a chimerical objective and the English knew this. Who is to guess what will be relevant to a student's interests in ten years' time? Even in the applied sciences, it is not relevance that forms and transforms the curriculum, but knowledge. A relevant technology is one that is relevant to us, here, now. To concentrate on teaching such a technology is to ensure that we remain locked in techniques that will soon be useless.

The collegiate approach to education was based on the view that knowledge advances because it is pursued for its own sake. Those who make discoveries frequently have no use for them. But almost invariably a use is found, and that which was most useless, and perhaps even valued for its pristine futility, like the theory of the transfinite cardinals, is suddenly revealed to be an indispensable asset of mankind. Who would have supposed that Boole's algebra and Frege and Russell's logic would lead to anything more than the rarefied speculations of philosophy? In fact they led in time to the computer revolution.

The same was true of the classical curriculum. How were those romantic students, destined for government offices in London, to

[1] Correlli Barnett: *The Collapse of British Power*, London, 1972; *The Audit of War*, London, 1986; *The Lost Victory: British Dreams, British Realities, 1945–50*, London, 1995.
[2] *The Collapse of British Power*, p. 37.

know that the dead languages and ancient literatures which were the sum of their learning would suddenly be precisely what they needed in governing an empire acquired in a fit of absence of mind? Homer and Virgil endowed them with an instinctive sympathy for pagan cultures, and their knowledge of ancient history prepared them for their encounter with the African tribe. And out of their experience of applied ancient history arose the new science of anthropology.

But of course, those beneficial results of the old education were not the purpose of it, but happy by-products of an activity whose true purpose was itself. Education was an induction into the life of the mind, a way of becoming familiar with and living through ideas. And for what life of the mind would Correlli Barnett have us prepare? Certainly not one that offers what has been offered to him: namely a synoptic vision of a national history.

If we examine the complaints made by Barnett, we cannot fail to be struck by the fact that they contain no comparative judgement. Set beside which élite did the English élite fail so badly? In which country of the modern world do we find the educational system which compares so favourably with the English college? Which European nations, unhampered by the code of the gentleman, have shown us the way to successful empire building and retreated with credit from their colonies? All such comparisons point to the amazing success of the English. By devoting their formative years to useless things, they made themselves supremely useful. And by internalising the code of honour they did not, as Barnett supposes, make themselves defenceless in a world of chicanery and crime, but endowed themselves with the only real defence that human life can offer – the instinctive trust between strangers, which enables them in whatever dangerous circumstances to act together as a team. It was not only the battle of Waterloo that was won on the playing fields of Eton: the entire imperial adventure was settled there.

But this raises another question: to what extent was the English élite closed to newcomers, and to what extent did it stifle the process of social renewal? Anthony Sampson and others have written book after book against the 'old boy network' which allegedly dominated and destroyed the country, and their complaints are of a piece with Correlli Barnett's, in supposing the English to have succumbed to the wrong kind of elitism – not the elitism of talent and industry, but that of class, connections and snobbery.

Once again, it seems to me, the complaints stem from a shallow view of human nature. Not only was English society in fact one of the most socially mobile in the modern world,[1] but the class system acted as a stabilising force. Élites composed entirely of self-made men are dangerous: for their members are in competition with one another and usually owe nothing to each other's help. The English élite was a slowly forming, slowly changing and yet mobile society of people whose connections, formed through school, college and regiment, were of the kind that fostered trust while maintaining distance. Its ethos was collegiate rather than familial, and this gave it enormous power to withstand external shock, to reform itself under threat, and to guarantee honest and trustworthy behaviour from its members. The comparative success of the City – as compared with the Paris Bourse or the Frankfurt stock exchange, for example – is to be explained by the habit of fair dealing that is the natural result of collegiate habits of association.

The working of this system can be seen in the gentleman's club, an institution created by the English in order to perpetuate the sense of belonging that they acquired in college and school. For reasons which should be evident, the English had need of another sphere of membership than that provided by the family. This was true of all classes of society, but especially of the upper-middle class, who had spent their childhood in spartan boarding schools, and who had learned to 'play up, and play the game' among boys who were not brothers but fellow initiates in a common rite of passage. They took with them into later life a deep need for that collegiate order and a desire to return to it – to rediscover a sphere where competition was

---

[1] See A.D. Harvey, *Britain in the Early Nineteenth Century*, London, 1978.

moderated by a code of decent behaviour, and where friendships were formal, dutiful and cold. Such was the gentleman's club, and it was through the club that so many Englishmen refreshed their vision of community, exercised their sense of honour and formed those ties which sustained them in their working lives.

The club was a corporate person, housed in a sacred precinct and known through its style. For the English gentleman it was not merely his true home, but also his moral and aesthetic tutor. His manners, his style, his sense of beauty and decorum were all derived from the club. The rich Turkey carpets, the mahogany and leather chairs, the regency dining tables, the walls lined with leather-bound books and musty portraits of forgotten worthies, the quiet smoking room, where old colonels slept behind their newspapers and younger members browsed over maps and diaries – all this had an atmosphere and an authority which the English gentleman tried to recreate wherever he was, be it the City of London, the Australian outback or the hills of Simla. And perhaps the most important component of this atmosphere was silence: 'not,' as Čapek beautifully put it, 'the silence of a man in solitude, nor the silence of a Pythagorean philosopher, nor silence in the presence of God, nor the silence of death, nor a mute brooding, it is a special silence, a society silence, a refined silence, the silence of a gentleman among gentlemen.'[1]

And here we come to the essence of the English experience of class. It was not snobbery but a kind of decorum that motivated the English people to seek out their separate spheres of belonging. My father's Ancoats, my mother's and John Betjeman's Surrey suburb, the City and the London club, the country house and its estate – all these were places hallowed by membership, where people grouped together in mutually cooperating and competing circles, and established order, civility and a durable form of human kindness. English law facilitated the formation of these autonomous societies and

---

[1] *Letters from England*, pp. 60–1. Czech has an active verb (*mlčet*) for the state of being silent (the equivalent of German *schweigen*). In Czech, therefore, the sentence captures more exactly *what goes on* in a club: *mlčení* – a *keeping* of silence.

protected them from the state and the sovereign. In so doing it personalised the landscape and townscape of the English. The 'little spot of earth' became a person, with a face of its own.

Chapter Eight

English Government

Nothing is better known about the English than the fact that they developed over the centuries a unique political system, and then planted it around the globe. Yet the nature of this system is widely misunderstood. The reason for this, I believe, is that commentators have misidentified the fundamental principle on which the English constitution rested. Almost all popular historians and political analysts see the English system as an experiment in parliamentary democracy. In fact, however, the key notion was not democracy but representation, and it was as a means to represent the interests of the English people that we should understand the institutions of Parliament.

Democratic election can, in the right circumstances, lead to the representation of the interests of the voters. But not all legitimate interests can be catered for by voting, and the large hereditary components in the English constitution were in part an acknowledgement of this. How, for example, can you represent the interests of dead and unborn Englishmen, merely by counting the votes of the living? And how, in a system where important issues are determined by majority voting, do we protect the dissident minority, the individual eccentric, the person who will not or cannot conform? One of the great achievements of the English system of government was that it fostered a society in which no real conformity was required, except the conformity to law. It is not by design, but by the invisible hand of tradition and compromise, that this tolerant system arose.

This is not to say that democracy was a late arrival in England, or a mere appendage to a fundamentally undemocratic constitution. On the contrary, the seeds of democracy can be divined in the Anglo-Saxon moots and witenagemots, and the long process of reform, which began in the thirteenth century and continued with one or two interruptions into the twentieth, was driven at every point by the desire of rising classes and emerging interests to gain a voice in the government of the country. The 'common people' appear from the earliest times as a powerful force in English religion and culture, and from Langland and Chaucer to George Eliot, Dickens and Thomas Hardy some of the most popular characters in English literature have sprung from the lowest social class, so placing the interests of that class on the agenda of the fiction-reading public. Nevertheless, the populist spirit of English culture down the centuries should not lead us to overlook the fact that the English constitution contained not merely an attempt at democracy, but also an attempt to resist it.

Representation is a fiduciary relationship. To represent someone is to be under an obligation to defend his interests. Thus a barrister represents a client by making the best case for a judgement in the client's favour. Representation here is a relation with three terms: the client, the barrister and the court of law. The barrister has an obligation to defend his client; but he also has an obligation to the court of law, to obey its procedures, to deal openly and honestly with its officers, and to respect the law which the court applies.

Legal representation is only one kind; but it provides the model for political representation as the English conceived it. The common law evolved through the search for remedies. As people found their interests threatened, they sought redress before a judge. And when they could not obtain redress, they appealed to the sovereign through the court of chancery, so giving rise to equity as a distinct branch of the law. This appeal to the sovereign was based on an underlying feudal idea of the monarch. The king was representative of his people – before foreign powers, before any domestic power that sought to assert itself against the common interest and, in a sense, before God (for he was head of the Church, and also crowned by it). The king was bound to the people in a fiduciary relationship, and the relationship had three terms: sovereign, subject and the law of the land. The sovereign had an obligation to defend his subjects; but he also had an obligation to respect the law of the land, upon which his own claim to legitimacy was founded.

Needless to say, these obligations were often violated. And it is not as easy for subjects to depose their monarch as it is for clients to dismiss their barristers. Nevertheless, from the moral and political standpoint, the Crown was a representative institution, and owed its authority to the inherited ties of obligation which bound subject to sovereign and sovereign to subject in mutual support. Hence, whenever their monarchs notoriously and repeatedly transgressed the underlying conditions of their office, the English *did* depose them.

Parliamentary representation emerged within the context of this over-arching representation of the subject by the sovereign. The member was under an obligation to promote the interests of his constituents in accordance with the procedures, limitations and expectations of the court where he sat. Burke distinguished representation from delegation,[1] arguing that the duty of the representative is not merely to convey the opinion and desires of his constituents, but to consider each issue on its merits. But the fundamental point, which Burke took for granted, is that representation, unlike delegation, is a relation with three terms, and therefore that the representative has a duty not merely towards his constituents, but towards the institution in which he sits. His concern is not to promote the interests of his constituents come what may, but to promote those interests which can be brokered and resolved by Parliament, in the way that Parliament requires. As in the case of the law courts and the sovereign power, the search is for a *ruling*, a decision in which all the relevant interests have been given a hearing, and which has the authority and the impartiality of law.

[1] Edmund Burke, 'Appeal to the Bristol Electors 13th Oct. 1774', in Paul Langford, ed., *The Writings and Speeches of Edmund Burke*, Oxford, 1996, vol. III, p. 61.

Representation requires respect towards the forum in which it occurs – whether a judicial court, the council of the sovereign or the chamber of Parliament. The representative sees the forum as an honourable and authoritative judge, who must be addressed in formal and quasi-liturgical terms. The English were not merely experts in this kind of thing: it was the very image of their social existence. The forum was that thing to which they most immediately responded: the corporate person, elevated by ritual, in whose shadow human relations became formal and objective. It was the very negation of those warm and partial feelings which are the glue of Mediterranean life. It was also the guarantee that all interests could be heard, even the interests of one's enemy, who thereby ceased to be an enemy and became an opponent. From the earliest days, therefore, English representative institutions made room for opposition, and the discovery in the early nineteenth century of 'His Majesty's opposition' was merely the joking recognition of something that had been essential to Parliament from the beginning. In Bagehot's words: 'England was the first administration which made criticism of administration as much a part of the polity as administration itself.'[1]

One consequence of this approach to parliamentary government was that the political process was seen in quasi-legal terms – an adversarial contest, in which interests were brokered and judgement given. Parliament began life as a kind of court of law, and its procedures and officers were conceived on the model of a high court of justice. The monarch acted not as supreme commander but as supreme judge. Parliament did not issue edicts or 'directives'; it adjudicated petitions, whether from sovereign to subject in the matter of taxation, or subject to sovereign in the matter of grievances and remedies. Its jurisdiction ensured that the monarch was treated as an office, rather than a person, and that his powers were limited by the conditions of his tenure. For this reason, the English could acquire a

[1] Walter Bagehot, *The English Constitution*, ed. R.H.S. Crossman, London, 1963, p. 72.

new sovereign from some foreign country (as happened with William of Orange, for example) without any fundamental change in their settlement, in the law which governed them, or in the rights of the subject and the Crown.

In an army, the supreme commander dictates to his officers who dictate to their men. That too is a possible view of sovereignty, and one that has often prevailed on the Continent. But it was never the English view. The purpose of politics, as the English conceived it, was to uphold the law of the land, and to resolve the conflicts of interest that arise within its borders, through a multi-layered process of representation. This view was made possible in part by the unusually demilitarised nature of English society, which, until Cromwell, had no standing army of its own and relied entirely on sea power to defend its borders. In a state based on sea power, only a small minority takes part in the necessary business of aggression. Armies, when needed, were raised by calling upon those residual feudal ties which enabled local lords to bring battalions and regiments from the shires. English conquests abroad were more the work of tradesmen and lawyers than of soldiers, and for much of England's history the countryside was kept in order by local magistrates rather than by the soldiers of the king.

And here we should note something that is often said, both by those who praise and by those who condemn the English way of doing things. The institutions of government in England were often criticised as irrational, with no clear chain of command, no constitutional provisions and no procedure for settling what was required of the subject, in advance of a legal consideration of his case. If you looked for the centre of power it appeared now in the sovereign, now in Parliament, now in the Cabinet, now in the judiciary, now in some quaintly named officer of the Crown, such as the Chancellor of the Duchy of Lancaster, the Lord Privy Seal, or the Master of the Rolls. If you sought to enumerate the rights of the Englishman, you would find yourself poring over hundreds of casebooks and commentaries, in which conflicting judgements seemed to hide far more than they showed of the constitutional limitations to the power of the state. If you were curious as to the rights, duties and powers assigned to any particular office, you would in all likelihood fail to find any document where they were officially defined. The Prime Minister – an informal title first used of Sir Robert Walpole, who held the office from 1721 to 1742 – was simply the first minister of the Crown, by convention the leader of the party that could command a majority in the House of Commons. His powers were undeclared and for the most part undiscovered, and in any case constantly changing. All matters which, in more rationalised arrangements, were explicitly laid down, were governed, in the English system, by custom and convention. It was a custom, for example, that the Lord Chancellor should appoint the judges, that he should sit as part of the judicial committee of the House of Lords, that he should be appointed 'by the sovereign on the advice of the Prime Minister' (i.e. by the Prime Minister), that he should enjoy the full legislative privileges of a member of the Upper House and that he should speak for the government in all matters relating to judicial policy. For many commentators this confusion of functions undermined the 'separation of powers' which had been discerned in the English Constitution by Montesquieu,[1] since it seemed to subordinate the system of justice to an officer nominated by the executive power. However, it was also a convention that no judge could be dismissed merely because a government was displeased with his judgement, that no Parliament could (unless in exceptional cases) legislate retrospectively, that the Lord Chancellor, sitting as judge, would have no more authority than any other law lord, and that, in conflicts between them, the government would yield to judicial opinion. Hence the judicial and executive powers were *de facto* separated, even if no rule existed to ensure this.

To the outsider all this looked like so much muddle. It was as though the English had acquired everything – even their constitution

---

[1] *De l'esprit des lois*, 1748.

– in a fit of absent-mindedness, with nothing considered, laid out or decided, and everything no more than a residue of decisions made long ago and for purposes now forgotten. However, to see things in that way is precisely to overlook what was distinctive in the English approach, not only to government, but to all other matters of social organisation. Although the English procedures were not rational – in the sense of laying down precise goals and adopting exact plans for their realisation – they were reasonable, in the sense of attempting to find reasonable solutions to social problems. The common law was an illustration of this: not a set of rules, but a set of cases, from which rules could, with patience, be extracted, but which were esteemed as just and reasonable solutions to concrete human conflicts, even if no *ratio decidendi* had been found.

We know from the work of the Austrian economists and game theorists that clear goals and rational plans are not necessarily the friends of reason. And it is worth rehearsing the argument.[1] To act reasonably in a social context we need information about the desires and needs of other people. In a family this information is explicit, because emotions, aims and needs are shared. But in a political community – and especially one like England, which is defined by territory rather than kinship – the information cannot be made explicit, since the community is a community of strangers, whose desires change unpredictably in response to the desires and actions of people whom they do not know. Nevertheless, in a free market there is a vital and dynamic source of information about the wants and needs of others: namely the prices at which goods exchange. In a planned economy, where prices are fixed by central policy, this information is destroyed. Hence, however rational the planned economy may seem, it will never be reasonable; for it destroys the information without which it cannot respond coherently to changes caused by itself.

---

[1] The interested reader can find the argument spelled out at length in Ludwig von Mises, *Socialism: Economic and Sociological Analysis*, tr. J. Lane, London, 1951, and F.A. Hayek, *Law, Legislation and Liberty: A New Statement of the Liberal Principles of Justice and Political Economy*, London, 1982.

The market is only one among several devices whereby people adjust their behaviour to the needs of strangers, and so maintain social equilibrium. The common law is also such a device, which does not try to predict the needs of people, or to forestall their conflicts, but rather to restore equilibrium when conflict occurs. It has no great plan or scheme, and its judgements are shaped by the concrete situations in which they are delivered. Its principles and rules emerge over time, marked by the history of a particular community and adapted to its social and geographical circumstances.

Think about this, and you will see why the English constitution was so durable – durable precisely because it was never written down, because it never tried to anticipate conflict but only to remedy it, because it never set up an absolute standard or an all-comprehending power but only a network of courts and chambers and councils, in which individual interests could be represented and reconciled. It grew as the common law grew, in answer to the local needs of an intensely localised community. And in place of abstract principles and clear chains of command, it established mysterious offices with yet more mysterious names, wrapping all its doings in a veil of ceremony that made them alternately sublime and ridiculous, so that the English both admired and laughed at them, as they admired and laughed at themselves.

Power in England was dispersed through many institutions, whose relations to one another were governed by custom and habit rather than by hierarchical rules. Power was also dispersed geographically, and took its nimbus of authority not only from the sovereign as final court of appeal, but also from the land itself. I have already remarked on the extent to which justice was administered locally, by courts in which local magistrates and local juries dealt with local matters. But locality was deeply entrenched in the whole system of government. England was divided into counties or 'shires', each of which had its own sheriff, its own law-enforcement officer (the coroner) and its own courts of law. This dispersed system of administration and adjudication, inherited from the Anglo-Saxons, was reconciled with

unified sovereignty by the writs and rulings of Royal Courts, and
ultimately by the King's Bench Courts centred on London, whose
judgements were binding on all lower courts. The history of these
remarkable institutions lies beyond my scope. What is important is
that they had been entrenched by long usage in the English attitude
to government, and served as a barrier against the turmoils of high
politics. Constitutional crises at the centre therefore often made no
impact on the provinces – as at the deposition of Richard II, when
the country continued its unbroken rhythm of government even
though there was no one at the head of it.

The dispersal of power also meant that the administration of day-
to-day affairs was largely in the hands of unpaid amateurs. Justices of
the Peace (whose function was already recognised in the Justices of
the Peace Act, 1361) were local people of standing, whose office was
rewarded by status rather than money. Their duties were constantly
expanding to answer new social needs, and it was the JPs who were
required to administer the two poor laws of 1597 and 1601,
establishing what was perhaps the first effective welfare system in the
modern world. By 1640 they had become the backbone of the
constitution, administering all those functions which were suddenly
and fatefully taken from them by the Local Government legislation
of 1888. Appointed by the Lord Lieutenant, and remaining unpaid
officers of the Crown, they were effectively irremovable by Parliament, and therefore able to stand up for the rights and interests of
localities against centralising tendencies in national politics.

Not that Parliament was inherently unsympathetic to local
administration. On the contrary, it was from the same body of unpaid
amateurs that its members – whether peers or commoners – were
recruited. Perhaps the greatest mistake that Oliver Cromwell made
was to centralise the administration of the country in himself, so
outraging a Parliament that spoke for local interests and eventually
causing him to dismiss Parliament altogether. Cromwell was the first
and last absolute monarch that the English had known, and one
destined for failure.

Schools, the police force and emergency services were all administered locally. The organisation of the Anglican Church was dispersed through sees which had their principal seat in cathedral cities, most far smaller than the industrial towns which grew up to overshadow them. Regiments were originally county militias, and the experience of Cromwell's New Model Army made the English people for a long time hostile to the idea of an army which served the interests of a centralised state. When finally the necessity for a standing army was acknowledged, regiments were raised locally and drew upon local loyalties and historical ties. During the nineteenth century the practice arose of naming the regiments after the counties from which their members came.

My first lessons in geography, at Priory Road Primary School in High Wycombe, required me to draw and memorise the map of Buckinghamshire, to pick out its principal towns and rivers, and to understand the different soils and crops and industries that were responsible for the variety of our local landscape. The object was to teach me useful facts, and also to tell me where I was and why. It was an education in loyalty as much as in knowledge. Our town's schools competed in the county championships, and our local football team – Wycombe Wanderers – was recruited from local amateurs, who measured themselves against rivals from Aylesbury, Buckingham and Marlow.

This delicate organism, which balanced town against town and shire against shire, which fed national identity from local ties, which identified patriotism with the love of land and roots, became conscious of itself in art. Hardy, Housman and Edward Thomas; Elgar, Vaughan Williams and Holst offer the last plaintive invocations of a regional England, in which people were united by the history that divided them. Theirs was a country of varied agriculture and localised building types, of regional accent and folk song, of local fairs and markets and shows. Even the offices, rights and charters of the towns differed from county to county, and local government was (from the reign of Elizabeth I onwards) the charge of parishes and boroughs, whose duties were inextricably mingled with the pastoral presence of the church.

With the passage of the Local Government Act 1888 and the advent of modern administration all that was destined to decay. During the course of the twentieth century local government became politicised, corrupted and prodigal of its tax-raising powers; the national political parties invaded and cancelled the local identity of the councils, and the parishes lost all say in their future. The names of the shires were eventually scrubbed from the map, England was carved up for the convenience of bureaucrats and local administration became just another form of government from elsewhere – the elsewhere often bearing the name of a river ('Avonside', 'Thameside', 'Humberside') in order to emphasise that the old ties to the land had now been flushed away into the ocean.[1] Addresses too were bureaucratised: once a steady descent from shire to town to street to the plot of English earth so haloed, they were reduced to 'postcodes', whose impenetrable symbolism effectively wiped away the sense of place, and reinforced the common perception that the English are really living nowhere.

Until those changes, however, the sense of locality was one of the most powerful forces in English politics, and was responsible for the unique system of representation in the Lower House of Parliament. According to this system, each Member of Parliament represented his constituency, which was defined as a portion of English (or Welsh or Scottish or Northern Irish) territory. He was the voice of a place and of the people who resided there. His duty was to represent that place, and he was therefore obliged by convention to reside there and hold weekly surgeries, so that his constituents could convey their grievances to him. His responsibility towards his constituents did not depend upon whether they had voted for him. Nor did it depend upon their opinions, party affiliations or social standing. It was an

---

[1] The original instance of this vandalism was perpetrated by the French revolutionaries, who abolished the old counties of France and replaced them with *Départements* named after rivers.

immovable obligation which grew from the locality itself. Of course, this system had been subject to many abuses – as the 'rotten boroughs' of eighteenth- and early nineteenth-century politics remind us. But in the wake of the first Reform Act of 1832 these abuses were gradually remedied, giving rise to that characteristically English phenomenon of which almost everyone of my generation knew an instance: the 'good constituency MP', for whom party affiliation and a career in government were far less important than the interests of a place and the people who lived there.

Such a form of representation reveals the gentleness of England and the conciliatory nature of its politics. The purpose of English institutions was to mobilise consent. The two Houses of Parliament arose because consent for levies and for legislation had to be obtained from two quite different sets of people – from the peers and bishops, who administered large estates, and from the towns and shires (or commons), which administered themselves. Magna Carta had been signed by King John in 1215 and reissued by Henry III in 1225. It required the sovereign to govern with the consent of the Great Council (consisting at the time largely of peers), and reaffirmed the rights and freedoms of the English people. It did not create the rights that it describes, but declared them to be part of the ancient law and custom of the land. Feudal tenure was effectively abolished by the statute of *Quia Emptores* 1290, and it was established shortly afterwards that no sovereign could raise taxes without the consent of the Commons. By the late Middle Ages, England was a free, mobile, property-owning society, governed by a common law founded on the search for remedies. Important interests were represented in Parliament, and the sovereign was both duty-bound to uphold the law and dependent on the consent of his subjects for his right to do so. The sovereignty of Parliament (or 'the King in Parliament') was conceded by Henry VIII, under the creative guidance of his Chancellor Thomas Cromwell, and affirmed by Sir Thomas Smith, Secretary of State to Queen Elizabeth, in 1589.[1]

---

[1] Thomas Cromwell has found a tireless advocate in our day in Sir Geoffrey Elton,

The English returned constantly to this style of politics, and troubled times were seen as interruptions of a natural constitutional order, which had never been spelled out, largely because it was assumed to be common property – part of the consciousness of the people and the law of the land. The relation between the two Houses of Parliament therefore remained undefined. Nevertheless, the Commons was the forum in which coalitions could be most rapidly made and unmade, and in which new interests could most effectively find a voice. Hence, after the 'Glorious Revolution' of 1688, the House of Commons gradually became the primary legislative chamber, finally achieving precedence in 1832, after a show of force over the Reform Bill in which the Lords were eventually compelled to back down. Thereafter the House of Lords acted more to ensure respect for parliamentary procedures and the Crown than to introduce new legislation. Thus, when democratisation came in the nineteenth and twentieth centuries, it came without damaging the structure.

In 1867 Walter Bagehot wrote his famous book, *The English Constitution*, in which he tried to make sense of what was by then, after eight hundred years of spontaneous development, an all but unfathomable mystery. He distinguished the 'effective' parts of the constitution, which initiated change, from the 'dignified' parts, which made change acceptable by endowing it with a ceremonial veneer. For Bagehot the House of Lords, like the monarchy, belonged to the 'dignified' part of the constitution – it was there to grace the proceedings of Parliament with a ceremonial flourish from the past, so easing the passage of bills not only into law but also into the hearts of the English people.

However, there was more to it than that. The English constitution was influenced not only by democratisation but also, as I earlier suggested, by the attempt to resist its excesses – and in particular the

who has portrayed him as the true artificer of the English form of sovereignty. See G.R. Elton, *Reform and Renewal: Thomas Cromwell and the Common Weal*, Cambridge, 1973.

attempt to resist the constant appeal to the short-term interests of current majorities. Complete democratisation was seen by many people as a threat to the principle on which everything rested – the principle of representation, in which every Englishman had a voice. And every Englishman means not the living only but also the unborn and the dead. It is precisely the interests of those absent generations that are jeopardised by too much democracy.

Mention of the dead seems quaint to modern ears: after all, they are no longer with us, and therefore, you might suppose, have no interests which are affected by what we do. That is not how Burke saw the matter, however, and his way of putting the point corresponded exactly to the English vision of political order.[1] The dead, he believed, have an enduring interest in our respect for them. Hence the law obliges us to carry out the will of a testator, whether or not it is in anyone else's interest. Hence we protect monuments, shrines and historic towns. Hence we respect graveyards and ancestors and ancient ceremonies.

Moreover, from the beginning of time, it is reverence towards the dead that has formed the basis of institution-building. Schools, universities, hospitals, orphanages, clubs, libraries, churches and institutes began life as private foundations, dependent on property given or bequeathed by people no longer alive. The present holders of that property are, morally speaking, the temporary trustees. Respect for the dead forbids the arbitrary use of their bequests, and compels the trustees to further the purposes which the founders and donors would approve. By honouring the dead, the living trustees are safeguarding the interests of their successors. Respect for the dead is the foundation of the attitude of trusteeship upon which future generations depend. Remove the dead from the equation, and you remove the unborn.

If democratic choice is to be rational, therefore, it must take place in the context of institutions and procedures that give a voice not merely to minorities, who would otherwise be vulnerable to

---

[1] *Reflections on the French Revolution*, 1790.

oppression from majority opinion, but to past and future majorities. These institutions and procedures would, in effect, urge on the representatives an attitude of trusteeship, whereby the immediate demands of the living could be moderated or deflected in the interests of the long-term future of society. The English constitution was an attempt to stand as a bulwark against the demands of living people, and to ensure that the voice that sounded through the legislature was the voice of the land, with all its burden of corpses and all its promise of future life.

The constitutional monarchy is the light above politics, which shines down on the human bustle from a calmer and more exalted sphere. Not being elected by popular vote, the monarch cannot be understood as representing the interests only of the present generation. He or she is born into the position, and also passes it on to a legally defined successor. The monarch is in a real sense the voice of history, and the very accidental way in which the office is acquired emphasises the grounds of the monarch's legitimacy, in the history of a place and a culture. This is not to say that kings and queens cannot be mad, irrational, self-interested or unwise. It is to say, rather, that they owe their authority and their influence precisely to the fact that they speak for something *other* than the present desires of present voters, something vital to the continuity and community which the act of voting assumes. Hence, if they are heard at all, they are heard as limiting the democratic process, in just the way that it must be limited if it is to issue in reasonable legislation. It was in such a way that the English conceived their Queen, in the sunset days of Queen Victoria. The sovereign was an ordinary person, transfigured by a peculiar enchantment which represented not political power but the mysterious authority of an ancient 'law of the land'. When the monarch betrays that law – as, in the opinion of many, the Stuarts betrayed it – a great social and spiritual unrest seizes the common conscience, unrest of a kind that could never attend the misdemeanours of an elected president, or even the betrayal of trust by a political party.

Monarchy and the hereditary peerage were both ways in which past and future acquired a voice in present politics. The hereditary peerage, as traditionally understood, caused political office to go hand in hand with enhanced social status, and with a title attached directly or indirectly to a piece of England. People coveted peerages, not for the wealth attached to them – for they were in fact expensive to maintain in the style expected, and were sometimes refused (as by Winston Churchill) for that very reason – but for the romance and dignity of the title. This dignity was awarded not to an individual but to a family: it was passed from father to son, and constituted a permanent endorsement of a family's social status, while crowning it with real political power.

The Upper Chamber of Parliament therefore consisted largely of people whose interests were not the short-term interests of a living human being, but the long-term interests of a territory. First among such interests is a deep-seated desire for social and political continuity. A privilege enjoyed by inheritance can be safeguarded only if the social and political arrangements which confer it are maintained. Inevitably, therefore, a hereditary Upper House will see itself as guardian or trustee of a social and political legacy, and to that extent a brake on the democratic process.

Heredity is not sufficient in itself to generate aristocrats who are worthy of the privilege. Nevertheless, 'the hereditary principle', as Burke called it, is one of the few proven ways to place the long-term point of view at the heart of politics. And, thanks to the educational practices and self-renewing sentiment of class that I discussed in the last chapter, the English aristocracy did, in its heyday, prepare itself as an instinctive political class, which offered effective statesmen to the country in times of need, and which also endowed social and political institutions with a permanent nimbus of authority. Perhaps the last and greatest of these amateur statesmen was the third Marquess of Salisbury, whose greatness consists precisely in the fact that nobody knows anything about him.[1] This wise statesman made

---

[1] I exaggerate, of course. Andrew Roberts certainly knows a lot about Lord Salisbury,

one great error of judgement, under pressure from the prevailing parliamentary cartels. This was the Local Government Act 1888, which, in Maitland's words, sacrificed the Justice of the Peace, who is 'cheap, pure and capable' on 'the altar of the spirit of the age'.[1] In other matters, however, he delayed the onset of the modern world by twenty years, and perfected the dream of empire before it was blown away in the ensuing storms.

Salisbury was animated by the knowledge that it is easier to lose good things than to create them, and that the task of politics is to understand an inheritance of laws and institutions, and to protect it from unnecessary experiment. That vision of politics is perhaps peculiar to the English-speaking world. And it comes to us precisely from our great tradition of political amateurism. It is ambition and the lust for power that inspires people to march to the drum of progress. The person who acquires political power by the accident of birth, who has nothing to gain from its exercise in the way of money, status or recognition, and who regards the business of government as the wise disposition of inherited goods, is a great force for stability. If an explanation is needed of the peace that prevailed in England, when the whole of Europe was eager for revolution and war, then it is to be found in people like Lord Salisbury.

The 'dignified' part of the constitution owed much of its character to something that Bagehot did not sufficiently understand, which was the role of the English Church in conferring legitimacy on secular institutions. What to a foreigner must have appeared to be the height of English absurdity, seemed to the English themselves wholly reasonable – namely, that one and the same person should be both head of state and head of the Church. Moreover, his or her legitimacy as sovereign was confirmed by a coronation in which the Archbishop of Canterbury played the part once assumed by the

as is shown by his biography of the statesman (London, 1999); but such an exception proves the rule. It is not that Salisbury has been forgotten along with the rest of English history; it is that he was never very much noticed.

[1] H.A.L. Fisher, *Frederick William Maitland*, London, 1910, pp. 63–4.

popes, anointing the sovereign's head, and consecrating him to God and country in a gesture that could only be understood in sacramental terms. Like all monarchical ceremonies, that of coronation was viewed by the English with a mixture of scepticism and awe. They knew that they were the cause of this enchantment; but they also experienced it as real, shining on them from a higher sphere like a light at the top of a Christmas tree, which they themselves had climbed up to put there.

In similar vein, most of the bishops of the Anglican Church were also peers of the realm, entitled to speak and vote in the House of Lords and to introduce legislation. This was not a right that had been granted to them, but a right that they had never lost – a survival of those immemorial customs to which the English have always referred when at a loss to understand the oddities of their government. It is almost as though nonsense sanctified by custom is not nonsense at all, but common sense.

None of this should be seen merely as a structure of committees, like the German *Bundesrat* or the Soviet Party machine. The representational function of English institutions depended upon their ceremonial embellishment. Titles, forms, procedures, traditional dress and diction, religious byways and theatrical spectacles were all integral to the authority of Parliament and Crown, and greeted by the people with the same sceptical awe as the coronation. By confounding the religious and secular spheres as it did, the Anglican Church helped to preserve the magic of the monarchy and the ceremonial authority of Parliament. It encouraged the process whereby the English came to see the Queen in Parliament as yet another corporate person, a form of membership raised higher than the clubs and societies of ordinary people, enjoying some of the authority claimed by the popes, which resides in an unbroken tradition of mystery. The reference to ancient laws and customs had some of the unimpeachable status of the apostolic succession.

The emphasis on ceremony served another function too. It effectively separated the offices of government from the people who occupied them, so ensuring, as Aristotle required of all true constitutions, that the rights and duties of an office should not be the personal property of its tenant. Much of the dutifulness of English politicians (compared, that is, to their continental equivalents) stemmed from this fact. They had something to live up to, a role defined by history and shaped by the great theatre of Parliament into dignities which must be earned and endured. This was made clear by their quaint and impenetrable titles: Black Rod, Lord Privy Seal, First Lord of the Treasury, Lord President of the Council, Lord Steward of the Household, Lord Keeper of the Great Seal and so on – titles which generally described functions that had died, but which were perpetuated in this way as odourless mummies in the gallery of ancestors. Holders of high political, legal or ecclesiastical office would be appointed to the Privy Council – an institution which derives, via the *Curia Regis* of the Norman kings, from the Anglo-Saxon witenagemot. The Privy Councillor bears the title Right Honourable, and is summoned to attend meetings of the Council or standing committees thereof, whenever the sovereign has need of advice on some matter outside the normal purview of Parliament.

This ceremonial aspect of English politics spilled over into English society, thanks in part to the honours system, whereby titles and dignities were periodically scattered over those judged worthy to receive them, so confirming the Crown as the fount of honour and the source of authority, and reinforcing the perception that authority is one thing, power another. England was one of the few countries with a recognised route to the top through some other means than wealth, intrigue or intimidation. In theory at least honours were earned through service: they were a reward for the fulfilment of duty, and could be acquired through charitable work, military prowess or the furtherance of public-spirited causes. They added grace and glamour to drudgery, and both perpetuated the class system and moralised it, by making virtue a route to social status. They therefore contributed to the English gentleness, in all senses of that necessary word.

An important illustration of this benign process is given by the legal profession. Judges earn less than the senior barristers from whose ranks they must, under the common-law system, be recruited. By convention, however, High Court judges are knights, and enjoy through this title the high social prestige which compensates for their loss of earnings. They can also aim for promotion to the House of Lords, so becoming peers of the realm. So long as these honours and titles are esteemed, therefore, it is possible to recruit the very best legal minds to the benches. In America, where promotion to the rank of judge indicates a vast drop in salary and no compensating gain in social standing, we find that, with a few exceptions, the judges are far less able than the barristers who address them; hence the growing theatricality of the American courts, as the barristers run rings around bewildered judges, appealing directly to the jury and mocking the idea of objective law.

Common law and equity, which between them secured the place of the judiciary at the nub of British politics, and ensured that the subject was never without defences against those – including the sovereign – who might otherwise oppress him, also had the effect of protecting civil society from the state. Hence, although Parliament and Crown appropriated the full powers of legislation, many institutions upon which government depended for its functioning owed their identity and structure to civil initiatives. Even when founded by a monarch – like the Royal Chelsea Hospital or the Royal Society – these institutions remained private, with their own constitution and criteria of membership. Others, like the Inns of Court, or the Law Society, established a collegiate identity which gave authority to their decisions, and status to their members, without the need for any Royal Charter to establish their right. Or they were founded as private initiatives, like the British Academy, before petitioning for a Royal Charter to give added authority to their decisions. The proliferation of these institutions, each with its corporate personality, and each protected by the law of trusts from the squandering or pillaging of its assets, was in part responsible for the dispersal of power in the English settlement. They could successfully resist legislation that ran counter to their interests, and also cooperate with the government on terms that gave them a voice. They formed the background to that peculiarly English thing called the Establishment[1] – a network of vested interests and autonomous institutions, which every government was obliged to respect, and which was responsible for some of the social initiatives which changed the face of England. The National Health Service was brought into being by government; but it was possible only because private hospitals, universities and medical schools had created the necessary store of expertise, and only because the British Medical Association (founded as the Provincial Medical and Surgical Association in 1832) and Florence Nightingale had carefully prepared the ground.

Government initiatives in education likewise called upon the rich profusion of civic institutions, and the betterment of the industrial working class was as much due to trade unions, working-men's clubs, the Workers' Educational Association and the Mechanics' Institutes (the first of which was founded by George Birkbeck in 1824) as it was to the efforts of parliamentarians like Shaftesbury. Whenever they encountered a problem, the instinct of the English was to join together to solve it – to found a club or society, a gathering of strangers united by their common cause, which within no time would have its funds, its rituals, its criterion of membership and its premises. Even in the military sphere this was true.

It is thus that the empire was acquired. It was not the English Crown which established English rule in India, but the East India Company, which, though established by Royal Charter in 1599, acted independently, creating in due course not merely the trading links which were its initial purpose, but a panoply of English institutions and English laws, and eventually obliging the Crown to step in and administer the territories where it had established itself.[2] Similar

---

[1] Term first used by Kingsley Martin, then editor of the *New Statesman*, in 1952.
[2] The contrast with the French East India Company, established by Colbert in 1664,

initiatives – many of them by the merchant adventurers described in Hakluyt's *Voyages*, or the 'forgotten worthies' celebrated by J.A. Froude[1] – spread English habits of association and institution-building around the globe.

But these habits took root only in those places – Australia, Canada, America and South Africa – where English settlers formed the social élite. The collapse of the empire was due not so much to the antiquated education and crusty sense of honour ridiculed by Correlli Barnett, as to the fact that English politics and English law could work only in the context of English civil society – a society based on private initiative, corporate personality, and discipline between strangers. Transplanted to a culture where religion, family and tribe counted for more than law, the English institutions lost their enchantment and their prescriptive right. What had maintained itself by its intrinsic authority must now be maintained by force; authority declined to power, and honour to a badge of membership. The result, as Kipling saw, was a spiritual unease, a loss of the instinctive belief in legitimacy, and a longing for the island home, where the hysteria, disorder and 'Hobson-Jobson' of the natives would never be heard, and where all would be cool and calm and moderate.

It is not merely fashionable to denigrate the empire; it is heresy to praise it. But the cruelty, the snobbery, the caste system, the sheer arrogance of those officers in the Colonial Service who imagined themselves to be governing people of some lower species than themselves, should not blind us to the real achievement of the English in their attempt at world government. Thanks in part to the public-school spirit, the Victorian administrators of this ramshackle structure believed themselves to be in many ways the servants as well

---

is illuminating. From the beginning the French company was regarded as an instrument of French foreign policy, backed by military power, whose primary purpose was to secure French-protected princedoms and so prevent the British from profiting from their already established trade.

[1] 'England's Forgotten Worthies' in *Short Studies on Great Subjects*, London, 1905, pp. 443–501.

as the masters of those whom they governed.[1] Tradesmen and adventurers may have founded the empire, but once brought under the jurisdiction of the Crown it was the policy to adjudicate disputes with the native population through impartial courts, and to encourage the emergence of native legal systems adequate to modern commerce and modern administration. There may have been self-deception in this; but nothing that I have been able to glean from the literature of colonialism, or from the old colonials whom I encountered, has given me reason to believe that, in the last days of the Colonial Service, Mr Chapman was not typical. Virgil's idealised model of the Roman Empire was always before them – for, thanks to their blessedly irrelevant education, they had no other: 'To rule the nations under your sway, to impose peace with law, to spare the vanquished and to put down the proud'.[2] When atrocities occurred, as at Amritsar, they held each other to account for them, and if they offended the susceptibilities of their subject peoples this was due as much to stupidity as to malice.

I have found much to praise in English political institutions. For my purpose is to praise. But of course there was much to criticise too. The mystery that surrounded the great offices of state led of its own accord to habits of secrecy and concealment, and hence to government which, while pretending to be accountable to Parliament and thence to the people, was really only accountable to itself. Although no law prescribed this, the prime ministers began in the late eighteenth century to form Cabinets, which would meet behind closed doors and take collective responsibility for decisions the real reasons for which might never be discussed in Parliament. Ministers of the Crown very soon ceased to be answerable to the sovereign and looked instead only to the Prime Minister for preferment.

With the decline of the Upper House, and the gradual exclusion of

---

[1] See the well-documented account by Jan Morris, *Pax Britannica*, Faber edition, London, 1998, p. 122f.
[2] *Aineid*, Book VI.

the aristocracy from politics, politicians became professionals, with no other claim to fame or status than their success in drawing attention to themselves. The rise of parties amplified their actions, and made legislation into the first priority of every Parliament. Even the House of Lords became professionalised, as prime ministers increasingly used it to confer political power on cronies who could never have acquired it by election. The voice of the amateur was less and less heard in Parliament and the old conception of government – encapsulated by Lord Salisbury in the phrase 'delay is life' – gave way to a new and more activist alternative. The purpose of politics, under the old dispensation, was to manage change when it was necessary, and to prevent change when it was not. All the mystery and the careful petitioning for consent pointed to this end, since civil peace seemed to require it.

Under the new dispensation, however, Parliament increasingly saw itself as the originator of change, the instrument for reforming the English people, regardless of their desire to remain the same. Mountains of ill-drafted legislation passed through the Commons, to be bull-dozed through the Lords by Parliament Acts which expressly arrogated to the Commons the powers demanded by its self-opinion. The old equilibrium was disturbed, and Parliament remade, not as a court of law, but as an instrument of social engineering. The rise of political parties, instead of alleviating social conflict, exacerbated it, by encouraging the electorate to divide along party lines. And the old idea of representation, in which Members of Parliament represented places and their interests, gave way to the continental system, according to which members represent not their constituents but aspects of the political process itself. The wholly un-English idea of proportional representation, now regularly put forward as a solution to the conflicts which party politics have caused, points to the effect of this. No longer does Parliament represent the people to the government; it represents the government to the people, and receives its orders from a Cabinet that it can do nothing to control.

With the expulsion of the hereditary members of the House of

Lords, with the use of honours, quangos and committees to promote cronies to positions of influence, with the reliance on media presentation rather than political judgement, and with the presidential style of Mr Blair, who ensures that the monarch is merely someone who tags along behind him, rather than the person who appointed him and who is the true representative of the people whom he serves, we have effectively reached the end of the English system of government. One more step and England will become in law what it already is in fact – a secular republic, governed by conspiratorial élites, most of them resident elsewhere.

Chapter Nine

English Culture

When anthropologists write of culture, they mean the rituals, customs and beliefs that bind people together in a single community. When critics write of culture they mean the works of imagination and speculative thought which occupy the leisure of the educated. It is culture in this second sense that will concern me in the present chapter. In this area generalisation is more than normally dangerous, since it is in the nature of high culture to be open to outside influence, to change and adapt itself to what it perceives of the larger world. English art, architecture, literature and music have been shaped by continental forces from the earliest Middle Ages, and by the eighteenth century our national culture, influenced by classical education, Italian art and architecture, French literature, German music and the obligatory Grand Tour, could fairly be described as cosmopolitan.

Indeed, the very idea of national character is often shaped from outside. Our modern image of Spain is less the creation of Lope de Vega, Velázquez or Goya, than it is of Prosper Mérimée, author of *Carmen*, of Bizet, who set the story to music, and of Chabrier, whose 'España' transplanted the rhythms of Spanish popular music to the modern concert hall. Nor were the Spaniards unaffected by this. When Mañuel de Falla came to write his *Nights in the Gardens of Spain* – one of the greatest attempts by a Spanish composer to convey the essence of his country in music – it was to Ravel and Debussy that he turned for inspiration, and in particular to the

'Puerto del vino' from Debussy's second book of Preludes. Yet Debussy, who had been to Spain only once in his life and only for a day or two, found it more satisfactory to create the country in his imagination than to visit it in fact.

English culture has also been transformed from outside, not once but several times. Shakespeare has been esteemed as the poet who typifies English virtue ever since Ben Jonson's encomium, and the Shakespeare cult was well established by 1740, when Peter Scheemakers' monument was erected in Westminster Abbey. Nevertheless, it was Goethe, Lessing and Herder who remade Shakespeare for modern uses. Under the influence of the German proto-Romantics, Shakespeare lost the character bestowed on him by Johnson, of the guardian of moral order, and became the universal poet of the inner life. It was in the subjective sphere, Herder believed, that national consciousness is born, and the Herderian vision of Shakespeare was to be adopted by the Romantics as canonical.[1] It was not Edwin Muir or Walter de la Mare who made modern English poetry but two Americans – Ezra Pound and T.S. Eliot – and an Irishman – W.B. Yeats. The Anglican vision of England was recreated for our century by Eliot in *Four Quartets* – surely the greatest work of homecoming in the English language, and all the greater in that its author was returning after many centuries. The ideal of the English gentleman and his code has never been better expressed than by Henry James and Joseph Conrad – two foreigners both of whom were to become 'naturalised' Englishmen, having been seduced by their own invention of England.

Even the pastoral tradition in English music owes much to foreign perceptions – for its leading exponent, Frederick Delius, was not of English extraction, and it was while living at Grez-sur-Loing that he conceived his most evocative studies of the landscape of England. The impact of continental Europe on modern English culture is well

[1] See, for example, Wolfgang Stellmacher, *Herders Shakespeare-Bild: Shakespeare-Rezeption im Sturm und Drang*, Berlin, 1978, and Hans-Jürgen Blinn, ed., *Shakespeare-Rezeption: Die Diskussion um Shakespeare in Deutschland*, 2 vols, Munich, 1982.

symbolised by that ever-popular Christmas carol, 'In the Bleak Mid-Winter', words by Christina Rossetti, daughter of an Italian immigrant, music by Gustav Holst, descendant of Swedish merchants. It was a German refugee, Nikolaus Pevsner, who made the first attempt to analyse the Englishness of English art in a book of that title. And the very success of the English, in extending their civilisation over all the world, had the reciprocal effect of internationalising their language, so that many of the most important works of English literature were written by Irishmen, Scots, Americans, Australians, Indians and Africans. Maybe the last full flowering of Englishness in literature was in the novels of V.S. Naipaul, a Trinidadian of Indian extraction. And it was an Irishman, Edmund Burke, who best articulated the English conception of political order.

The English were often attacked as 'philistines', people of boorish tastes and uncultivated judgements, isolated from the culture of Europe by a puritan dislike of elegance and a preference for the high moral tone. It was Matthew Arnold who first made the charge, and he himself was proof of its falsehood. Until destroyed by the universal dumbing down, English high culture was a model of catholicity, and the English education system as open to outside influence as any other in the modern world.

At the same time, the high culture of England had a robust and indigenous core, in which the peculiarities of the English and their island home were given philosophical foundations and artistic expression. It is possible that no people on earth, apart from the ancient Greeks and Hebrews, has built such a monument to itself in literature. And in the literature of England we find not only the distinctive mark of national character, but also a poignant recognition of its impermanence and fragility.

In science and philosophy the English character showed itself clearly: sceptical, practical, resourceful, more interested in concrete details than in airy speculation, and reaching for theories only when these were required by the facts. At the same time the English accomplished, through Newton and Darwin, two of the greatest achievements of the scientific imagination: theories which emerge from behind myriad observations like the dawning of radiant suns. Perhaps no scientific writing is more English in this respect than *On the Origin of Species* (1859). The opening pages, in which the author reflects on his time as a 'pigeon fancier' and shows some of the soothing inwardness of that peculiar English hobby, the sense of adventure as he sets out across the globe in search of evidence, the evocative descriptions of species and their variety and the delight in concrete detail – all these are marked by the love of life that characterised Victorian England. And the theory itself, so shocking to orthodox religion, and so indifferent to the fact that it is shocking, has the mark of English scepticism stamped firmly upon it. It is the theory of an individualist, addressed to fellow eccentrics and adventurers, put forward calmly and as an invitation to dialogue.

Darwin's studies began at home, in response to a reading of *An Essay on the Principle of Population* by Malthus (himself a scientific amateur, and curate of a rural parish). He continued his researches as unpaid naturalist aboard HMS *Beagle*. Darwin was not an academic, but a private obsessive, an enthusiast, working alone, but in eager communication with his kind. The English scientific community was more like a club of gentlemen than an academy of specialists. The Royal Society, which was the clearing house for scientific thought during the great days of discovery, began as an informal weekly discussion club in 1645, though its work had been anticipated by the circle of amateurs who gathered around the Earl of Arundel in the earlier part of the century. In 1675 the Royal Observatory was founded at Greenwich, and with it the office of Atronomer Royal, so founding a centre of scientific enquiry outside the universities.

Ingenious amateurs figured prominently among the scientists, inventors and discoverers of the eighteenth and nineteenth centuries, and great names like Dalton, Davy, Faraday and Rayleigh made many of their advances in private, discussing their results among themselves. The amateurish quality of English science meant that anybody with means could join the club, thereby vastly increasing the quantity of research – both useless and useful. The growth of empire conveyed these amateurs to far-off regions, where they observed and catalogued the species, languages, customs and gods that aroused their curiosity. Their classical education did not impede their researches – indeed, in the case of the budding science of anthropology, it greatly aided them, and the greatest work in that subject, Sir James Frazer's *The Golden Bough* (1890–1915), owes everything to an imagination raised on the poetry of Greece.

Indeed, it is the very amateur quality of English science which caused science to occupy its central place in the intellectual life of the country. It was a scientific amateur who spelled out the fundamentals of inductive method, in a book which was to destroy the Aristotelian legacy of the schools. Sir Francis Bacon was a judge, an essayist and a courtier, whose *Novum Organum* gave an outsider's view of scientific enquiry, at a time when it was exactly an outsider's view that was needed. Thanks to Bacon science became the *lingua franca* of intellectual debate, and there was scarcely a subject that did not seem amenable to the method of induction and experiment.

Nor, *pace* Corelli Barnett, were the English so behindhand in technology. The Royal Society for the Encouragement of Arts, Manufacture and Commerce was founded in 1754, and continues to hold its meetings in the original clubhouse, built by the Adam brothers behind the Strand. Its publications, exhibitions and connections did much to further technological experiment, especially after the purely artistic side of its activities was taken over by the Royal Academy, when that institution was founded in 1768. The installation of a centralised system of state education in Bismarck's Germany, with the *technische Hochschule* expressly devoted to technological training, doubtless did much to remedy Germany's previously backward performance.[1] But this did not alter the fact that amateur resourcefulness and curiosity, acting in conjunction

---

[1] See Michael Sanderson, *Education and Economic Decline in Britain, 1870 to the 1990s*, Cambridge, 1999.

with collegiate institutions in which eccentrics could pursue their researches wherever they led, produced in England those key inventions (the tank, for example, and radar) which led in two world wars to the defeat of Germany. Even the jet engine, which was anticipated by the Germans though in a far inferior version, and which was developed by the RAF in its own laboratories, was the invention of an amateur – Frank Whittle, then serving as an officer in the RAF.

The sceptical and enquiring spirit that gave such strength to English science was also displayed in English philosophy – though in both spheres the achievements were as much British as English, with the Irish (Boyle and Burke) and the Scots (Hume, Reid and Adam Smith) often taking the lead. Empiricism – the philosophy which holds experience to be the root of all knowledge, and the 'truths of reason' to be no more than quibbles – characterised English philosophy from medieval times. It predisposed the English to adopt highly individualistic and atomised theories of society. If the human mind is made up of discrete sensations, and if the soul or self is, as Hume claimed, nothing more than an illusion, then something similar ought to be true of society. Society should be seen not as an organic whole but as a collection of individuals, bound together in pursuit of their common good.

And here arose a vast tension in the English view of things, which emerges clearly in the philosophy of Thomas Hobbes, but which animated many of the more destructive conflicts to which the English psyche was given. The English were individualists, who prized the rights and privacy and freedoms of the individual above all political gifts. But they were also instinctive joiners, who were incomplete until they had found the club, team or regiment that gave shape to their projects and meaning to their solitude. Hobbes reflected the tension between these attitudes in the political vision expounded in his *Leviathan* (1651). On the one hand society is nothing over and above the individuals who compose it, and exists for their convenience. Without society, however, they may enjoy a certain freedom –

but life would be 'solitary, poor, nasty, brutish and short'. Natural freedom is therefore incomplete, and needs to be amplified and secured by the artificial freedoms that come through membership of a political community. Political organisation creates a 'leviathan', a corporate person which is something greater and more worthy than its parts, and whose nature is expressed in the right to command. If we value the individual, therefore, we must value authority more.

Throughout the nineteenth century English philosophers wrestled with this conflict. For Maine, Dicey and Maitland, offices, institutions and traditions were the foundations of social order, without which there could be no individual liberty and no legal rights. For Bentham, Mill and the utilitarians, the invocation of social organisms and collective persons was dangerous nonsense, which could only serve the cause of tyranny. Society, for them, was not an end but a means – whether to individual liberty or to the general happiness (of which liberty was surely a part).

The emphasis on liberty was, however, common to both sides in this conflict. Traditionalists and conservatives praised the freedom to associate, which is the foundation of civil society. Individualists and liberals praised the freedom to detach oneself and to engage in the 'experiments in living' defended by Mill. This freedom to do your own thing in private, they argued, is the pre-condition of government by consent. In the contest between conservatives and liberals, we encounter again the English approach to conflict, in which what is most important is not the local disagreement but the shared assumptions. Whether collectivist or individualist, Burkean traditionalist or Benthamite utilitarian, the English political thinker would take for granted that liberty was all-important and not to be exchanged for some other, and invariably lesser, good.

The German Romantics were surely right in their view of Shakespeare, who was not merely the greatest of English writers, but also the most English among them. Perhaps it is always the case that a great writer bears the marks of national character, if only because the national language lives so strongly in his imagination. Goethe without Germany is inconceivable, as is Baudelaire without France. But Shakespeare seems to touch on what is deepest and most important in the English experience – which is England itself. Four themes receive in his works a profound dramatic and lyrical exposition, and each of them goes to the heart of English culture.

The first is the theme of the common people. Chaucer and Langland in one way, Wycliffe and Tyndale in another, made this theme fundamental to English literature. In the medieval passion plays, and the drama of *Everyman*, the theme was also made part of popular culture, England being unique in its continuous tradition of popular theatre, of which the Elizabethan stage was the high point. In Shakespeare this theme takes on a wholly new aspect: ordinary people intrude into both tragedies and comedies as the repositories of moral sentiment. Their conversation is a continuous background murmur of judgement, a morally charged sifting of the facts, which sets the drama in the context of normal life – as between the two coarse murderers of the Duke of Clarence, or between Cornwall's servants during the blinding of Gloucester. Here and in a hundred other places, Shakespeare makes adroit use of ordinariness, as the sign of our common humanity and the final court of moral appeal. Friar Lawrence and Lear's Fool, the Merry Wives, the slobbering court of Falstaff, Hamlet's memory of Yorick, the fickle crowds in *Julius Caesar* – in all these glimpses of the common people Shakespeare is at his most searching, showing freedom, guilt, judgement and responsibility to be not luxuries of the court, but the root of our condition.

The Everyman theme both preceded Shakespeare's plays and also survived them, taking on, in Milton and Bunyan, a religious and defiant tone that profoundly influenced the national consciousness. It resurged in the eighteenth century in the engravings of Hogarth, in the writings of Goldsmith and in the ever-popular *Beggar's Opera* of John Gay, resurrected in our time by Benjamin Britten, and made un-Englishly political by Brecht and Weill. It led on through Wordsworth, Surtees and Dickens to Kipling, Lawrence and Orwell, to provide a touchstone of authenticity in English prose. In all its variants it treated Everyman not merely as an object of respect, but as the test against which morality and ideals should be measured. The implication was that reality, truth and virtue lie buried in the human heart, but can be discovered anywhere, and especially in those orders of society which have learned to hide their joys and sufferings from the false light of fame.

The second theme is one that was also to influence all subsequent literature in English – the theme of the individual. It is not just that Shakespeare's characters are individuals – for that is true too of Racine's, of Goethe's, of Balzac's and Tolstoy's. It is that the poet goes to the root of their individuality, and sees the mark of free choice in every emotion, every word and every action that he attributes to them. Even when surrendering to destiny they do so with an inimitable will – typified in Richard III's pointedly ambiguous declaration, 'I am determined to prove a villain'. Each feature that distinguishes a Shakespearean character is amplified by the flood of language that expresses it, and the result is so prodigious a record of the varieties of human existence as to render commentators dumb with amazement. Creations like Falstaff and Lear, Hamlet and Leontes, Rosalind, Juliet and Portia, Coriolanus and Cleopatra are not larger than life, but life itself realised and completed. Every word that they utter is inimitably theirs, and seems to flow from a centre of being that could not have been borrowed or imitated by another. They are as far as they could possibly be from caricatures – further, in a way, than any real human being. Their individuality is also a kind of wild celebration of our freedom to be. And, the poet implies, it is by being fully and completely yourself, that you justify being anything.

Subsequent writers – notably Smollett, Fielding and Dickens – have added to our repertoire of national characters. Dickens, at his histrionic best, almost matches Shakespeare for the detail with which he brings a character to life, and with which he makes the extraordinary seem natural. But only Shakespeare seems to capture the metaphysical core of individuality – the selfhood that presses into words and is only ever half-revealed in them. In Hamlet, Cordelia and Ophelia he shows us this thing that even Proust, in the relentless glare of introspection, could never quite discover: the I that gives and withholds itself in love, the inscrutable selfhood, which is the true centre of human existence, but which always seems to elude our attempts to observe it. It is this very elusive nothing that comes to the fore in Shakespeare's verse, and shows itself there to be everything. And that is what Herder, Lessing and the Schlegels perceived in our national poet and which they identified as his greatest glory: his ability to give outward form to the inner life.

The third theme is that of England. Although Shakespeare would set his plays in any part of the world and at any time where his imagination had set foot, England was self-evidently the focus of his social and political interest. The history plays are sometimes dismissed as Tudor propaganda, a brilliant attempt by a socially ambitious upstart to gain favour with monarchs whose title was far less secure than they wished it to be. But this view involves a shallow reading of the plays. Shakespeare's histories dramatise the English constitution and present the Crown as its core idea. For Shakespeare the Crown is not the piece of jewelled metal that perches on the heads of kings – though there are kings, like Richard II, who assume it to be so, and who therefore promptly lose it. The Crown is the mysterious corporate person which is the spirit of England. It is the 'corporation sole' that endures from year to year and century to century, even when there is no living monarch, and even when all is in turmoil in the world of power. Its concrete representation sits firmly only on the head that bows to it – for only such a head matches power to authority, and so rules legitimately over the land and its people.

We find in the history plays an extended meditation on the distinction between power and authority, and on English sovereignty as a union of the two. Shakespeare's Crown is inherited: but it is rightly earned only by those who exchange power for authority, and who identify with the land and laws of England. This transformation we observe in Prince Hal, as he finally frees himself from his riotous attachments, and tells Falstaff to 'presume not that I am the thing I was'. And the sequel, with the great battle of Agincourt, became for Englishmen of my generation (and not only educated Englishmen) the paradigm expression of what the Crown meant to its subjects, at the end of a war fought against evil powers with evil weapons, in which neither motive nor goal had been clear. Of course, Laurence Olivier and Sir William Walton gave edge to the message. Nevertheless, if there is one work of art that crystallised the ordinary English sentiment of loyalty, at the moment when it was about to dwindle, it is surely Olivier's film of *Henry V*.

Themes from the history plays are taken up and expounded in other dramas, where they are given full elaboration unhampered by didactic purpose. In *Troilus and Cressida* Shakespeare presents, in the character of Ulysses, his ideal of political authority, as standing above and beyond the exercise of power, and residing in inherited institutions, laws and 'degree'. Ulysses' famous speech summarises the class system as the English conceived it. 'Degree' involves the whole system of honour and preferment which gives sense to people's lives; it creates the distance between people that is necessary for their harmonious union, and the rewards which make virtue profitable and vice abhorred. Take degree away and

> Force should be right; or rather, right and wrong, –
> Between whose endless jar justice resides, –
> Should lose their names, and so should justice too.
> Then everything includes itself in power,
> Power into will, will into appetite;
> And appetite, an universal wolf,
> So doubly seconded with will and power,
> Must make perforce an universal prey,
> And last eat up himself . . .

Seldom has the distinction between power and authority been more forcefully presented. Authority, Ulysses tells us, is a social artefact. It depends upon the distance between people, and upon the collusive work of social construction whereby ranks and offices and honours are printed on human hearts. This idealised vision of class was the vision that animated England in its greatest times, and the loss of which has indeed led to the collapse of authority into mere power, and power into appetite.

The fourth Shakespearean theme is the one closest to my argument in this book: the theme of enchantment. This was not a new theme in English literature. The Arthurian legends, which had fired the romantic imagination of King Edward III and been glamorised by Malory in *Morte d'Arthur* (one of the books chosen by Caxton to introduce the craft of printing to his countrymen), had planted in the culture of England the image of a land watched over and haunted by departed heroes, whose reappearance would herald the restoration of virtue and the return of ancient rights. There is an old and widespread spiritual need reflected in such legends, whose equivalents can be found all over the world, from the Huron Indians to the Aborigines of Australia. In England, however, they had a special significance, as vehicles of an ethical idea. England was idealised as a legendary place, where justice, law and the mystical authority of kingship reign undisturbed. This legendary England lay, as it were, just out of sight, over the horizon of daily life. But by summoning it in words and deeds, the English could incarnate it in themselves and so repossess their country. Shakespeare's near contemporaries Sir Philip Sidney and Edmund Spenser conveyed some of this, the first in his *Arcadia* and the second in *The Faerie Queene*. Both were educated in medieval Platonism, and wished to clothe the gentleman in Platonic robes, a visitor from some higher sphere who inherits the land and also transfigures it. The Spenserian vision is there in Milton's *Comus* and inspired the greatest of English composers, Henry Purcell, to write masques for the stage which would insinuate the legendary England into the consciousness of fashionable London.

Spenser was also significant in another way. His *Faerie Queene* helped to animate the new sense of English nationhood, and to focus it upon Queen Elizabeth, the Virgin Queen who arrived on the scene just in time to replace the Virgin Mary, whose cult had been suppressed. In Spenser the English idea of sovereignty is written into the landscape and given the timeless authority of myth.

But it was Shakespeare who sealed the connection between legitimate order and the enchanted land, and who showed how ennobling and reconciling this enchantment could be. In *A Midsummer Night's Dream* and *The Tempest* we are granted visions of supernatural order, in which the whole world is animated by personal forces and ruled by ethical ideas. Shakespeare's genius was to transcribe this supernatural order into concrete characters, to recruit the natural world to his moral purpose, and to show the great aims and conflicts of the human spirit as entwined with the place and time in which they occur. Through these two plays Shakespeare shifted the focus of English literature, giving to the moral ideas which composed the legend of old England a 'local habitation and a name'. To the last days of England, Puck and Ariel exerted their magnetic force over its national culture, sometimes appearing in person – as in Kipling, or in Britten's brilliant operatic version of *A Midsummer Night's Dream* – sometimes represented in their more modern progeny – as in Tippett's *Midsummer Marriage*, in the landscape poetry of Ted Hughes, or in the paintings of David Inshaw.

John of Gaunt's speech from *Richard II* has been so often used to invoke a fake and sentimental patriotism that I hesitate to refer to it. However, there remains no better expression of the idea of England as Shakespeare explored and in part created it, and it interestingly brings together the themes that I have identified. England appears in this speech first and foremost as a place, a land transfigured by nature and history, and personalised and moralised by the Crown. It is to the land that the English loyalty is owed, and from this loyalty there grows that 'happy breed of men', whose kings are distinguished by their wanderings 'far from home', and by their 'Christian service and true chivalry'. Shakespeare is invoking here not only the kings of England, but the common people, and the ideal of the gentleman which their island safety made real to them and, so to speak, a national possession:

> This royal throne of kings, this sceptered isle,
> This earth of majesty, this seat of Mars,
> This other Eden, demi-paradise,
> This fortress built by Nature for herself
> Against infection and the hand of war,
> This happy breed of men, this little world,
> This precious stone set in the silver sea,
> Which serves it in the office of a wall,
> Or as a moat defensive to a house,
> Against the envy of less happier lands,
> This blessed plot, this earth, this realm, this England,
> This nurse, this teeming womb of royal kings. . .

Those last two lines contain in a nutshell the idea of England, as I have described it: not a race or a people, but a place – a place that is 'blessed' (enchanted) yet nevertheless real and here and now ('this earth'), and also a 'realm' (i.e. a corporate person defined through a Crown), and so 'this England', the birthplace and nurse of its kings (well, some of them at least), and of the sovereignty that authorises them.

The love of the land and the landscape, and the desire to personalise and domesticate its charm, was a long-standing theme of English poetry, which began to acquire its familiar modern form with Ben Jonson and Andrew Marvell. But it was not a theme confined to literature. The peculiar sense of place that we find in medieval and Elizabethan literature was a permanent inspiration to English architects. The English Gothic cathedrals, which constituted the greatest native achievement in the sphere of architecture, were not heavenward-tending, earth-discarding feats of the imagination like the cathedrals of Beauvais and Chartres, but settlements, continuous ribbons of stone, with cloisters, chapter houses, refectories, monastic halls and libraries, all set within a 'close' where grass and trees and houses nestled in quasi-rural calm. They were symbols in stone of the unity between a country and those who dwelt in it, and in the leaf-mouldings of Southwell Minster we find the beauties of English nature, represented as Paradise.

Pevsner has pointed to the 'horizontal' tendency in English cathedral architecture – its tendency to grow outwards, rather than upwards in the manner of the French or German Gothic.[1] But the 'settled' and landscaped character of the English Gothic has other and perhaps more significant aspects. Even at its most ornate – as in the angel choir in Lincoln – the English Gothic maintains a quiet and earth-bound rhythm, in which the arches unfold towards one another like the branches of trees, and the sculpted figures peer from the foliage with serene and downturned glances. The emphasis is on windows and the passage of light, on the dialogue of light and shade and on the movement away from the centre to the surrounding cloisters and the open land beyond. Every detail seems to imply that this is a holy place, but no more holy than the land on which it is built or the close that stretches away from its porches. The cathedral endorses, so to speak, a sanctity that already attaches to the place in which it stands. And the close surrounds it with a quotidian and domestic ordinariness, as though the day-to-day life of the English were of a piece with the prayers and harmonies that fill the space within.

The feeling of sanctity promotes the secret desire for sacrilege, which is the revenge of the self against its gods. Traumas in the experience of English sovereignty would therefore turn quickly into assaults on the holy places. Thomas Cromwell made astute use of this tendency in diverting attention from his modernising politics; the emergence of 'the King in Parliament' as our national sovereign was

---

[1] Sir Nikolaus Pevsner, *An Outline of European Architecture*, Seventh edn, Harmondsworth, 1963, pp. 118–28, and *The Cathedrals of England*, Harmondsworth, 1985.

therefore accompanied by the destruction of the greater part of our Gothic legacy. A later Cromwell added to this sacrilegious frenzy, and as a result the great monuments of medieval England now lie ruined or mutilated in the landscape whose spirit they shared.

The Gothic was also a vernacular style in England. This happened three times – once in the Middle Ages, once at the Renaissance and finally in the great days of industrial expansion and imperial government. The schools and colleges of medieval England adopted the ecclesiastical idiom, as did the houses of merchants and prelates in the market towns. The Gothic window became the trademark of English architecture, its mullions permitting a wide expanse of glass, and its mouldings and dripstones securing the house against the weather. Later, with the emergence of the perpendicular style, church roofs, church windows, church porches and church towers reappeared as part of the repertoire of secular architecture. And because these details retained their sacred character, and reinforced the perception that a place, a landscape and the house itself have a soul of their own, the English were reluctant to change them, and vented their iconoclastic rages only in church. Hence the classical style brought from the Continent by Inigo Jones came late and was slow to take root. When it did so the result was the country house in its Palladian splendour, a splendour enhanced by the enclosures that were to change the face of England.

Of the third appearance of the vernacular Gothic I have already written. The Gothic revival was of Romantic inspiration, manifest first in Regency Gothick, a diversion of the wealthy. And it had German, Polish and French advocates as well as English – the most influential of whom, Pugin, was of French descent. Eventually, however, it was to be identified with Victorian England, where it became the architecture of industrialisation. The Gothic revival both facilitated and reacted against the displacement of the common people from the countryside which was their birthright and their home. Hence it became here what it never became elsewhere: a comprehensive vernacular style, in which whole cities and suburbs could be conceived. It was promoted as a spiritual antidote to migration – an attempt to reconsecrate a land that had been desecrated by industry and by the unsettling of its native population.

The efforts of the Gothic revivalists were later sneered at by modernists. These fairy-tale office blocks and warehouses, turretted factories and ecclesiastical counting houses were so much hypocrisy, their critics said, part of the ideology of capitalism, designed to soften in thought a tyranny that they only hardened in fact. Such criticisms ignore the peculiar nature of the English religion, in which hypocrisy, compromise and a half-conscious scepticism were essential to the deal. Alone among the peoples of the modern world, the English were able to entertain simultaneously the thought that the sacred is a human invention, and the thought that things really are sacred. Hypocrisy in this context is only another word for grace – the gentle and complicitous pretence whereby we establish a new order of things, an order which so changes our intentions that, once established, it ceases to *be* a pretence. This grace lies at the heart of manners, of ceremonies, of formal dress and social dignity, and no gentleman could fail to see the point of it. The important thing is not to look behind it, as one looks behind a mask to find the face. For it *is* the face, and behind it there is nothing – or at any rate, nothing human, but only that 'universal wolf' against which Shakespeare warns us.

All that ought to be obvious to the reader of Ruskin; still more obvious to someone who compares Victorian industrial towns like Leeds or Bradford as once they were, with their terraced streets and Gothic chapels, their skylines of spires and turrets and pitched slate roofs, with the modernist equivalent, such as Karl-Marx-Stadt (now once again Chemnitz) in the former East Germany, where honesty is all-apparent, and merely directs our eyes and minds to the boundless desecration all around.[1] The Victorian architects did not wish to give

[1] Although the Communists were particularly adept at razing cities to the ground, it should be said that the excuse offered by the Communist town council of Chemnitz – namely, that war damage had made repairs impracticable – was offered also by post-war planners in Britain, with results almost as disastrous.

a religious colouring to their towns – for they knew that religion cannot *be* a mere colouring. Rather, they saw the antique styles as sanctified by history, and by the collegiality of medieval life. By using these styles they hoped to reinvent the community of strangers which the Industrial Revolution had threatened. It is an irony of history that, in setting out to restore the mutilated and neglected Gothic churches of England, they obliterated the remaining traces of a pious handicraft that they affected to admire but failed to notice.

Comparable to the ecclesiastical tradition in English architecture was the love of gardens. Although gardening is not normally counted among the high arts of a civilisation, it is nevertheless a distinctive expression of the love of land, and therefore had a special place in the culture of England. It is also an art within the compass of every man and woman, an art of Everyman, which united the classes in a common attempt to transform nature into artifice, and the real world into its legendary image. Events like the Chelsea Flower Show were celebrations of a common culture, and received both the royal blessing and reams of idiotic commentary. Behind them was a tradition of vegetable sculpture which goes back to the Middle Ages, and which led, with enclosures and the sudden freedom of the landlord to take nature under his wing, to the landscape gardens of Capability Brown and William Kent. The landscape garden soon became picturesque – part of an all-embracing cultural movement which was the true initiator of the Gothic revival and the Romantic novel. The country house now began to take its inspiration from Fonthill Abbey and Strawberry Hill. The Palladian villa and the half-ruined 'abbey' were both affirmations of private sovereignty over the landscape, and in each we see the workings of an Arcadian attitude whose roots lie deep in the English experience, and in a social and political order based on rights of possession. Even when busy, as at Stow or Blenheim, in reshaping the landscape and disinheriting the peasants who had farmed it, the English aristocrat was shaping his territory according to an image of the real (in other words legendary) England. And the last attempts at a country-house architecture –

those of Sir Edwin Lutyens, designer of New Delhi – were also set amid gardens, designed by the great horticulturalist Gertrude Jekyll, with whom Lutyens created one of the finest and most jewel-like glimpses of idyllic England at the Deanery in Sonning (1899–1902).

The greatest flowering of English painting was part of this same Arcadian movement. The Puritans had confined English painting to the production of portraits, and forbidden any religious iconology. For two centuries after the Reformation the art had been dominated by foreigners – Holbein, Rubens, Van Dyck, Zoffany and Kneller. The landscape appeared as a background to society portraits and only gradually detached itself as a subject in itself. Gainsborough's landscapes are continuous with his portraits of aristocratic families – attempts to give legitimacy and permanence to a family and to vindicate its possession of an 'ancestral' (though often recently appropriated) territory.

Within a decade or two, however, painting had freed itself from aristocratic patronage, and we encounter the first visual records of the personality of the English landscape and of the moral force that animates it. Although Poussin and Claude Lorrain had attempted something similar in their studies of the Roman Campagna, their charmed landscapes were also inhabited by the gods and spirits of a defunct mythology: Poussin's Arcadia is explicitly mythical, and draws attention to its universal meaning at the same time as to its inaccessibility. The painter shows us sudden glimpses of another and idealised world, which glimmers in the twilight of a countryside that has fallen irremediably out of history and time. In Crome and Constable, however, we find the here and now of Arcadia – England as it is, but subtly remodelled in the light of its own ideal. The religious use of painting has been rediscovered – not in order to present the defunct Catholic icons, but so as to celebrate the created world, and to bear witness to the godliness of England.

The original inspiration of English landscape painting was as much literary as visual. By explaining the natural world in terms which made no reference to God, science had posed a threat to religion. But

by making nature mysterious, writers countered the scientific claim
to explain it, and reconstituted the religious sense. Addison's essays
on 'The Pleasures of the Imagination' in the *Spectator*, Burke's short
treatise on the *Sublime and the Beautiful* and William Payne Knight's
Essays on the Picturesque, were among the most influential works of
the eighteenth century. In them nature is internalised, reclaimed for
the inner life, as something not explained but imagined. By endowing
nature with mystery, such writers re-enchanted it, as a subjective and
personal possession. Influential too were the improving road
networks and the habit of journeying to remote areas of Britain in
lieu of the Grand Tour abroad. These and many other factors fed the
Romantic search for a prelapsarian order, and helped to create a
hunger for Nature – not Nature as she is, but Nature re-imagined as
the source and the object of our religious yearnings.

Religion is a spiritual homecoming, and the charm of Constable,
both for his contemporaries and for all Englishmen since, lies in his
depiction of the English landscape as a home. In his images of
Dedham and the Stour he was revisiting childhood haunts, and
works like the famous *Haywain* involve a conscious attempt to
recapture the Edenic experience of his own early years. His
landscapes are bounded, tamed, hemmed in by human uses, with
prominent parkland and sheltering trees. They radiate safety and
completion, as though everything undertaken comes without trouble
to fruition. And in his pictures of Salisbury, Constable evokes the
Anglican cathedral as an aesthetic idea – a temple rooted in the
landscape, as much part of the visible order as the arch of trees
through which it is seen, and dappled with precincts of light that
move across its surface with the slow untroubled motion of the
clouds.

It is perhaps true, as left-wing writers remind us, that the common
people were often painted out of the English landscape, or allowed in
only if they did not disturb its domestic charm.[1] But this was

[1] See John Barrell, *The Dark Side of the Landscape: the Rural Poor in English Painting,
1730–1840*, Cambridge, 1980.

because the landscape was seen as shaped by personal relations, belonging to the viewer as the viewer belonged to it. All those things that give permanence to the English experience of home – the changeable sky, the grey uncertain light, the meandering roads and rivers and the permeable boundaries – were singled out for emphasis, and the people portrayed, if at all, as integral parts of the landscape, not visitors but residents, too much settled to deserve a drama of their own.

Thanks to Thomson's *Seasons* – one of the most popular poems ever to have appeared in English – the landscape was a standard theme of English poetry when Wordsworth began his monumental attempt to portray it as a thing with a soul. Wordsworth, like Constable, was concerned to re-enchant the haunts of his childhood, and to vindicate the life that had grown there – the life of shepherds and drovers and carters, whose occupations were destined to die with them. It was a landscape beyond the boundaries of ownership, enjoying some vestige of the ancient forms of cultivation which were elsewhere vanishing beneath the march of modern industry. For Wordsworth the lakes were the real England, the England of the common people whose traces could be read in its soil, but whose bodies were rarely found above its surface. It was by focusing on this land where solitude was the norm, that he was able to rediscover its spiritual meaning. But, as he well knew, the England that he discovered in the landscape did not correspond to the reality that he encountered in the towns. The ancient ways were disregarded, the old altars desecrated:

> Milton! thou shouldst be living at this hour:
> England hath need of thee: she is a fen
> Of stagnant waters: altar, sword, and pen,
> Fireside, the heroic wealth of hall and bower,
> Have forfeited their ancient English dower
> Of inward happiness.

This 'inward happiness' is what Wordsworth set out to rediscover, by communing with the England he loved not through its people or its institutions, but directly. His was a face-to-face, indeed person-to-person, encounter with scenery. Yet what he saw he also remembered: to see, for Wordsworth, was to reconstitute the present moment as a thing recollected, endowed with the invulnerability of things for ever gone. The landscape appears in Wordsworth's poetry as a kind of memorial to itself, and to the human life that has been brushed away from its surface.

The result was a triumph of meditative verse – a sustained attempt to endow the landscape with a soul, by mingling it with the soul of the observer. It should be compared to that other, equally English, monument to country living – *The Borough*, written by Wordsworth's contemporary George Crabbe. In the person of Crabbe we encounter an instance of one of the great English cultural inventions – the educated parson, appointed to a living far from the city, for whom pastoral duty and literary imagination become parts of a continuous redemptive endeavour. He is tutor and guide to his flock; his mission is to rescue them from oblivion, by seeing the work of Providence in all that they feel and do.

English Christianity never had a kinder or more modest voice than Crabbe's, and it is a voice that weaves together in a new way the themes that I have been discussing in this chapter. *The Borough* is a truthful, often disturbing, account of the common people of an English coastal town, in which the poet explores the individual self of each resident, and sees his soul and destiny reflected in the landscape. It is informed by a very English religion – a religion of order and continuity and biblical example – and it celebrates the local community, its inwardness and personality. The poem also gives us, in the character of Peter Grimes, a remarkable representation of the outsider in literature – remarkable precisely because the poet so vividly invokes the English togetherness from which Peter is excluded.

English art and literature were not exclusively pastoral – far from it. The birth of the novel, the growth of the argumentative essay and the satirical journal, the art of caricature and social comment – all these express the new spirit of eighteenth-century London, in which the court and its intrigues have been marginalised, and a thriving culture of enterprise has peopled the streets and the clubs with eccentrics. Defoe and Richardson, Addison and Steele, Pope and Burlington, Hogarth and Rowlandson, Reynolds and Soane and above all Dr Johnson represent a disputatious urban culture acutely aware of its own modernity, and eager to embrace the varieties of life that thrive in an outward-looking and commercial city. Even in the newest and most urban of art forms, however, those of the novel and the satirical engraving, the image of country life would constantly return. The country had become a symbol of moral order and belonging – of the true and inviolable England against which the artifice of the city must be measured and found wanting. Hogarth's series of engravings recounting the Rake's Progress, Richardson's *Clarissa*, Fielding's *Tom Jones* and countless lesser works are variations on the theme of rural innocence, corrupted by city life. The country is seen as the natural place of residence, and the journey to the city has the character of an initiation into a life that has been turned from its natural course. It was the Wessex-born Joseph Addison, founder of the *Spectator*, leading light of literary London but also Member of Parliament for the rotten borough of Malmesbury, who gave us, in the character of Sir Roger de Coverley, the first full portrait of the innocent country squire.

Country life remained a central theme of English literature throughout the nineteenth century, with the Brontës, George Eliot and Jane Austen giving unforgettable portraits of the dramas which occur when people live together in isolated communities, under the tutelage of the Anglican Church and the dispersed English sovereignty, and struggling always with the illusory promise of escape. This literature is a literature of acceptance – though acceptance after temptation, strife and moral victory. The early Victorian novel is laden with sadness, invaded by dark forces and a sense of doom, yet winning through, as a rule, to a peaceful reconciliation with the surrounding order. Later in the century the picture changes. Trollope gives us acid portraits of people shorn of human kindness. Dickens's eccentrics spring from the crannies of a city beneath which the land has been buried in darkness. And in Thomas Hardy the traditional countryside appears for the last time, mourned in deep sorrow, but still the home of that 'darkling thrush', and the source of 'Some blessed Hope, whereof he knew / And I was unaware'.

The internal migrations of the English and their Celtic neighbours had less effect, at first, on the high culture of the country than they had on the popular culture. The rise of Nonconformism in the cities, the growth of literacy and the renewed popularity of the Bible and Bunyan, in a population that could now help itself to its spiritual legacy, changed the outlook of ordinary people, and prompted them to invent their own forms of entertainment. Theirs was a culture of amateur songwriters and musicians, amateur performances and semi-professional repertory theatres. The folk song began to die out and the parlour song came in its place. The displacement of people to the towns, where they had to create their own sense of belonging, led to the discovery of childhood, as the only enchanted state remaining, and the one that suffered most in these new conditions. Stories for and about children therefore took a central place in the new popular culture. Few were more influential than *The Water Babies*, by the Rev. Charles Kingsley – still a favourite book in my own early days. Kingsley was a hunting parson, who lived in the shires, basking in the old enchantment. But his works were read by my grandmother, whose son's hopes were fixed on Mr Dickson's door beyond the alleyway.

The brass band and the amateur choir began to occupy a central place in the life of the towns. The Three Choirs Festival, held annually in rotation at the cathedrals of Gloucester, Hereford and Worcester, had existed since 1724; now it took on a new and more encompassing life, to be imitated by festivals and competitions between amateur music-makers all over the country. Above the polluted streets of the industrial cities there arose a hullabaloo of popular song, dance and declamation, the echoes of which can be heard in the novels, plays and serious music of the period. It is present even in Tennyson, if only because he is so obviously stopping his ears to it. The England that I knew bore the marks of this amateur culture. Every other household had a piano, and as like as not there was someone around who could play it. Books, of a self-improving kind, had a place in every living room, and evening entertainments would involve games like charades which drew on the histrionic talents of the family.

Our piano had come down to us from my grandmother, a memorial to her doomed and favourite child. It was such a piano that Lawrence recalls in his famous poem, one which had accompanied songs and hymns and choruses throughout my father's childhood days; and he too, when it was played, 'wept like a child for the past', recalling the futile hopes of his sister; eventually he forbad my mother to play it, and even her favourite piece – 'Marigold' by Billy Mayerl, with its excruciating parallel fourths – lay untouched in the music stool. I left Cambridge in 1965 and lived abroad for a while, first in provincial France and then in Rome. I was astonished to discover that nobody I met in either place had a piano, and that in almost no household were there books, other than untouched sets of Balzac or *I Promessi sposi* in a tooled leather binding.

In Victorian England popular culture and high culture were adjacent parts of a continuum, and music was the symbol of this. Although there was no great English composer between Purcell and Elgar, there was an unbroken tradition of music-making, in which amateur played side by side with professional, and popular song and dance vied with the symphony and the oratorio. As in other areas of English cultural life, private initiatives and spontaneous institution-building had enabled an eclectic and vital musical culture to flourish without the need for patronage from the state. Although the Reformation had, with its war on liturgical music, isolated England from the great achievements of Continental polyphony, the English themselves worked hard to reconnect themselves with their musical past. The Academy of Ancient Music was founded as a private initiative in 1710, in the Crown and Anchor tavern in the Strand. It was devoted to reviving the music of Byrd, Tallis, Purcell and Palestrina. An Academy of Vocal Music followed in 1726, devoted to restoring the tradition of English church music. Meanwhile, Handel had taken London by storm, and soon provided the English with the art form which brought their biblical culture and their clubbable spirit together: the oratorio, of which Handel's most famous example, *The Messiah*, became a kind of extended national anthem, following the decision, in 1750, to stage an annual performance for the benefit of the Foundling Hospital. In the England of my youth there was scarcely a town which did not attempt to mount a performance of *The Messiah* at Christmas, and we in Marlow were especially proud of the fact that we could scrape together most of the musicians required to use Mozart's re-orchestration.

The significance of *The Messiah* was not merely musical; nor was its protestant message of the first importance. Far more significant for the English audience of my youth was the fact that it set passages of the English Bible to music that was imbued with an English pastoral tranquillity. It was also an occasion for joining in, and one which had a moment of typically English patriotism, when we stood together for the Hallelujah chorus, to commemorate the time when George II had tottered to his feet in admiration, and a bewildered audience had deferentially done the same.

The Royal Philharmonic Society was founded in 1813, and during the nineteenth century the subscription concert became institutionalised all over the country, creating a new kind of audience which awaited impatiently the latest works from the Continent. The tradition of involving the widest possible audience in the propagation of good music culminated in another private initiative – the Promenade Concerts of Sir Henry Wood. These began in 1895 with the intention of making serious music available at the cheapest possible price to all-comers, and were taken over by the BBC in 1927 in order to broadcast the concerts to Everyman. Today the Proms are probably the only enterprise controlled by the BBC which that institution cannot pervert into some kind of anti-English satire.

The importance of amateur music-making in Victorian England meant that the distinction between high and popular culture was never as clear-cut as the aesthetes would have liked it to be: and the aesthetes themselves were satirised in those triumphs of middle-brow art, the operettas of Gilbert and Sullivan. At High Wycombe Royal Grammar School we performed one of those operettas each year, and the tunes and verses stuck in our memories, specimens of a lost joviality and an affectionate debunking of Old England.

Gilbert and Sullivan exemplify a general feature of the *fin-de-siècle* culture of England: that it mocked what was serious, and also affirmed it as serious. The same is true of the children's literature which reached its high point with Lewis Carroll. Gilbert's satirical verses, which show the institutions and offices of the English in all their artificiality, also normalise the pomp and ceremony at which they laugh. All this, they tell us, is both charming and harmless, and besides, there is no better way to be governed than by a long-standing joke.

Lewis Carroll is especially relevant in this respect, as is Edward Lear. Both writers sought and found an answer to scientific disenchantment in nonsense. And although, as I remarked in Chapter Three, nonsense has had a special appeal to the English in every period, it was seen by these writers as a way to spiritualise the world without *believing* anything. 'Jabberwocky', with its Keatsian rhythm, its mock-courtly language, its epic tone and its invocation of a medieval trope (the gaining of manhood through the slaying of a monster) is like a spell, an incantation, summoning the enchanted view of things without any commitment to its content or its truth. (Spells are, indeed, the original form of nonsense; the 'Alice' books are one long *abracadabra* thrown in the face of Victorian science. Their author, however, was a professional mathematician.)

A Shropshire Lad, with its valedictory invocation of the shires as they had been before the factories, and love as it had been before the railway and the bicycle, set a new trend in art and music – the invocation of a vanished folk culture, and of places as they appear in legend. Thus was reborn, *in extremis*, the Shakespearean theme of the haunted landscape. The growing perception that the empire was unsustainable, that European war was again on the cards, and that England's greatest hour had passed caused people to turn their thoughts backwards and inwards, to the still breathing memory of a homeland that had not offended the world. The greatest creations of this spiritual moment equal almost anything in the national culture – Elgar's symphonies and cello concerto, for example, and the paintings of Paul Nash, who came home from service as official war artist in the Great War to take a last glimpse at the English landscape, as it was before suburbanisation and agribusiness destroyed it.

Most impressive of those whose artistic life began in the sunset glow of the empire was the composer Vaughan Williams who, Welsh name notwithstanding, epitomised the national culture at this last moment when belief in it was possible. He died in my lifetime, just as I was discovering his music and wondering, in Leavisite fashion, whether it was permissible to enjoy it. His widow is living even now. Yet his art memorialises the English idea at its fullest, embracing and distilling all the elements of the national culture that could still be internalised, accepted and not quite believed. He was the son of an Anglican vicar, the editor of the English Hymnal and the co-editor of *The Oxford Book of Carols*. Vaughan Williams was also a lifelong admirer of Bunyan, whose *Pilgrim's Progress* he was to turn into a serene stage work, with music commenting on the spoken word. He epitomised the old religious culture of England – the more so in that, as time went on, he allowed scepticism to triumph over faith, and expressed in his later works the curious half-belief of the English, which is a belief not so much in the revealed truths of Christianity as in the English traditions which convey them. With Cecil Sharp he collected the folk songs of the English at the moment when they could last be heard, sung in pubs and markets in the dying fragments of Hardy's countryside. His *Fantasia on Greensleeves* brilliantly combines one of these songs ('Lovely Joan') with the most famous of Elizabethan courtly laments, in a piece which summarises, from the perspective of loss, the folk tradition of the English. A pupil of Parry and Stanford, he also studied with Ravel, and drew on his knowledge of Impressionist harmony in a setting of poems from *A Shropshire Lad*. The result (*On Wenlock Edge*) is surely one of the masterpieces of modern music, its unashamed romanticism notwithstanding. When serving, like Leavis, as an ambulance man in the Great War, Vaughan Williams encountered some of the worst of the suffering and destruction. His reaction, however, was a very English one – to compose the *Pastoral Symphony*, an invocation of the countryside for which the English imagined themselves to be fighting, and which they were soon, of their own initiative, to destroy.

Vaughan Williams overcame the nostalgia that inspired his early works, internalised the idioms of folksong and hymn-tune, and used his art to confront the reality of England, as it emerged from the Second World War, so finding the ghosts of old virtues and the inspiration for a life in decline. The Sixth Symphony already anticipates the bleak exhausted spirit of a nation that was to emerge from victory with the feeling of defeat. The *Sinfonia Antarctica* goes further, and endorses defeat as a form of spiritual achievement.

Since Anglo-Saxon times the English have been moved by futile heroism. *The Battle of Maldon* commemorates a typical episode, in which the warriors fight to the death after their chieftain has been slain, precisely because there is nothing now to be achieved by dying, and death has become its own meaning. In 1948 Ealing Studios decided to commemorate the virtues of the English with a film devoted to Scott of Antarctica, and Vaughan Williams was asked to compose the music. Scott's expedition had no motive other than the competitiveness of schoolboys; it was the ultimate futile gesture, in which the virtues of the English were put to their supreme test. Scott and his team were the transcendental image of the 'good loser': the player who sacrifices everything with a smile, and who lies buried far from home with no achievement apart from the honourable conduct

which led to this end. He was one of the last examples of those
explorers like Dr Livingstone, whose self-imposed and functionless
heroism lifted them above reproach, and somehow justified the
empire which arose by an invisible hand in the wake of their
adventures.

The intense feelings that Scott's journey to the pole inspired in the
English, as they emerged from a war in which they had gained a
victory but lost everything else, are easy to imagine. In the death of
Scott was the mystical proof that loss is gain. And Vaughan
Williams's invocations of the Antarctic wilderness are the musical
expression of a bleakness far more significant than that of the
uninhabited wastes displayed on the screen. In this and subsequent
symphonic works, Vaughan Williams looked back on Mr Chapman's
England without irony or sarcasm, but with a tender appreciation of a
doomed experiment in virtue.

English culture did not die with the empire. On the contrary, it
achieved a remarkable new flowering, in almost every art form, at the
very moment when the empire fell away. Only in architecture, which,
being a public art, requires a kind of self-confidence that no longer
existed, did the high culture of England fail to renew itself in the
wake of the Second World War. Two giants, who equalled in their
achievement almost anything in the history of England, gave form
and meaning to the post-war perspective: T.S. Eliot, who was an
American by birth, but an Englishman by conviction, and Benjamin
Britten. Eliot first made his mark with *The Waste Land* (1922), a
poem expressing a very English sense of the modern townscape, as a
place disenchanted and starved of spiritual meaning, but offering
glimpses, nevertheless, of a subterranean spiritual life. The references
contained in this work, to which Eliot draws attention in his notes,
became part of the culture. He adroitly conscripted the French
symbolists, Wagner, Jessie Weston and Sir James Frazer to give what
was in effect a negative theology of the City, and to invoke the
longing for a renewed and resanctified landscape, which would also
be the locus of a renewed and rededicated national culture.

Eliot went on to give a remarkable account of English literature, as it appears or ought to appear to an undeceived and modern sensibility. And then, before and during the war, he composed the poem which brought back everything that the English longed for: *Four Quartets* (1935–42), in which a still living Anglican holiness is rediscovered in the calm of country churches. The diction of the poem draws heavily on the English Bible and the English Book of Common Prayer. It evokes old communities and old forms of collegiality. And the Arthurian ghosts put in the most surprising of their recent appearances, emerging from their tombs illusionless but not disillusioned, and speaking with a serene and decorous conscious-ness of their invented nature.

Eliot typified a feature of modern English culture which stands in marked contrast to the Continental pattern. He was not merely conservative in his outlook; he was also thoroughly respectable. On arriving in England he had worked as a schoolteacher (as it happens, in High Wycombe Royal Grammar School), and then as a banker, before joining Faber & Faber, which he turned into London's leading modernist publisher. He wore three-piece suits and a tie, spoke with a quiet reserve, cultivating a meticulous bachelor manner that was scarcely affected by his two marriages. Eliot, who had insinuated the bohemian culture of Paris into the modern English consciousness, was entirely anti-bohemian in his values and his style. Similar examples dominated the culture of post-war England: the novelists Henry Green and Kingsley Amis, the poet Philip Larkin, composers like Vaughan Williams, Edmund Rubbra, Lennox Berkeley and John Ireland – all of them respectable citizens, often with conservative, even reactionary, opinions, upholders of the moral order and unassuming members of the long-suffering middle class.

This anti-bohemian respectability was not a novel feature of the national culture. The leading artistic spirits among Englishmen have almost always been prepared not only to belong to the respectable classes, but also to defend the values which make respectability respectable. Chaucer, Donne, Herbert, Dryden and Pope; Dowland,

Byrd, Tallis and Purcell; Austen, Crabbe, Thackeray, Tennyson and even the mercurial Browning; Elgar, Lutyens and de la Mare – the list is all but endless, and the exceptions (Blake, Morris, the Pre-Raphaelite brotherhood, Aubrey Beardsley, Wyndham Lewis and D.H. Lawrence) merely serve to emphasise the deep-seated normality and humility of the artistic temperament as the English displayed it. Nobody is more typical than Shakespeare, with his lifelong pursuit of gentility, his deeply conservative vision of social order, and his final retirement to Stratford, there to enjoy a bourgeois household and a grant of arms. The shabbiest of English eccentrics, Dr Johnson, was also the most dutiful of Tories, who abhorred nothing more than the libertinous affectations of the self-appointed wit. A great poet in his own right, he saw poetry as continuous with morality, a sphere not of licence but of restraint and judgement, the ultimate aim of which was to uphold the decencies which make life in society worthwhile.

Something of this survives in the last truly great artistic talent that England produced. In Benjamin Britten we find a revived – and sceptical – Anglicanism, together with a Shakespearean breadth of imagination, which looked well beyond the confines of English Christianity for its sacred places and holy characters. The love of the island home inspired Britten, in self-imposed exile, to compose the opera which made him famous. Crabbe's outsider is exalted by Britten into a symbol of loss – the loss of community and of the hope for it. The sublimated love of boys, which was such an important force in Victorian culture, emerges again in Britten's music, in which children occupy a central place, either as performers, or as the focus of a drama. Britten's disciplined self-purging of the erotic brings with it a chaste and lucid style – though one that is not without a wealth of romantic effect.

Britten produced the greatest of all arrangements of the English folk songs, as well as works for children and those who teach them which have proved to be a major contribution to the native tradition of amateur music-making. He recreated Aldeburgh, as a memorial to

Crabbe and all that Crabbe had represented. And he gave us, in the *War Requiem*, the final elegy for England. Yet even this impressive work does not reach the heights of the opera *Curlew River*, in which traditional Japanese devices are used, almost against themselves, to recreate an entirely English experience of belonging. The opera, composed in the sparse, evocative idiom of Britten's later years, is a 'church parable', designed by implication for performance in some High Anglican, monastic and perhaps subliminally pederastic establishment, in which all the parts are taken by men or boys. It tells the story of a mother who travels in search of her stolen child, and who discovers the spot where he died, beside the Curlew River. There she is visited and comforted by the child's ghost, who appears as a very Anglican and Pre-Raphaelite angel. Into this little drama Britten put all his longing for the old sources of holiness and community, and all his sense of loss. The work is elegiac, but without self-pity.

And this returns us to the point from which this chapter began. English culture was constantly adopting an outside view of itself, taking the perspective of the enlightened foreigner on its own inner life. In *Curlew River* Britten succeeds in recreating the Anglican vision of our destiny, with its sceptical but consoling acknowledgement that the place where we are, and the customs which are ours, are all that we know of the sacred, and also enough. He achieves this effect by borrowing a form perfected centuries ago and continents away – the form of the Noh play, devoted to the sacred times and places of the Shinto religion. *Curlew River*, like the *War Requiem*, is conceived in a humble spirit of reconciliation. Its tribute to the religious heritage of the English, nominal victors of the Second World War, is shaped by the religious art of the Japanese, who suffered the most terrible defeat. Such a work exemplifies what we mean, or ought to mean, by the gentleness of England. *Curlew River* is a work of forgiveness, a peace-offering to all mankind.

No view of English culture would be complete without mention of the constant praiseworthy attempt, which came to a climax in the early part of the twentieth century, to make high culture available to the man in the street. Victorian philanthropists had followed the example of Sir George Birkbeck in establishing 'Mechanics' Institutes' in the industrial towns, and these rapidly began to create the class of autodidacts like Mr Dickson, who did so much to transform my father's view from Ancoats. Birkbeck's own Mechanics' Institute was eventually to become part of the University of London, devoted to providing education to men and women in full-time employment; one of the happiest experiences of my life was that of teaching philosophy at Birkbeck College, as it is now known, to students who were volunteers and not conscripts.

The aim of such initiatives was not to invent a learning and culture suitable to the needs of the lower classes. It was to transmit to ordinary people the high culture of the university milieu – not by talking down to them, but by raising them to a higher level. The most influential of all the many attempts in this direction was the British Broadcasting Company (later Corporation), founded in 1922 as an independent institution operating under licence from the government. Its first General Manager, Lord Reith, set the tone for the BBC of my youth: decorous, civilised, reserved, with a meticulous respect for truth, a consciousness of authority and an acknowledgement of standards. It was a far-reaching expression of patrician values, respected everywhere for its objectivity and its quiet, stiff, sceptical tone. It had about it something of the high-toned irony of the Anglican Church, and indeed a Latin inscription above the entrance to Broadcasting House tells us that we enter a temple of the arts and sciences, dedicated to the glory of God and the propagation of knowledge. The old BBC was free from advertising and all commercial pressures; it was staffed by educated people who respected the culture that had given sense to their lives; it was objective in all matters of politics, while conveying a subdued but definite patriotism; and it offered to ordinary listeners (and subsequently viewers) not the things they wanted to hear or see, but the things that they *ought* to hear or see, on the understanding that, in a civilised society, these would be one and the same.

The culture which made such an institution possible has retreated from public life. The present-day BBC is a laughable caricature of the 'temple' conceived by Lord Reith, and worthy of mention only because it reminds us of the fact that most of what I have described in this chapter is no longer available to the ordinary person, and that the high culture of the English may soon be remembered and honoured only in private, by people ignored by the public media and regarded by the majority as cranks.

Chapter Ten

English Countryside

English loyalty was loyalty to a place domesticated by its indigenous law. Hence, when war or other crises forced the English into consciousness of their historic ties, it was the country that was the object of their intensest feelings of community. In and around the two world wars books began to appear, addressed to the general reader, devoted to this or that aspect of the rural way of life. In almost all of them the assumption prevailed that somehow rural England was the essential England, and urban England, by contrast, an accident, a concession to progress or even a spiritual sham. Wartime propaganda films dwell upon the countryside, as the most effective visual explanation of 'why we fight'. In such quaint works of quasi-propaganda as *Tawny Pipit* by Bernard Miles and Charles Saunders, and *A Canterbury Tale* by Michael Powell (both 1944), the landscape and the human life contained in it are portrayed as symbols of political stability and of unhurried order – antidotes to the tumult of war, and places to which we come home in imagination, as we hope to come home in fact.

The countryside forms the backcloth to the English religion. The Prayer Book and the Psalms, with their still rhythms and pastoral imagery, were the daily reading of Englishmen for centuries; the English Church, with its cathedral towns and rural deaneries, was designed to cater for a largely rural population, and never adapted itself to the new industrial towns, where dissent, Nonconformism and finally scepticism destroyed its old authority. The most influential

English evangelist, John Bunyan, set his parable in the country lanes of England, with the dangers and the comforts familiar to all who travelled there.

The place of the countryside in popular culture is exemplified by that most successful of middle-brow literary forms, the detective novel.[1] In Agatha Christie and Dorothy L. Sayers the setting is almost always rural, with murder conceived as an intrusion into Eden, the sudden fall into sin. *'Et in arcadia ego'* is the underlyng theme, and the solution of the murder brings with it the restoration of an other-worldy tranquillity. Death is vanquished through the plot which begins in a death.

The rural idyll had an even more important place in non-fiction. Izaak Walton published *The Compleat Angler* in 1653, so inaugurating a literary genre that was to enjoy three centuries of success – the nature documentary, simultaneously user's manual and dreamer's rhapsody. Gilbert White's *Natural History and Antiquities of Selborne* was a later and more learned instance, which has been reissued in every year since first publication in 1788. By the time of Richard Jefferies and W.D. Hudson, the rural documentary had become the most popular form of non-fiction among the reading public – a position that it has retained to this day. From *The Country Diary of an Edwardian Lady* to *Cider with Rosie*, from the pastoral films of Ealing Studios to *The Archers*, the rural theme has occupied a seemingly immovable place in the national culture, feeding illusions, soothing troubled hearts, and – let it be said – often preventing people from perceiving that the England of their dreams was no longer a reality.

Since 1945 a culture of lamentation has arisen, inspired in part by the writings of H.J. Massingham, and focused on the 'thoughtless' destruction of a rural heritage whose passing had already been lamented by William Cobbett in the early nineteenth century. Was this rural heritage a myth? The existence of the Council for the

---

[1] See W.H. Auden's essay, 'The Guilty Vicarage', in *The Dyer's Hand*.

Protection of Rural England, the National Trust, the Wildlife Trusts, the Countryside Restoration Trust, the Ernest Cook Trust, the Royal Society for the Protection of Birds and a hundred more – now including the Countryside Alliance, which sees the threat to field sports as the beginning of a final assault on rural England – suggests that, even if the idea is a myth, it is a widely accepted one. Moreover, since myths that are accepted become as influential as truths, it is a myth that we ought to examine.

The comparison with France is instructive. Rural France has been often described, and some of Balzac's most energetic novels are set there; so too is Flaubert's desolate masterpiece, *Madame Bovary*. In many cases, however, and in particular this last one, the theme is the *ennui*, the emotional and intellectual paralysis, the illusion-ridden incarceration, of life away from the capital. Thanks to the centralised culture that grew around the court in Paris and Versailles, and which remained even after the Revolution, the French have been more concerned with the privations of rural communities than with their fulfilments. Of course, they are as attached to their landscape as the English are to theirs – but attached in a different way. It is the home of a Catholic peasantry, priest-ridden, obstinate and canny; its character reflects the hardship and routine which wins a living from the soil. It moves like a sorrowing ghost through the pages of Mauriac's *Thérèse Desqueyroux*, and appears dark and forbidding in the background to Bernanos's *Journal d'un curé de campagne*. If Proust's Cambray occasionally recalls the evocative idylls of Victorian novelists, this is in part because it is a place of childhood and holidays, where drudgery occurs unobserved.

The dispersal of power in the English settlement ensured that the court never acquired the political, cultural and social status that it acquired in France. Centralising tendencies – such as those which appeared under Cromwell, or in the Restoration court of Charles II – did not endure for long, and the metropolitan wits who dominated eighteenth-century culture were acutely conscious that the metropolis was not the best place to be. Thanks to the system of representation by constituency, and the attachment of peerages to territory, the Houses of Parliament spoke as much for the villages as for the towns of England. Localised jurisdiction, parish councils, JPs, judicial circuits and the diocesan system ensured that law, administration and religion acquired a local voice, while remaining harmonious across the kingdom. The situation of the major public schools away from the urban centres, often in small market towns like Shrewsbury and Rugby or in rural settings like Eton, and the isolation of Oxford and Cambridge, enhanced the authority of the countryside, as a place not of 'rural idiocy', as Marx said, but of learning and instruction. London was frequented by the upper classes, but only for the 'season', in which social life and political manoeuvres were executed in the time required, but after which the town was deserted for those happier and quieter places where one really belonged – places which often bore one's own name and which therefore conferred their inimitable endorsement of status and power.

The country house came into being during the early Renaissance, and was already a thriving institution in 1616, when Ben Jonson celebrated the peace and harmony of Penshurst Place – the seat of the Sidneys and birthplace of Sir Philip. Here, the poet writes, the Sidneys had learned 'the mysteries of manners, armes and arts'. Jonson emphasises the domestic character of Penshurst: it is a place where people *dwell*, dispensing kindness and hospitality on visitors and dependants. And even if Jonson's picture is idealised, it corresponds to a feature of English country-house life that is repeatedly encountered in the literature – the conjunction of liberty and liberality that comes about when affluence coincides with a secure and localised social standing. The papers of the Verney family are sufficient proof of the day-to-day reality, and they display the seventeenth-century country house as a social, political and economic microcosm, autarkic, industrious, and providing in wise measure for all its many dependants.[1]

[1] These fascinating documents are summarised by G.M. Trevelyan, *English Social History*, London, 1944, pp. 250–3.

Following the Restoration the country house was to acquire an enhanced political importance, and improvements in transport facilitated the week-long parties on the great estates, where hunting and shooting by day were followed by elaborate formal dinners. A French political novel would perforce be set in Paris; but there are English political novels – notably those of Trollope – which take place almost entirely in country houses, or around dinner tables that might as well be in the country as in the town. To travel down to the country from London was to take a step up in the hierarchy of influence; and until very recently a weekend party in a country house would involve rituals once inseparable from the brokering of political power. People would dress for dinner, and the ladies would retire at dessert, leaving the men to settle their disputes and form their alliances over port and claret.

The country house was a sphere of limited sovereignty, which in turn limited the sovereignty of Westminster. It succeeded in capturing the political and social power that was already dispersed across the countryside, and in weaving it into a localised form of authority. In doing so it transformed not only itself but also the surrounding landscape. The ambition of the English gentleman was not to spend his money in London, still less to squander it in the colonies where so much of it was made. It was to bring the money home to his country retreat, and there to embellish the house, the landscape and the gardens with the trappings of peace and permanence, and perhaps also with the spoils of his Grand Tour abroad.

The peasantry were often victims of these aristocratic schemes, which could involve arbitrary dispossession, enclosure, and even the relocation or destruction of villages. The good landlord, however, would endeavour to improve the circumstances of his tenants at the same time as improving his own. He depended, then as now, on local goodwill for the enjoyment of his territory; and English law had the habit of siding with the tenant in disputes over possession. Whatever the justice of the process, it is undeniable that it remade much of the landscape in a form that is scarcely visible elsewhere, as a place of views and vistas, of parks and woods and monuments. Moreover, it scattered the artistic treasures of the nation – both architectural and pictorial – around the countryside, so that they became, not symbols of courtly civilisation and urban grandeur, but private possessions, signs and endorsements of a local sovereignty in which the land itself was the principal possession.

The country house was also the heart of local industry, employing farm-hands, house servants and every kind of ancillary worker in the maintenance of a labour-intensive and ecologically beneficent economy. With its home farm, its tenancies and its hospitable habits, the house promoted diversified agriculture, local distribution and thriving markets. The sporting interests of the squire required woodlands, copses and coverts; and the establishment of local packs of foxhounds brought neighbours of all classes together in a sport that could be successfully conducted only if each could cross the others' land.[1]

For those and many other reasons, the country house came to represent an ideal of English civilisation – one in which hierarchy was softened by neighbourliness, and wealth by mutual aid. The ideal was fortified by the long-standing, quasi-constitutional relation between the squire and the parson, who would often be a learned cleric like Gilbert White, bringing to country society the scholarly outlook of the university, taking charge of local education and recording his surroundings in diaries, poems and reports. Hence the ideal influenced the reality and, as we can see from Jane Austen and George Eliot, served to moralise the routines of country life and give order and decency to communities that were destined to survive on their own.

That is partly why the English felt such a strong attraction to the country house, and why writers have written so poignantly about its

---

[1] See David C. Itzkowitz, *Peculiar Privilege: a Social History of English Foxhunting*, Brighton, 1977.

demise – witness James in *The Spoils of Poynton*, Forster in *Howards End* and Waugh in *Brideshead Revisited*. And that is why the English would subsidise the efforts of the National Trust to keep the country house in being as a symbol and a replica, even while endorsing the taxation that was depriving it of life. The countryside is now scattered with aristocratic corpses, varnished over and preserved in their dying postures. And they are visited by hordes of curious tourists for whom these places, rather than any parliament or palace, breathe the mysterious magic whereby power becomes authority, and authority power. They are memorials to the force that maintained English society and English politics in being, and which became incarnate in them, as part of the landscape. They are the last signs of what England was like, when those who governed it also dwelled in it.

Thanks in part to the country house and in part to the tradition of the yeoman farmer, the English landscape was criss-crossed by visible boundaries – boundaries both permanent and permeable. Although it is often said that fields have been enclosed in recent times, as a result of the Enclosure Act, it seems that this is not so, and that much of the patchwork which is still visible from the air – though now much tattered and neglected – was already in existence in the early Middle Ages.[1] Primogeniture, and the abolition of feudal tenures, gave early reality to the small family farm, intact over generations and able to secure its boundaries.[2] It is on such farms that the 'yeoman stock' celebrated by Macaulay was raised.[3]

That the English countryside should be so intricately bounded, and so self-evidently owned, is in part a consequence of law and of the freedoms which grew from it. But it is also a consequence of the soil and the climate. Cattle and sheep thrive on English pasture, but

---

[1] See the illuminating account by Oliver Rackham, *The History of the Countryside*, London, 1986.

[2] See Alan Macfarlane, *The Origins of English Individualism*, Oxford, 1986, pp. 87–9 and 122.

[3] See Macaulay, *History of England*, Chapter 3.

can be kept secure there only if properly fenced – and hedges are the securest and most enduring form of enclosure. It is these hedges which have done most to soften and humanise the landscape, and to protect the animals which bring it to life. In Slavonic languages a hedge is a *zhivy plod* – a 'living fence' – though following Communist agriculture few of them are left in the places where Slavonic languages are spoken. Not only are hedges alive; they also *contain* life. Hedges have been, perhaps, the most significant concession that man has made to other species, in his relentless search for territory, and they are a primary source of the abundant wildlife which existed until recently in England.

After the last war it was government policy to subsidise the uprooting of hedgerows, in the misguided search for an efficient and competitive agriculture. The result was the sudden appearance in England of that previously unknown and deeply troubling thing: a landscape without boundaries. Faced with the desolate prairies of East Anglia and the Midlands, the English began to revolt against the destruction.

Where you see hedges that have grown straggly, with the trees wrestling upwards for the light, you know that the land is passing from the old grassland agriculture, in which sheep and cows were the main source of livelihood, to the new, in which horses, kept for the pleasure of urban refugees, have colonised the pasture. Horses can be confined with the flimsiest of wooden fences, while cows and sheep, which move in seething crowds, will break down any barrier that is not able to withstand the combined weight of the herd. Where hedgerows are maintained, therefore, it is because the old and unprofitable business of meat and milk still lingers. The hedge is there because of the old livestock economy, which was also the backbone of the small family farm, and of the rural communities that the English still love in the abstract, while regarding their actual fate with indifference.

The hedge became a symbol of Englishness, therefore, at the very moment when its function was being lost. It was a pointer to a dying form of life, and a reminder to the English that the thing which defines them – the land itself – is also being removed from them. It is now government policy to subsidise the planting of hedgerows, and to penalise those who grub them out: too late, of course, to save East Anglia, and too late to save the small farmers who, by treating boundaries as sacred, have lost out against the absentee agribusinesses that are erasing the landscape. But the gesture again illustrates the enchantment that lay over England, and which still mysteriously calls to those who live there.

As I have argued, English culture entered the modern era with an immovable commitment to the pastoral as its preferred tone of voice. There has been no greater effort by English intellectuals than that devoted to the conservation of the landscape, and the battle against roads, suburbs and unsightly development. But none of it has had any effect on those who make the important decisions, which is another way of saying that England is governed and controlled from elsewhere.[1] This love of countryside is seen by some writers not merely as the perpetuation of a mythical vision of England, but also as an impediment to social and material progress, the sign of an indolent and debilitating patrician culture.[2] But the first steps outside a university library would refute such a view. The fact is that the passion which educated English people devote to the *idea* of rural life is not matched by any creative interest in the *fact* of it. By saving the appearances – through such exercises in taxidermy as the National Trust – the English have enabled themselves to turn their backs on the reality. Insensibly, and without admitting it to themselves, they have become an urban people, extolling their countryside as the symbol of what they no longer are. The landscape where their ancestors dwelled is one which they are merely passing

[1] On the fate of the English country in the twentieth century, see Marion Shoard, *The Theft of the Countryside*, London, 1981, and Graham Harvey, *The Killing of the Countryside*, London, 1997.

[2] See, for example, Martin Wiener, *English Culture and the Decline of the Industrial Spirit*, Cambridge, 1981.

through. And sensing this, and sensing that they no longer truly belong in the land which made them, they have lost their self-confidence as a people.

Chapter Eleven: Epilogue

The Forbidding of England

England consisted in the physiognomy, the habits, the institutions, the religion and the culture that I have described in these pages. Almost all have died. To describe something as dead is not to call for its resurrection. Nevertheless, we are in dangerous territory. Valediction is permitted, but only 'a valediction forbidding mourning'. Anything else is greeted with a sneer. So you want to bring back maypoles, mummings, gaderyngs and morris dancing – or at any rate, Larry the Lamb, knee-length bathing trunks, steam engines, foxtrots, cigarette cards, all-male cricket clubs! To these familiar jibes there is only one response, namely to mourn, but privately. Without what Freud called the 'work of mourning' we are diminished by our losses, and unable to live to the full beyond them.[1] It is right that the heirs to English civilisation should commemorate its virtues, its achievements and its meaning. For dead civilisations can speak to living people, and the more conscious they are while dying, the more fertile is their influence thereafter. Roman civilisation, which understood itself so well in the Augustan poets and orators, endowed its successors with law, language, literature and an image of virtue, and in the moments when European civilisation has returned to these things for inspiration it has taken new heart.

Nevertheless, the reader may feel that I have been too lavish in my

[1] See 'Mourning and Melancholia', in *Collected Papers*, ed. Joan Rivière, London, 1925, vol. IV.

praise of England, and insufficiently conscious of the country's defects. The example lies before us of embarrassing self-deception uttered in England's name: those excruciating odes of Austin Dobson, W.E. Henley and Sir Henry Newbolt; the insufferable gibberish of E.F. Benson and Alfred Austin; the reams of imperial kitsch that accompanied the Boer War and the run-up to the war of 1914. Were the perpetrators of this drivel ignorant of the slave trade and of the oppression of the Irish, of the persecution of witches and the dire punishments of petty offenders in Old England, of the treatment of children in the Victorian factories, of the condition of women at the time when they wrote? Such are the questions which modern people ask, and they deserve an answer. And my answer is to invite comparisons. In contrast to which country, nation, political system or colonial venture is England to be judged so harshly? To what extent were the terrible punishments of Renaissance England a peculiarity of the English, rather than of the times? Just which European country entered the modern world with less bloodshed, less turmoil, less cruelty, less injustice than England? And when it comes to that late imperialist literature, just where, in the Europe of the time, do we find a culture unpolluted by kitsch and free from the false sentiment that arises when religion wavers and declines? Pondering those questions, and the history of modern Europe since the French Revolution, I find myself confirmed in the desire to praise the English for the virtues which they once displayed, and which they were taught even in my youth to emulate.

This does not alter the fact that these virtues are rapidly disappearing. Having been famous for their stoicism, their decorum, their honesty, their gentleness and their sexual puritanism, the English now subsist in a society in which those qualities are no longer honoured – a society of people who regard long-term loyalties with cynicism, and whose response to misfortune is to look round for someone to sue. England is no longer a gentle country, and the old courtesies and decencies are disappearing. Sport, once a rehearsal for imperial virtues, has become a battleground for hooligans. Sex, freed from taboos, has become the ruling obsession: the English have the highest rate of divorce in Europe, regard marriage as a bore, are blatantly promiscuous and litter the country with their illegitimate, uncared-for and state-subsidised offspring.

Gone are the congregations and the little platoons. Gone are the peaceful folkways – the children's games, parlour songs, proverbs and sayings – that depended on a still remembered religious community. Gone are the habits – the stiff upper lip, the aloof sense of duty, the instant assistance to the stranger in distress – that went with imperial pride. Gone are the institutions – the village shop, the market, the Saturday-night dance, the bandstand in the park – through which local communities renewed themselves.

None of that should surprise us. The loss of traditional virtue and local identity has occurred throughout Europe and its diaspora.[1] England was part of Christendom, one branch of a spiritual tree which was struck by enlightenment and died. The global economy, the democratisation of taste, the sexual revolution, pop culture and television have worked to erase the sense of spiritual identity in every place where piety shored up the old forms of knowledge and local custom fortified the moral sense.

Nevertheless, the new media culture has been a particular misfortune for the English. When your fundamental loyalty is to a place and its *genius loci*, globalisation and the loss of sovereignty bring a crisis of identity. The land loses its history and its personal face; the institutions become administrative centres, operated by anonymous bureaucrats who are not *us* but *them*. The bureaucratic disenchantment of the earth has therefore been felt more keenly in England than elsewhere. For it has induced in the English the sense that they are really living nowhere.

---

[1] The lament over Spain began in earnest with Ortega y Gasset's *España Invertebrada* in 1921, some fifteen years before the lament over England. The lament over France, which began at the same time with Charles Maurras and Gustave Thibon, achieved devastating expression in *Les Orphelins*, the novel published by Louis Pauwels in 1994, shortly before his death.

The institutions and customs that I have described depended on England being a somewhere and a home. They have therefore been dismantled, either by corruption or decree. What is curious, however, is not the decay of England, which is matched by the decay of France, Germany, Italy, Spain and Ireland. It is the fact that England has been forbidden – and forbidden by the English. Venerable customs and wise institutions are under threat or already abolished: the grammar schools, the old House of Lords, the Prayer Book and the English Bible, English weights and measures, English currency, local regiments, the Royal Tournament – every practice in which the spirit of England can still be discerned seems fated now to arouse contempt, not in the world at large, but in the English. Moreover, the growing licentiousness of the English has gone hand in hand with a loss of liberty, and the country which first made toleration into a public virtue has espoused a new form of intolerance, which, while permitting and even encouraging breaches of traditional morality, seeks to enforce a common code of 'political correctness'. Any activity connected with the hierarchy and squirearchy of Old England is now likely to be persecuted or even criminalised: not only hunting and gentlemen's clubs, but uniforms, exclusive schools, old ceremonies, even the keeping of national customs and the display of the national flag.

In June 1999, during the elections to the European Parliament, seventy-eight-year-old George Staunton, who was putting up posters for the UK Independence Party in Liverpool, painted on the wall of a derelict building the words 'Don't forget the 1945 war' and 'Free speech for England'. He was arrested by the Merseyside Police, and has since been charged with 'racially aggravated criminal damage' – an offence which carries a maximum sentence of fourteen years. The damage was 'racially aggravated' on account of the gratuitous reference to England, the country for which Mr Staunton fought in the Second World War and which has since been forbidden.

A district council in the Home Counties last year refused to extend the opening hours of a pub which wished to celebrate St George's

Day, since this would be provocative and jingoistic; the same council automatically grants extensions to pubs which wish to celebrate St Patrick's Day, since that is the expression of a valid ethnic identity. The Metropolitan Police have ruled that London taxis may not sport the English flag, while saying nothing about the Welsh, Irish or Scottish emblems, all of which can be seen whenever a sporting event invites them.

Peter Hitchens has written, in this connection, of the abolition of Britain.[1] The story he tells, however, is a specifically English story, and it is doubtful that the same fervour of repudiation has been heaped on their institutions and their culture by the Scots, the Welsh or the Irish. English history is no longer taught in English schools, or taught as a tale of crime and exploitation; Scots and Irish children learn, by contrast, self-vaunting national legends, as well as the intricacies of national history. Unlike the Celts, English students come to university with no knowledge of their national heroes, and only the vaguest awareness of what happened before their time. Nelson, to the majority of them, is Nelson Mandela, and Wellington no more than a boot. They have learned that Englishmen were involved in the slave trade, but not that England, the country, set an example to an astonished world by outlawing it. Nor do they learn about the thing which made this possible – the heroism of a Royal Navy devoted to its sovereign and able through its fortitude to 'rule the waves'.[2]

The forbidding of England is a strange phenomenon and one that is hard to explain. The country was always victorious in war, and was not impoverished even by the loss of its empire. No outside force compelled it to relinquish its national pride and culture. The process came from within, and seemingly without resistance. George Orwell commented on the disloyalty, the anti-patriotism and 'intellectual sabotage' that had helped to weaken England during the 1930s.[3] He

[1] Peter Hitchens, *The Abolition of Britain*, London, 1999.
[2] See R. Anstey, *The Atlantic Slave Trade and British Abolition, 1760–1810*, London, 1965, and S. Drescher, *Econocide: British Slavery in the Age of Abolition*, London, 1977.
[3] 'England, your England', and elsewhere.

attributed the phenomenon to the fact that the old imperial society excluded the intellectuals, and therefore drove them to take up a negative posture towards it. But that seems a shallow explanation. The most subversive of our modern intellectuals have often been those most pampered by fashionable society: Lytton Strachey, for example, whose *Eminent Victorians* (1918) set the pattern for the *de haut en bas* debunking of the loyalties of ordinary Englishmen; the Bloomsbury Group; the fellow-travellers; the 'homintern', as Auden called it, whose last prominent member, Anthony Blunt, enjoyed every privilege that an art historian could acquire, including knighthood and appointment as Keeper of the Queen's Pictures, before being finally exposed as a traitor. Nor were these intellectuals a novelty on the English cultural scene – Charles James Fox and his circle had set the pattern in the eighteenth century, and Tom Paine achieved international eminence on the strength of his self-righteous anti-patriotism.

Moreover, we should always set the privileged rebels against the far greater number of less prominent, more modest and more worthy intellectuals who have become priests, civil servants, dons and schoolmasters, humbly accepting their place in the *status quo*. It is just that, when this happens, you don't hear about them. Intellectuals all seem to be seditious bigots only because seditious bigots do the most damage or at any rate make the most noise. The 'forbidding of England' cannot be explained merely as a result of this noise, which is no more part of the national culture than the background crackle is part of a radio programme.

It seems much more as though the English emerged from two world wars in a condition of moral fatigue. An inheritance is a burden that must be taken up. An overwhelming sense of guilt seemed to paralyse the country – guilt at its own successes, and an awareness of their cost. A culture of repudiation arose not only among intellectuals, but in every area of civil life, and those like Mr Chapman, who lived according to the old virtues, the old customs and the old religion, were subjected to humiliating scorn by the makers of public opinion. This book too will be scorned – not for its manifest imperfections as an elegy, but for such little success as it might have, in praising the virtues of Old England. English opinion-makers laugh at the culture and institutions that might have been theirs, and regard with cool amazement the old fuddy-duddies who still respect them. Of no body of opinion-makers is this more true than the BBC, heir to the most remarkable experiment in popular education that was ever undertaken by the English, and now devoted to abolishing what remains of the national culture.

This does not mean that nobody regrets the passing of England. On the contrary. The post-war London stage has given us an unceasing stream of regrets – most of them (from Alan Bennett's *Forty Years On* to Tom Stoppard's *Arcadia*) ironical and humorous, but all of them depending for their effect on the last flickers of the old enchantment. Many of the customs and institutions that I have described have societies which stand in lamentation at their deathbeds – the Prayer Book Society, the Victorian Society, the Council for the Protection of Rural England and so on. Yet the regret leads nowhere and will, under the slightest strain, change from regret to repudiation.

The impulse to repudiate has also led to far-reaching constitutional 'reforms'. The political institutions of the English, based in the corporate Crown, in hereditary succession, in representation and the formalities of office, have been rejected from within, by people who compare them unfavourably with Continental or American practices, and call for 'more democracy', more transparency, more openness to social and cultural change.[1] Precisely those aspects of the constitution that I have singled out for praise are now the objects of distrust – and the distrust has triumphed. The hereditary parts of parliamentary government will now disappear, and the professionalisation of politics will quickly follow. It was regarded as the greatest scandal of

[1] For two particularly intelligent critics of the English settlement see Anthony Barnett, *This Time*, London, 1997, and Jonathan Freedland, *Bring Home the Revolution*, London, 1998.

Lloyd George's premiership that he sold honours and peerages; today the practice is routine. The old settled Establishment, identified with the land and the customs of the English, is now replaced every four or five years by the cronies and toadies of the latest clique in power. The delicate mechanism which amplified authority while restricting power, has been replaced by a system of levers, controlled and operated in secret by a Cabinet that recognises no purpose more important than remaining where it is.

The result of this has been the effective disenfranchisement of the English. The old order of England depended upon the rural communities. Those who maintained the landscape also sanctified the common home. They were eventually outnumbered by the city-dwellers and the industrial workforce; but the Upper House would speak for them. Hereditary titles were attached to landed estates; rural England was thereby woven into the *authority* of Parliament, even though the urban majority had the greater share of its *power*. With the loss of a hereditary House of Lords, rural England has been silenced.

So too has urban England, though in another way. This has resulted from two extraordinary changes, both the outcome of sustained mendacity and subterfuge: the transfer of sovereignty to European institutions and the devolution of political power. It is only with a measure of irony that English law could now be described as the law of the land. Not only has endless legislation effectively marginalised the common law, English courts are required to apply European directives, regardless of native precedent. For the first time in their history, the English are ruled not by judgements but by decrees. Devices which, from the beginning, ensured that nobody could gain sovereignty over England without becoming subject to the English law, have been finally set aside. The English are no longer a sovereign people, and their law is no longer their own.

Again, the pressure towards this outcome has come from within – from businessmen wedded to the global economy, from bureaucrats in love with administrative power or programmed to carry out some defunct project of 'reform', and from progressive intellectuals who regard national loyalty as a crime against enlightenment. Those who have voiced opposition to the unaccountable bureaucracies and tinpot tribunals of the European Union have been dismissed as chauvinists, reactionaries or 'Little Englanders', while the process of union itself has been decked out in the same trappings of 'historical inevitability' with which Communism was imposed on the Russians and National Socialism on the people of Germany. Vague talk of 'subsidiarity' does nothing to alter the fact that the English are finally, after a millennium of resistance, subject to jurisdiction from abroad. And this political disenfranchisement is also a disenchantment of their country.

England was part of a union, the other members of which were divided from it by race, history, religion, culture and to some extent law. The English were not a criminal people. Nevertheless, they committed crimes, and the worst of these was against the Irish. And although their union with Scotland was a more or less inevitable long-term consequence of the fact that King James VI of Scotland inherited the English Crown, it too was the occasion of oppressive acts and attempted rebellion. The Labour Party, whose ideology grew out of Nonconformist religion, working-class discontents and the advocacy of trade-union rights, would never have come to power, had it not been for its support in Scotland and Wales, where it was seen as an anti-English force. Many of its parliamentary members openly sneered at the monarchy, and none of them had much time for the hereditary principle, the Anglican orthodoxy, the class system or the mysterious workings of the English law. Around the Labour Party, partly associated with it and partly opposed to it as insufficiently radical, there gathered a powerful establishment of intellectuals and academics, devoted to undermining the authority of Old England, and making it faintly ridiculous in the eyes of the young.

Devolution, when it came, was not so much a gesture in favour of the Welsh and the Scots as a gesture *against England*. The Scottish and Welsh Members of Parliament kept their seats at Westminster, so retaining full power to legislate for the English even though the English have only a diminished ability to legislate for Scotland and Wales. This radical disenfranchising of the English is also a political interdiction. In the revised United Kingdom there simply *is* no English part, and the official map of the European Union, issued by the European Commission in Brussels, which divides the Continent into 'regions', makes no mention of England. England has been finally disposed of. When Poland was partitioned, and the name of a country that had existed for eight centuries as a sovereign state was removed from the official maps of Europe, the English were appalled. Two centuries later what was done to Poland by force is being done to England by subterfuge, and the response of the English is a guilt-ridden silence.

It is important to understand the vehemence of the feelings that led to the destruction of the union. Exemplary was the Scottish writer Tom Nairn, whose *The Break-up of Britain* (1977) was a seminal text among left-wing academics at the time when I first began to puzzle over the question of England and its future. Here is a representative passage:

> 'Moderate', 'orderly', 'decent', 'peaceful and tolerant', 'constitu-
> tional'; 'backward-looking', 'complacent', 'insular', 'class-ridden',
> 'inefficient', 'imperialist' – a realistic analysis of the British state must
> admit these two familiar series of truisms are in fact differing visages
> of the same social reality. That arcadian England which appeals so
> strongly to foreign intellectuals is also the England which has, since
> the early 1950s, fallen into ever more evident and irredeemable
> decline – the United Kingdom of permanent economic crisis, falling
> standards, bankrupt government, slavish dependence on the United
> States and myopic expedients . . . [1]

Leaving aside the falsehood of most of that, it is evident from the style that whatever could be said in favour of England would be

---

[1] *The Break-up of Britain*, London, 1977, pp. 44–5.

treated by such a writer as a yet more damning criticism. It is true of all of us, that our virtues are hateful to our enemies, and perceived by them as faults. And that is significant, for it brings home to us that Tom Nairn is writing as an enemy. It was the tragedy of England to have accumulated such a weight of internal enmity – in the case of the Irish a justified enmity. In the twentieth century English patriotism seemed almost to be as Dr Johnson half jokingly described it: the 'last refuge of the scoundrel'. Rather than risk the accusation that they were so bellicose and xenophobic as actually to believe in themselves, the English preferred to apologise. One of their most endearing traits became their nemesis.

But surely, you will say, the *country* remains – the place called England, admitted on your own account to be the real focus of national loyalty? If the country exists, then so does England.

I sympathise with that response; but it fails to convince me. Of course, the rough contours remain and could be altered only by some calamity which would also destroy the destroyers. But the landscape that was inscribed upon those contours has been scrubbed away. The old England for which our parents fought has been reduced to isolated pockets between the motorways. The family farm, which maintained the small-scale and diversified production that was largely responsible for the shape and appearance of England, is now on the verge of extinction. The towns have lost their centres, which are boarded up and vandalised; and the cities have been all but obliterated by vast steel structures which at night stand empty amid the wastes of illuminated concrete. The night sky is no longer visible, but everywhere blanketed with a sickly orange glow, and England is becoming a no-man's-land, an 'elsewhere', managed by executives who visit the outposts only fleetingly, staying in multinational hotels on the edges of the floodlit wastelands. And nature has responded, as is her habit, to culture. The species that helped to consecrate the English countryside – the firefly, the nightingale, the barn owl, the eagle, the roadside reptiles and hedgehogs, the newts of the ponds and skylarks of the meadows, even the 'darkling thrush' – are now rapidly disappearing. They too have their societies of defenders, like the Royal Society for the Protection of Birds, whose contribution to the well-being of birds is to report ineffectually on their disappearance.

In his revolutionary sermon at the outbreak of the Peasants' Revolt in 1381, John Ball asked 'When Adam delved and Eve span, who was then the gentleman?'[1] His rhetorical question was aimed at the heart of the English settlement, and at the ideal which had served both to unite the classes and to divide them. The class resentment which I was brought up to regard as the true (as opposed to the sycophantic) form of national loyalty was simply the latest incarnation of an enduring historical force. This force had often been domesticated, it is true, by the conciliatory pressure of the English law; but it could burst out in violent, intemperate and implacable forms, whenever questions of sovereignty were at stake. De Tocqueville wisely observed that revolutionary sentiments are born not from oppression, but from the sense of bravado that comes when the old order loses its power.[2] As the religious basis of the English loyalties declined, so did resentment establish its empire. The sneering and jeering at Old England was caused not by the country's strength but by its manifest weakness, which meant that it could be despised with impunity.

When I look back at my father's early lessons in discontent, however, I am impressed by a feature that is seldom mentioned by the historians of radical thought, and unnoticed by our modern reformers. The proof that England is in the hands of her enemies, my father told me, can be found by looking out of the window. Behold the desecrated townscape of High Wycombe, once a thriving market town, with streets of half-timbered houses in which the people lived and carried on their lawful businesses, now a soulless waste of empty office blocks, each with a sign saying 'For rent'! Ask yourself how it came about . . . Who controls planning? The council. Who controls

---

[1] Ball was adapting verses from the earlier English mystic, Richard Rolle de Hampole.
[2] *De l'ancien régime et la Revolution.*

the council? The local Tory Party. Who controls the Tory Party? The capitalists, the grandees and the landowners – in short, people from elsewhere. Who is profiting from the work of destruction? The capitalists, the grandees, the landowners – people from elsewhere. Add a few additional premises – the Anglican Church (= the Tory Party), village Hampdens, trade-union martyrs, bits of folklore, H.J. Massingham, articles from *The Countryman* – and you come quickly, my father thought, to the conclusion that the old Establishment of England was an alien presence, a usurping class of hypocrites, who had stolen the birthright of the English people and treated it as their private goods. Their fine ideals of the good sport, the brick and the gentleman were just so much 'ideology', designed to pull the wool over the eyes of people like Roger Scruton – people who must live in the ruins of a country whose squandered capital funded yachts in the Bahamas, grouse moors in Scotland and villas in Nice.

Take away the mythopoeia, the resentment, the sense of helplessness, and you will find in this argument the very enchantment that I have been describing. My father loved what was local, collegial and attached to the land. His protest was a protest against the forces that were disenchanting England; and if he identified these forces with big business, and big business with the Tory Party, was he wholly wrong? Deep down his passion was a religious one, a protest against a world which placed material prosperity before spiritual need, and which ignored the fact that the soul of man is a local product, rooted in the soil.

I don't say that this was the only motive behind the dissenting tradition in England. But it was an important one. The coal miners, protesting against the closure of their mines, were fighting the same cause: namely the local community against the global economy, somewhere against nowhere. Many people shared my father's belief in the Labour Party, as the sole institution that would actually *stop* things. Only through the Labour Party, he thought, could we safeguard an England which belonged to the people, who in turn belonged to it. The spectacle of a Labour Party committed to 'globalisation', indifferent to the fate of rural England, and managed by smooth 'consultants' who might next year be working for the other side, which is in fact only the same side under another description, would have appalled him. Even in his bitterest protests against the monarchy, the aristocracy and the class system, he was a patriot, who knew in his heart that England was not a nation or an empire or an enterprise but a country, whose law was the law of the land.

Acknowledgements

The author and publishers wish to thank the following for their kind permission to quote:

Bill Hamilton as the Literary Executor of the Estate of the Late Sonia Brownell Orwell, Martin Secker & Warburg Ltd for an extract from *The Lion and the Unicorn* by George Orwell (Copyright © George Orwell, 1941); Constable & Robinson Publishing Ltd for an extract from *Soliloquies in England* by George Santayana; Faber and Faber Ltd and Farrar, Straus & Giroux for an extract from 'Home is so Sad' in *Collected Poems* by Philip Larkin; Marvel Press for an extract from 'Church Going' in *The Less Deceived* by Philip Larkin; John Murray (Publishers) Ltd for an extract from 'How to Get On in Society' in *Collected Poems* by John Betjeman.

Every effort has been made to trace the holders of copyrights. Any inadvertent omissions of acknowledgement or permission can be rectified in future editions.

Index